Truth at the Gate

Truth at the Gate

A Trial of History's Giants and the Nazarene

Dan LaBarbera

RESOURCE *Publications* • Eugene, Oregon

TRUTH AT THE GATE
A Trial of History's Giants and the Nazarene

Copyright © 2026 Dan LaBarbera. All rights reserved. Except for brief quotations in critical publications or reviews, no part of this book may be reproduced in any manner without prior written permission from the publisher. Write: Permissions, Wipf and Stock Publishers, 199 W. 8th Ave., Suite 3, Eugene, OR 97401.

Resource Publications
An Imprint of Wipf and Stock Publishers
199 W. 8th Ave., Suite 3
Eugene, OR 97401

www.wipfandstock.com

PAPERBACK ISBN: 979-8-3852-5891-8
HARDCOVER ISBN: 979-8-3852-5892-5
EBOOK ISBN: 979-8-3852-5893-2

02/06/26

Unless otherwise indicated, all Scripture quotations are from The ESV® Bible (The Holy Bible, English Standard Version®), © 2001 by Crossway, a publishing ministry of Good News Publishers. Used by permission. All rights reserved.

For those who sought truth even when it cost them everything.

Contents

Acknowledgment — ix
Author's Note — xi
Preface: A Word Before We Begin — xiii

The Weight of Evidence: Setting the Standard — 1

Part I. Legends Without Witnesses — 11
Alexander the Great: The King of Echoes — 13
Hannibal Barca: Rome's Phantom Enemy — 25
Cleopatra VII: The Empire's Siren — 39
Buddha (Siddhartha Gautama): The Man Without a Manuscript — 50
Confucius (Kong Fuzi): The Ghost of Virtue — 61

Part II. Echoes Without a Voice — 73
Socrates: The Man of Many Voices — 75

Part III. Documented Bureaucrats and Emperors — 85
Julius Caesar: The Emperor's Illusion — 87
Tiberius Caesar: The Forgotten Emperor — 99
Pontius Pilate: The Man Who Stood Before Truth — 109

CONTENTS

Part IV. The Prophet and His Community   121
Muhammad: The Prophet and the Pen   123

Part V. Singular Among History   135
Jesus of Nazareth: The Carpenter in the Records   137
The Double Standard of Truth   156

The Five Pillars of Historical Confidence   165
Bibliography   171
Index   189

Acknowledgment

To God, who still pursued and found me when I was lost. To my wife, Julia—my constant companion. To my mother, Kerry, and my father, Larry—thank you for never letting go of me, even when I stumbled. In you, I have seen God's hand at work. Through you, I have learned the meaning of grace.

Author's Note

I DID NOT WRITE this because I thought the world needed another book, or because I imagined myself clever enough to out-think centuries of scholars. I wrote this because I could not escape it. Everywhere I turned, I saw men and women lifting up the names of history's giants, kings, conquerors, philosophers, as if they were the pillars holding the world together. And yet when I placed Jesus among them, I found that He did not shrink beside them, He rose above them. The more I looked, the clearer it became: if we can honor Caesar for his empire, Alexander for his campaigns, or Socrates for his questions, then we must at least admit that Jesus of Nazareth stands in their company. And if He stands there, He surpasses them.

This book cost me something. It cost me hours of doubt, fear, and the weight of asking whether I was setting myself up for failure, or worse, setting Him up for it. More than once I almost walked away. But I could not. Not because I am strong, but because the truth pressed too heavily on me to remain silent. So read this book not as the final word, but as one man's witness. I cannot solve every riddle, I cannot silence every critic, but I can tell you what I have seen: that Jesus endures when others fade, and that His name belongs not in the footnotes of history but at its center. If I stumble in my telling, may you look past me and see Him more clearly. That is all I ask.

Preface
A Word Before We Begin

This book is not written to claim mastery over history, nor to pretend that I can solve every question left to us by time. History is complex, messy, and often contradictory. Records are incomplete. Sources disagree. Even the earliest witnesses wrote through the lens of their own lives and cultures. I know this. I do not ignore it. And yet, within that uncertainty, we continue to weigh, to compare, to measure. We do this with every figure we call "great": Caesar, Alexander, Socrates, Cleopatra, and countless others. We examine their words, their deeds, their legacies, and we still dare to say something about who they were and what they left behind.

This book is my attempt to do the same with Jesus of Nazareth. Not to strip Him of His mystery, nor to reduce Him to mere "evidence," but to show that even when weighed by the standards of history, He does not falter. In fact, He surpasses the giants of the past. I write not as a conqueror of truth, but as a witness to it. My aim is not to win arguments, but to give readers a fair chance to see Jesus as He is: not only the subject of faith, but also a figure who stands firmly within history itself.

If there are cracks in the record, they are not His fault. If there are distortions in the telling, they belong to us, not to Him. If anything, the very mess of history only makes His endurance more astonishing. So take this work for what it is: one man's effort to set Jesus alongside history's giants, and to show that He still towers above them. If I succeed, it is because truth has a way of shining through. If I fall short, I pray you see past my weakness to the strength of the One I am writing about.

The Weight of Evidence
Setting the Standard

I REMEMBER THE WEIGHT of what I was told was certainty. The feeling of confidence, of assurance that the past had been conquered by the pen. And yes, some stories were written by the victor, but more than that, we moderns, perhaps even unconsciously, infer that history recorded then is like history recorded now. As if everyone once had a pen, the way everyone today has a phone. But no, nothing could be further from the truth.

The floor we are standing on is loose, patched together with half-rotted boards fastened with rusty nails. Press hard enough, and you will fall through. By this I mean history, not conspiracies, not aliens or secret cabals. No, the distortion is subtler, woven into the arch, brewed into the mix. Because of this, every day brings a fresh distortion: a misquote repeated until it hardens, a date shifted, a battle claimed for the wrong flag, a line between record and legend blurred until it flatters the teller. This is not noise. It is the predictable result of three pressures on how the public inherits its past.

- **First**, selection and presentism: fragments are chosen to suit today's concerns, and yesterday is forced to speak through today's lens.[1]
- **Second**, narrative compression: dramas and documentaries must supply arcs, dialogue, and composite figures; what resists the script is pared away or invented.[2]

---

1. Carr, *What Is History?*, 9–12; Wineburg, *Historical Thinking and Other Unnatural Acts*, 3–10.

2. Rosenstone, *History on Film/Film on History*, 1–15, 72–75; Toplin, *Reel History*, 1–10, 35–37.

The Weight of Evidence

- **Third**, market incentives: what spreads is what provokes, novelty, certainty, conflict, not the slow discipline of context and qualification. The outcome is memory dressed in the garb of history.[3]

The combined effect is subtle but devastating. Each of these pressures is another uneven board laid beneath our feet. Step lightly, and it feels solid enough. But the weight of certainty rests on timbers that shift the moment they are tested. What begins as interpretation becomes assumption; what begins as entertainment becomes authority. The past, which ought to stand as a check on the present, is conscripted into its service instead. Characters become symbols, centuries are bent into parables, and entire civilizations are remade to fit the questions of today. The reader may not notice the shift; indeed, that is the danger.

It is here, in this narrowing corridor between fact and fable, that something like Spartacus is recast to answer modern quarrels.[4] Rome is retold as a mirror of contemporary politics.[5] The Middle Ages become a morality play for the present.[6] The Wars of the Three Kingdoms are trimmed to fit a season order.[7] None of this is malicious. Narrative is how humans remember. But when narrative outruns evidence, audiences inherit confidence without foundation.[8] We walk across a floor built by others, patched with their planks and nailed down with their motives. This book will not take the floor for granted. It will test whether the boards hold. We will slow down. We will name our sources. We will test every claim by standards any fair-minded reader can apply.

Before we turn to the Five Pillars themselves, it is worth asking why these particular measures were chosen. They are not theological tricks or apologetic shortcuts, but standards that can be applied evenly to any figure of antiquity. I did not include categories like "embarrassment," because while modern scholars sometimes lean on them, they depend too heavily on psychology and shifting notions of shame. Ancient writers were not bound by such concerns: they freely invented speeches, embellished scandals, and

---

3. Nora, "Between Memory and History," 7–24.

4. Plutarch, *Life of Crassus* 8–11; Wyke, *Projecting the Past*, 70–95; Futrell, *Roman Games*, 132–36.

5. Edwards, *Politics of Immorality in Ancient Rome*, 1–12; Morley, *Roman Empire*, 145–50; Cyrino, *Rome Season One*, 3–18.

6. Cantor, *Inventing the Middle Ages*, xv–xxi; Bartlett, *Making of Europe*, 1–10.

7. Hughes-Warrington, *History Goes to the Movies*, 165–72; Cressy, *England on Edge*, 3–5.

8. Evans, *In Defence of History*, 77–94; Fischer, *Historians' Fallacies*, 3–15, 134–35.

mingled myth with fact. What endures across cultures and centuries are not feelings but facts: when something was written, how many bore witness, whether outside voices confirm it, whether the ground itself agrees, and whether the record was faithfully carried forward. These are the tests that kings, conquerors, prophets, and philosophers must all face. And when the Nazarene is weighed on the same scales, the result is unlike any other.

- **First,** contemporaneity. How close is the witness to the fire he describes? Time erodes memory; distance breeds myth. Testimony must still feel the heat of the moment.[9]
- **Second,** multiplicity. One voice may falter. Two may conspire. But when many speak apart and yet echo the same truth, the chorus cannot be ignored.[10]
- **Third,** external corroboration. A claim without witness beyond itself is vapor. Truth must leave echoes, in rival scrolls, in hostile tongues, in the stones themselves.[11]
- **Fourth,** archaeology. The earth remembers what men forget. Fragments pulled from dust and monuments raised from ruin testify with a voice no empire can silence.[12]
- **Fifth,** chain of custody. Words endure only if they are carried. Who bore them, who copied them, who bled for them? Trust rests not in abstraction but in faithful transmission.[13] Where the evidence is thin, we will say so. Where it is strong, we will show why.[14]

---

9. Thucydides, *History* 1.22; Bauckham, *Jesus and the Eyewitnesses*, 5–9; Licona, *Resurrection of Jesus*, 68–74.

10. Meier, *Marginal Jew* 1:xx–xxi; Sanders, *Historical Figure of Jesus*, 88–92; Keener, *Historical Jesus of the Gospels*, 185–90. Each stresses the importance of multiple independent witnesses as a standard criterion of historical authenticity.

11. Tacitus, *Annals* 15.44; Josephus, *Antiquities* 18.3.3; Greenleaf, *Testimony of the Evangelists*, 16–20.

12. Mykytiuk, "Archaeology Confirms," 42–50; Evans, *Jesus and the Remains*, 25–27; Dever, *What Did the Biblical Writers Know*, 123–26.

13. Metzger and Ehrman, *Text of the New Testament*, 52–58, 276–80; Wallace, "Majority Text and the Original Text," in *Majority Text*, 157–73; Gurry and Hixson, *Myths and Mistakes*, 13–34, 215–20. Together these works demonstrate the faithful transmission of the New Testament text through centuries of copying and preservation.

14. Bauckham, *Jesus and the Eyewitnesses*, 5–9; Ginzburg, *Clues, Myths, and the Historical Method*, 96–125.

The Weight of Evidence
Today and Tomorrow and Yesterday

Of course, today's world is not the only culprit in terms of how we inherit our collective past. This has been happening since man first grasped the idea of comprehension. We have been telling stories, fiction, myth, explanation, since the dawn of time: since we could stare one another in the face and gesture with our eyes what we meant before speech gave shape to intent. Story came first; words only followed.

Think about this: art, cave art to be exact. Before there was a written alphabet, before there were chronicles or epics, there were images scratched in stone, ocher on walls, hands traced in negative against rock. It was story, not in letters but in symbols. Hunters drawn with spears, animals in motion, figures in ritual—the earliest record was not about precision but about meaning, memory, and awe.[15]

From there, myth was born. Oral cycles gave shape to the world, explaining thunder, sea, and harvest. When writing emerged, it did not begin as history in our sense, but as tally and transaction: grain, flocks, debts. Only later did men turn script to song, epic, and annal, attempts to preserve in words what art had first tried to capture in pigment and form. And even then, the line between memory and invention, between chronicle and myth, was porous. Storytelling was always there first; writing was simply a new medium.[16]

It has now come full circle. Where the ancients called them gods, we call them societal policies, injected into character and narrative. Arrian, Plutarch, even Cassius Dio, men we call historians, admitted to "dressing up" accounts to fit the expectations of their age, their audience, and their rulers. Plutarch, beginning his *Life of Theseus*, confesses that "myth must be mingled with history," aiming not for certainty but for plausibility.[17] Arrian, in the preface to his *Anabasis of Alexander*, justifies reshaping Alexander's life into a model narrative, explicitly comparing himself to Xenophon.[18]

---

15. Lewis-Williams, *Mind in the Cave*, 42–45; Eliade, *Myth and Reality*, 1–5. Lewis-Williams shows that Paleolithic cave art functioned as symbolic storytelling—a way to preserve meaning without words. Eliade stresses that myth was the earliest human attempt to order experience, long before writing developed.

16. Goody, *Logic of Writing*, 74–82; Schmandt-Besserat, *Before Writing* 1:120–38; Eliade, *Myth and Reality*, 1–15; Van Seters, *In Search of History*, 12–20, 45–60.

17. Plutarch, *Life of Theseus*, 1.

18. Arrian, *Anabasis*, 2–7.

The Weight of Evidence

Dio is even blunter: "I often insert speeches, sometimes what was said, but more often what ought to have been said."[19]

They were subject to the same three pressures we face now: selection and presentism (choosing what to include based on what flatters the moment), narrative compression (reshaping events until they fit into a story), and market or political incentives (serving empire, pleasing patrons, reinforcing gods or ideals).[20] Some things never change. Only the tactics do; the style and appearance shift, but the mechanism is the same.

Why do these pressures exist at all? Because memory is fragile, and human beings cannot bear to leave it untended. To remember is always to arrange.[21] Events are too many, too vast, too contradictory to preserve whole; the mind itself selects and reshapes before the scribe ever puts ink to papyrus. We do not merely recall, we interpret. And once an interpretation is offered, it competes in the marketplace of memory, where survival belongs not to the truest account, but to the one most useful.[22]

So in the ancient world, myth gave thunder a name, story gave heroes a lineage, and history gave empires their legitimacy. Each pressure arose not by accident but by necessity. Selection and presentism emerge because the past must serve the present, or else it is discarded. Narrative compression arises because the human mind will not hold chaos; it needs shape, arc, and consequence. Market and political incentives surface because memory is never neutral: it is currency, wielded by rulers, poets, priests, and patrons alike.[23]

They also say that history is selective, that only a privileged few had the ability to read, write, and preserve the record, and therefore what survives must have passed through the sieve of importance. And that is true, but we must be careful about what "importance" meant. To us, receipts and ledgers may look like trivial paperwork. To the ancients, they were survival. Clay tablets from Mesopotamia are filled with tallies of grain, lists of flocks,

---

19. Dio, *Roman History* 53.19.

20. Carr, *What Is History?*, 9–12; Rosenstone, *History on Film/Film on History*, 1–15; Nora, "Between Memory and History," 7–24.

21. Halbwachs, *On Collective Memory*, 37–40.

22. Assmann, *Cultural Memory and Early Civilization*, 25–30.

23. Hesiod, *Theogony*, 147–210; Herodotus, *Histories* 1.1; Plutarch, *Life of Theseus* 1; Polybius, *Histories* 1.1–2; Carr, *What Is History?*, 9–12; White, *Metahistory*, ix–xii; Ricoeur, *Time and Narrative* 1:3–9; Nora, "Between Memory and History," 7–24; Assmann, *Cultural Memory and Early Civilization*, 25–30.

records of rations distributed to workers.[24] These were not afterthoughts; they were the backbone of kingship, taxation, and empire. They mattered enough to be pressed into wet clay and baked for posterity because without them armies could not march, temples could not function, and cities could not feed themselves.

By contrast, ordinary lives, the laborer's conversation, the small quarrel between neighbors, the birth of a child outside royal lineage, rarely found their way into the record. Why? Because the record was expensive, laborious, and controlled. Papyrus, parchment, clay tablets, all were scarce and consumed time, money, and trained scribes. The result was inevitable selectivity: extraordinary events, political crises, royal decrees, and monumental battles took precedence, while routine life faded unrecorded.[25]

So when they say "History preserves only the extraordinary," it is not that the ancients ignored receipts and records of grain, they preserved them, but because to them, those were extraordinary. To us, the priorities are reversed: we want cultural texture, individual voices, the ordinary made visible. They wanted survival, legitimacy, and memory of what affected the whole. And so, the historian's hand was guided by necessity as much as by choice.[26]

From Herodotus declaring that he wrote so that "the great deeds of men may not be forgotten," to Polybius insisting that only events of world consequence deserved record, to Tacitus preserving the "memorable deeds" of emperors, ancient historiography openly privileged the extraordinary over the ordinary. Modern scholars such as Moses Finley and Arnaldo Momigliano have observed the same tendency: history was reserved for kings, battles, and statesmen, while the lives of the common and the trivial passed into silence.[27]

---

24. Kramer, *History Begins at Sumer*, 20–23. Kramer notes that the earliest written tablets are largely administrative: tallies of grain, livestock, and rations.

25. Finley, *Ancient History: Evidence and Models*, 12–16. Finley observes that ancient records overwhelmingly privilege elites, political events, and economic necessities, leaving ordinary life largely invisible.

26. Thucydides, *History of the Peloponnesian War* 1.22. Thucydides lays the ancient benchmark: historians should record only what is worthy of remembrance, focusing on the extraordinary rather than the ordinary; Momigliano, *Classical Foundations of Modern Historiography*, 8–10. Momigliano notes that ancient historiography consistently privileged "great men" and political/military events over the lives of common people.

27. Herodotus, *Histories* 1.1; 7.152; 8.144; Polybius, *Histories* 1.1–2; Tacitus, *Annals* 1.1. Across centuries, ancient historians frame their craft as the preservation of greatness: Herodotus writes to prevent the loss of "great and marvellous deeds" (1.1), reaffirming

The Weight of Evidence
Setting the Stage

If history truly spares no thought for the insignificant, then the record of Jesus Christ should never have survived. He was no emperor commanding legions, no king seated in marble halls, no philosopher founding academies. By their logic, He should have been forgotten, a wandering Galilean preacher swallowed by the dust of a restless empire. But the opposite is true.

The kicker is also this: you will often hear, "During the time of Jesus, there were multiple people walking around preaching, claiming to be god." That may be so, but where is their story? Josephus mentions Theudas, Judas the Galilean, and a host of unnamed "impostors" who led followers into the wilderness, but their memory is confined to a line or two.[28] Tacitus recalls messianic uprisings and self-proclaimed prophets, but none with detail beyond their suppression.[29] By contrast, the life of Jesus has left a record unparalleled for any obscure figure of antiquity.[30] So the claim that "others were walking around claiming divinity" is a red herring. It proves the point; it doesn't dismiss it: if many voices clamored for godhood, why is history silent about them yet unrelenting about Him? Why, out of all who could have been forgotten, is Jesus the one name history refused to bury?[31] So I put this to you plainly. "There is more written about Jesus Christ than Alexander the Great, Tiberius Caesar, Cleopatra, Buddha, Confucius, and more."[32]

---

at Thermopylae and Salamis that his duty is to record valor "for remembrance" (7.152; 8.144). Polybius likewise insists history must concern itself with "the greatest and most splendid events ... which embrace almost the whole world" (1.1-2). Tacitus continues the same tradition, pledging to recount deeds "of great importance, done in peace or war" (1.1); Finley, *Ancient History: Evidence and Models*, 12-16; Carr, *What Is History?*, 9-10; Bloch, *Historian's Craft*, 27-31; Momigliano, *Classical Foundations of Modern Historiography*, 8-10. Modern historians echo this tendency: Moses Finley stresses that ancient records overwhelmingly privileged elites and politics; E. H. Carr highlights the historian's selective hand in determining which facts survive; Marc Bloch reflects on how significance shapes preservation; and Arnaldo Momigliano shows how classical historiography canonized the extraordinary while silencing the ordinary.

28. Josephus, *Antiquities* 18.1.1; 20.5.1; *Jewish War* 2.13.4-5.

29. Tacitus, *Histories* 5.9-10; Suetonius, *Life of Vespasian*, 4.

30. Bauckham, *Jesus and the Eyewitnesses*, 5-9; Meier, *Marginal Jew* 1:57-59; Habermas, *Historical Jesus*, 31-38.

31. Sanders, *Historical Figure of Jesus*, 239-42; Wright, *Resurrection of the Son of God*, 28-31.

32. Fox, *Alexander the Great*, 32-33. The earliest surviving narrative of Alexander is written more than three centuries after his death; Grant, *Twelve Caesars*, 59-63. Tiberius's reign is chiefly preserved by Tacitus and Suetonius, both written generations later,

The Weight of Evidence

If He were a myth, a voice without substance, how has His name endured the fire of centuries? Why does it remain etched in human memory with more weight than kings and conquerors, philosophers and sages? I thought history had no time for what was not deemed important. And yet, the testimony of Jesus of Nazareth eclipses them all.[33] And this is the crux. Jesus defies the same pressures that plague the rest of our giants.

- **Selection and presentism.** By all logic, He should have been forgotten. He held no office, commanded no legions, left behind no monuments. Rome had little reason to preserve Him, and Jerusalem every reason to erase Him. And yet, His name appears in Josephus, a Jew writing for Roman audiences, and in Tacitus, a Roman senator hostile to the movement itself.[34] These notices are brief, even dismissive, but they prove the point: memory survived where none had motive to keep it alive.

- **Narrative compression.** Alexander became the conqueror, Caesar the martyr of empire, Socrates the voice of philosophy. Their stories were pared and shaped until each fit a type. Jesus resists this treatment. His teachings are too abrasive, His death too shameful, His resurrection too disruptive to collapse into parable. The Gospels preserve a figure who does not conform to expectation but fractures it.[35]

- **Market and political incentives.** Histories were written to please patrons, flatter empires, or reinforce gods. The Gospels came from persecuted communities with nothing to gain but suffering. They had

---

with significant gaps; Schiff, *Cleopatra*, 4–6. Cleopatra's memory comes filtered through Roman propaganda, not abundant Egyptian records; Armstrong, *Buddha*, xiii–xv. Buddha's life is reconstructed from traditions centuries removed from his time; Nylan, *Five "Confucian" Classics*, 1–3. Confucius's teachings come to us not in contemporary transcripts but in records assembled long after his death; Habermas, *Historical Jesus*, 28–33. In contrast, the historical attestation for Jesus begins within a generation of His death and multiplies across independent sources.

33. Bauckham, *Jesus and the Eyewitnesses*, 5–9. Bauckham argues the Gospels are rooted in direct eyewitness testimony, not mythic invention; Keener, *Historical Jesus of the Gospels*, 185–90. Keener stresses the unparalleled multiplicity of Gospel sources compared to other ancient figures; Bruce, *New Testament Documents*, 16–17. Bruce notes that the New Testament documents stand far closer to their events than most sources for classical history.

34. Josephus, *Antiquities* 18.3.3; Tacitus, *Annals* 15.44.

35. Bauckham, *Jesus and the Eyewitnesses*, 7–12; Wright, *Resurrection of the Son of God*, 28–31.

no empire to serve, no audience to impress, no patron to reward them. Yet they carried His story anyway, copying and spreading it at the cost of their lives.[36] What incentive explains this transmission? None but conviction that it was true.

Where the pressures of history explain why most voices are lost or distorted, they cannot explain why the voice of Jesus remains. His testimony runs against the current of every filter that should have erased Him. The record should not exist, yet it does, and it has endured the fire of centuries. Some turn away from this not because the evidence is thin, but because it is too much. Belief in Alexander asks nothing of you; belief in Jesus asks everything. That, perhaps, is the only distinction that keeps Him shelved under "theology" instead of "history." For to concede His reality is to face His words, His death, and the claim of His rising, and that demands more than assent to facts. It demands a reckoning.

Now history stands in the dock. Empires rise from their graves, their crowns dulled with dust. Philosophers shuffle their scrolls. Kings await their summons, thrones trembling beneath them. And at the center stands one man, the Nazarene. To judge Him is to judge the world. Yet judgment requires order. Evidence must be weighed on scales strong enough to bear the weight of eternity. There can be no shifting measures, no private definitions, no sleight of hand. The law is set. Let us use the Five Pillars of Historical Confidence to weigh not only Jesus, but the giants of history beside Him.

From the moment man painted on cave walls, we have chosen what to preserve. Ocher handprints, animals in motion, hunting scenes, these were not decoration but meaning pressed into stone. When writing emerged, the first words were not poetry but receipts: grain tallies, flocks, debts, and rations. To us, such fragments appear mundane. To the ancients, they were vital. They preserved order, sustained armies, and held empires together.[37] This is the paradox: what survives is not an even mirror of the past, but what a society could not afford to lose. Daily lives went unrecorded while ledgers of barley endured. Ordinary quarrels vanished while decrees of kings were etched in bronze. The written word was costly, and so it was reserved for the extraordinary, not in our sense of fascination, but in their sense of survival.[38]

---

36. Metzger and Ehrman, *Text of the New Testament*, 52–58; Gurry and Hixson, *Myths and Mistakes*, 13–34.

37. Kramer, *History Begins at Sumer*, 20–23.

38. Finley, *Ancient History: Evidence and Models*, 12–16.

The Weight of Evidence

So when we look back, we are not seeing "all that happened," but only what passed through this sieve of importance. We inherit not the voices of the many, but the choices of the few, scribes, rulers, storytellers, and historians who decided what mattered. And yet, despite this ruthless selectivity, the name of Jesus of Nazareth broke through the sieve. His words were preserved with more urgency than decrees of emperors, His deeds remembered in more detail than the triumphs of kings. By every logic of ancient recordkeeping, He should have vanished. Instead, His voice endured. And the question that follows is unavoidable: why?

The same pressures that warped the record of giants, selection and presentism, narrative compression, political and market incentives should have consigned Him to silence.[39] They bent kings into symbols, philosophers into parables, and conquerors into myths. But they could not erase Him. The planks of memory that splinter under the weight of every other life still hold beneath His name. Here, at last, the trial begins. The law is set. The evidence must be tested. And we will use the Five Pillars of Historical Confidence to weigh not only Jesus, but the giants of history beside Him.

---

39. Carr, *What Is History?*, 9–12; Rosenstone, *History on Film/Film on History*, 1–15; Nora, "Between Memory and History," 7–24.

PART I

Legends Without Witnesses

BEFORE THE NAZARENE STANDS at the gate, we must first examine the giants, those whose shadows stretched across continents, yet whose voices were captured only by others, long after the dust had settled. These are the kings and sages, the conquerors and mystics. Each revered. Each remembered. Yet none directly heard. Their legacy, as we shall see, stands not on the solidity of firsthand testimony, but on layers of recollection, revision, and reinterpretation.

1. Alexander—known by echoes and myth-makers.[1]
2. Hannibal—remembered not by Carthage, but by his enemies.[2]
3. Cleopatra—her story retold through the lust and politics of Rome.[3]
4. Buddha—enshrined in silence for centuries before pen touched page.[4]
5. Confucius—a philosopher reconstructed by students and successors.[5]

This section is not an attack on their existence. It is a confrontation of how little we truly know.[6] Before Christ is held to the flame, let us see how the world's icons fare when judged by the same standard.

   1. Arrian, *Anabasis* 1.1; Plutarch, *Alexander* 1; Bosworth, *Alexander and the East*, 1.
   2. Polybius, *Histories* 3; Livy, *Ab Urbe Condita* 21–30.
   3. Plutarch, *Antony* 1; Dio, *Roman History* 51; Roller, *Cleopatra*, 1.
   4. Gethin, *Foundations of Buddhism*, 1.
   5. Creel, *Confucius*, 1; Brooks and Brooks, *Original Analects*, 1; Makeham, *Lost Soul*, 1–2.
   6. Bauckham, *Jesus and the Eyewitnesses*, 1; Ehrman, *Jesus*, 1.

Alexander the Great
The King of Echoes

ALEXANDER III OF MACEDON (356–323 BC), better known as Alexander the Great, was king of Macedonia, pupil of Aristotle, and commander of one of the most ambitious military campaigns in recorded history. In just over a decade, he overthrew the Persian Empire, marched his armies from Greece to the edges of India, and founded cities that still bear his name. His image was struck on coins, carved in marble, and woven into the political mythology of kings for centuries after his death. Yet much of what survives about Alexander comes not from his own hand, nor from those who marched beside him, but from writers working centuries later. The Alexander we know is shaped by their choices by what they preserved, what they ignored, and what they invented. Before we can decide who Alexander was, we must first ask: who told his story, when did they tell it, and why did they want us to believe it?

Arrian: Face Behind the Legend

The man most responsible for shaping the image of Alexander the Great lived nearly four centuries after Alexander's death. Lucius Flavius Arrianus, remembered simply as Arrian, was a Greek from Nicomedia and a Roman citizen. He wrote in the early second century AD during the reign of Emperor Hadrian. His *Anabasis of Alexander* is often treated as the most authoritative account, yet it is not a biography in the modern sense. It is a retrospective reconstruction drawn from earlier narratives, composed at a time when Alexander had already passed from living memory into legend.[1]

---

1. Arrian, *Anabasis* 1.1.1–2

By contrast, the earliest accounts of Jesus were written within the living memory of those who knew Him, preserving voices that had not yet faded into legend.[2]

Something else of note is that Arrian was not a professional historian in the modern sense, but a statesman, soldier, and philosopher. He served as consul in Rome and later governed the province of Cappadocia. He was a student of the Stoic philosopher Epictetus,[3] whose teachings he recorded and preserved. His life and career were steeped in both Greek cultural heritage and Roman political order, giving him a unique vantage point from which to write about a pan-Hellenic conqueror like Alexander. He admired military discipline, valued moral character, and approached history with an eye for leadership and strategy.[4] When he turned to Alexander, he claimed his aim was to tell the truth as it could best be recovered, and for that, he chose to rely on two earlier accounts that he considered the most reliable.

The first of Arrian's two principal sources was Ptolemy I Soter, one of Alexander's generals and later king of Egypt. Ptolemy fought alongside Alexander in many of his campaigns and was entrusted with his body after death, an act heavy with political symbolism.[5] As ruler, he secured Egypt's borders, founded the city of Alexandria, and established the Ptolemaic dynasty that would last nearly three centuries. Ptolemy wrote his own history of Alexander's campaigns, a work Arrian repeatedly praises for its reliability.[6] Yet no copy of Ptolemy's text survives. It has been erased by time, preserved only in fragments quoted by later authors. What we know of it comes entirely through Arrian's retelling. This loss leaves us in a precarious position: the "most reliable" source on Alexander is one we cannot read, verify, or weigh for bias. The opposite is true for the Gospels, whose original witnesses are lost to time, yet whose words have survived in thousands of early manuscripts.[7]

---

2. Bauckham, *Jesus and the Eyewitnesses*, 7–11; Blomberg, *Historical Reliability of the Gospels*, 41–42.

3. Epictetus (c. AD 55–135) was a Greek Stoic philosopher, born a slave in the Roman Empire, whose teachings, preserved in the *Discourses* and *Enchiridion*, emphasized virtue, self-control, and aligning one's will with nature.

4. Arrian, *Anabasis* 1.8–12, 1.13–17.

5. Diodorus, *Library of History* 18.27–28, on the elaborate funeral carriage and procession for Alexander's body which Ptolemy intercepted and took to Egypt.

6. Arrian, *Anabasis* 1.1.2.

7. Metzger and Ehrman, *Text of the New Testament*, 51–53; Comfort and Barrett, *Text of the Earliest New Testament*, 17–19.

ALEXANDER THE GREAT

As king, Ptolemy had every incentive to portray Alexander not merely as a conqueror but as a god. His legitimacy as ruler rested on inheriting Alexander's divine aura. In Egypt, Ptolemy didn't just govern, he canonized. He enshrined Alexander in temples, issued decrees proclaiming his divinity, and began the Great Library of Alexandria as a monument to Hellenistic culture. For Ptolemy, Alexander's myth was inseparable from his own authority. To diminish the conqueror was to undermine the throne. Likewise, in the Roman world, to deny Jesus's resurrection was to threaten the very foundation of the Christian movement, and yet its earliest followers preserved it at the cost of their lives, not their thrones.[8]

Aristobulus is even murkier: he exists only because Arrian said he did. He served under Alexander, likely as an engineer or architect, and was once tasked with restoring the tomb of Cyrus the Great in Pasargadae.[9] He never commanded armies, never shaped imperial policy. His account, now lost, survives only in fragments quoted by later authors, especially Arrian[10] and Plutarch.[11] What emerges is a gentler storyteller: one who downplayed Alexander's excesses, softened his faults, and left us with a portrait polished by admiration.

Arrian is often hailed as the "best" source for Alexander's life, yet he wrote nearly four centuries after the events he describes. His work depends on earlier histories, chiefly those of Ptolemy and Aristobulus, which have not survived. What we have, then, is Arrian's selection of their narratives, filtered through his own judgment, literary aims, and the reverence of his age. No corroborating manuscripts of these eyewitness accounts exist; no fragment allows us to test his fidelity to them. In the case of Jesus, multiple eyewitness-based accounts still survive in independent form, allowing modern historians to test their harmony and divergence.[12]

We have to remember and consider that by the time Arrian wrote, the men who had marched with Alexander were not only dead, they had been dead for centuries. The memories had passed through generations of retelling, translation, and political repackaging. His chosen sources could not be cross-examined; their works no longer existed. All that remained

---

8. Habermas and Licona, *Case for the Resurrection of Jesus*, 54–56; Hurtado, *Lord Jesus Christ*, 99–103.
9. Arrian, *Anabasis* 6.29.7–11.
10. Arrian, *Anabasis* 1.1.2.
11. Plutarch, *Alexander* 35.3.
12. Licona, *Resurrection of Jesus*, 202–6; Bauckham, *Jesus and the Eyewitnesses*, 124–47.

was Arrian's assurance of their reliability. To put it into perspective, Arrian writing about Alexander is like someone in the year 2400 publishing the definitive biography of George Washington, claiming to use lost personal diaries and eyewitness accounts, but refusing to show a single page. And yet we teach it as fact. For us, Arrian remains the number-one source, second only to Plutarch, whom we will meet in a moment. If the same evidentiary standard were applied to Jesus, whose life is recorded in far earlier and more numerous sources, the classroom would look very different.[13] Perhaps then, any of us could recite the Sermon on the Mount by heart, if that classroom looked different.

The Apologists for Arrian

Even among skeptics who scrutinize every line of the Bible, Arrian receives an unusual reverence. His defenders tend to repeat three predictable arguments.

First: "Arrian used good sources, both Ptolemy and Aristobulus." But those sources are gone.[14] What we have is Arrian's claim that he used them. This is hearsay by any historical standard, and you cannot cross-examine a ghost. Even if Ptolemy's writings survived, they would be steeped in bias. He was not a detached historian; he was an heir to Alexander's mythos, a ruler whose political authority and divine legitimacy depended on portraying Alexander as a man touched by the gods.[15]

Second: "But Arrian was a soldier. He understood warfare." Military service does not grant access to the past. Arrian lived centuries after Alexander. His own experience may have helped him narrate tactics, but it could not verify motives, speeches, or truth. In fact, his Roman soldier's lens likely pushed him toward glorification, because Rome celebrated conquest, heroic generals, and the ideal of the "just war."

Third: "He wrote with a historian's eye, measured, calm, unsensational." But Arrian patterned his *Anabasis* on Xenophon's work of the same name, not as a sterile chronicle, but as a heroic memoir in which the author himself is cast as noble leader, moral exemplar, and warrior-philosopher.[16]

---

13. Bruce, *New Testament Documents*, 16–20; Sherwin-White, *Roman Society*, 187–88.
14. Arrian, *Anabasis* 1.1.
15. Arrian, *Anabasis* 1.1; Polybius, *Histories* 6.350–55.
16. Arrian, *Anabasis* 1.1–2; Xenophon, *Anabasis* 2.2–7.

Arrian was not reconstructing a man; he was resurrecting a myth, following a literary blueprint designed to inspire, not to document.

Voices in the Void

Arrian was not alone. Behind the constructed image of Alexander stands a small pantheon of Roman and post-Hellenic writers, none of whom knew him, and none of whom seemed concerned by that absence. Collectively, they functioned less as historians than as architects of legend. Let's consider again the earliest accounts of Jesus, penned within living memory of His ministry, driven more by the preservation of truth than the construction of legend.[17] The caliber and motive of the Gospel writers stand in stark contrast to those crafting the image of Alexander.

Plutarch (AD 46–119) is one of the most frequently cited sources for Alexander's life, yet his *Life of Alexander* was never intended as a factual chronicle. It belongs to his *Parallel Lives* series, a collection of paired biographies meant to draw moral comparisons between Greek and Roman figures, in this case Alexander and Julius Caesar. Plutarch's stated aim is not to catalog every event, but to capture "the signs of a man's soul," much as a painter captures the eyes and expression rather than every feature of the body.[18] This guiding principle shapes the entire work: campaigns are compressed, chronology is fluid, and stories of uncertain origin are included if they serve the moral portrait he is painting.

A philosopher and priest at Delphi, Plutarch viewed history as a tool for moral instruction. He did not sift events for forensic precision; he arranged them to reflect the virtues, or cautionary vices, he wished his readers to see. In his pages, Alexander is as much a vehicle for reflection on ambition, leadership, and self-control as he is a historical figure. Such shaping is not inherently a flaw if one reads it as moral literature. But the problem lies in how the work is received: modern readers often inherit Plutarch as if he were a reporter on the ground when in fact he was a moralist writing four centuries after Alexander's death. Without that context, the "biography" risks being taken for something it was never meant to be: direct historical testimony.[19] Again, by contrast, the Gospels were written within the same

17. Bauckham, *Jesus and the Eyewitnesses*, 7–11; Blomberg, *Historical Reliability of the Gospels*, 41–42.

18. Arrian, *Anabasis* 1.2–3.

19. Plutarch, *Alexander* 1.2–3.

PART I. LEGENDS WITHOUT WITNESSES

generation as the events they record, some by those who claimed to have walked with Him.[20]

Quintus Curtius Rufus (first century AD) produced his *Histories of Alexander*, a narrative rich in invented speeches, set-piece moral dilemmas, and vivid stagecraft. These are not incidental embellishments; they are the structural pillars of his work. Ancient readers expected speeches to reveal character and moral truth, but Curtius pushes them to the foreground, often allowing them to carry the historical moment more than verifiable events. His Alexander addresses troops with rhetorical flourishes unlikely to be verbatim, responds to crises with perfectly timed moral reflections, and moves through scenes described with the pacing and imagery of a Roman epic. Such techniques would have resonated in the imperial court, reflecting the virtues Rome wished to see in its leaders, decisive courage, magnanimity toward the defeated, and a readiness to moralize from victory.[21]

This matters because it shifts the purpose of the account. Curtius is not acting as an investigator assembling evidence from contemporaries; he is a Roman-era author shaping Alexander into a political and moral exemplar for his own time. The result is not a direct record of events but a mediated reconstruction, filtered through centuries of cultural expectations, literary convention, and the author's own moral agenda. What survives in his pages are not unaltered facts, but episodes retold to fit the Roman idea of what greatness should look like. Now by comparison, in the case of Jesus, the accounts emerge not after centuries of reshaping, but amid the very culture that sought to suppress them.[22]

When history goes unchallenged, we get things like Oliver Stone's 2004 epic *Alexander*, with Colin Farrell striding through scenes built not on verified history, but on Plutarch's moral theater and Arrian's polished legend. Alexander's battlefield speeches are lifted in tone and structure from Plutarch's idealized orations. His clemency toward Darius's family is played as saintly restraint and mirrors Arrian's moral framing, not the contested accounts. Even his grand vision of a "world united" comes straight from posthumous hero-crafting, not contemporary record. Marketed as historical drama, it was philosophy dressed as fact, propaganda sold as history.

20. Blomberg, *Historical Reliability of the Gospels*, 41–42; Bauckham, *Jesus and the Eyewitnesses*, 124–47.

21. Rufus, *Histories of Alexander* 3.9–10, 3.12.

22. Hurtado, *Lord Jesus Christ*, 99–103; Habermas and Licona, *Case for the Resurrection of Jesus*, 54–56.

What reached the screen was not Alexander as he lived, but Alexander as two millennia of storytellers needed him to be.[23] It is telling that Jesus's earliest followers preserved not the image the world wanted, but the message the world resisted, and later paid the ultimate price for doing so.[24]

Diodorus Siculus (first century BC) compiled his *Bibliotheca Historica* as a sweeping universal history, but when it came to Alexander, his foundation was Cleitarchus, a now-lost writer notorious even in antiquity for embellishment. Cleitarchus's Alexander was a creature of drama: banquet excesses painted in lurid detail, executions dripping with cruelty, and journeys into strange lands populated with fantastical peoples. Ancient critics accused him of privileging sensation over accuracy, crafting a version of Alexander's life more suited to entertain than to inform. Diodorus did not correct or temper these narratives; he transmitted them wholesale, lending them the unearned weight of inclusion in a "history." The result is not a vetted record of events, but an inheritance of unexamined spectacle, a vivid portrait with no guarantee of truth, preserved because it captured imaginations rather than because it captured reality.[25] Now, the Gospel portraits, by contrast, invite verification, rooted in public events and places where the earliest hearers could confirm or deny them.[26] That is the ultimate test: to proclaim such things within the lifetime of eyewitnesses, under the gaze of those ready to expose a lie, and yet to find the record corroborated not only by followers, but even by enemies.

What Did Rome Gain from Alexander?

Rome didn't record Alexander's myth—they absorbed it. By the time Arrian and Plutarch were writing, Rome wasn't just expanding its borders; it was building a theology of power. Alexander became the prototype: the warrior king, the divine ruler, the man-god.[27] He laid the foundation for emperor worship. If Alexander could be called the son of Jupiter, why

---

23. *Alexander*, directed by Oliver Stone (2004; Warner Bros. Pictures), drawing on Plutarch, *Alexander* 21–24; Arrian, *Anabasis* 2.11–14.

24. Bauckham, *Jesus and the Eyewitnesses*, 360–62; Wright, *Resurrection of the Son of God*, 28–31.

25. Siculus, *Library of History* 17.1–2; Arrian, *Anabasis* 1.1 (on Cleitarchus); Bosworth, *Alexander and the East*, 1.

26. Acts 26:26; Bruce, *New Testament Documents*, 31–33.

27. Rufus, *Histories of Alexander* 4.7.30–31.

not Caesar? His legend justified the imperial cult. By contrast, the earliest claims of Jesus as the Son of God did not arise from imperial decree or political necessity, but from the testimony of those who claimed to have seen Him alive after His execution, a claim made in defiance of both Rome and the temple authorities.[28] The practice of calling kings gods and gods kings made such rulers seem historical, empire feel like destiny, and set the standard for a new breed of god-king.

Additionally, as a "god-king," Alexander handed Rome a moral disguise for conquest: he had "civilized" the East, so Rome claimed the same mandate, and the same lineage. His myth became a mirror, reflecting the image of imperial domination draped in virtue, thanks to those who wrote him into that role and gave him that soul through the pen. Strip away the glory, and Alexander is a warlord. But to Rome, he was something else: a blueprint for power wrapped in divinity. Strip away the glory from the Gospels, and the divinity of Jesus does not collapse into conquest—it deepens into sacrifice, the very opposite of Rome's blueprint for power.[29]

Coins Are Not Testimonies

Skeptics might argue, "We have coins, busts, and mosaics, therefore Alexander must have existed!" I do not want to caricature the position, but that is often how the argument is framed. And yes, we do have such artifacts. But coins are not witnesses. They do not tell us who struck them, why they were minted, or whether the face stamped upon them bears any resemblance to the man himself. Coins are instruments of power, not impartial records. A ruler's image on a coin is a proclamation: "I reign here." It is branding. It is propaganda.

Alexander's coinage makes the point clearly. Many were minted long after his death, in cities he never set foot in, by successors and imitators eager to borrow his image.[30] Some depict him with the horns of Zeus-Ammon, a divine claim, not a biographical fact. Others present an idealized, ageless figure, crafted to make him appear as much god as man. These designs told subjects what to believe about their ruler, not what the ruler actually looked like. Likewise, the earliest Christian proclamation did not rest on symbols

---

28. Acts 2:32; Habermas and Licona, *Case for the Resurrection of Jesus*, 54–56.
29. Phil 2:5–11; Wright, *Resurrection of the Son of God*, 28–31.
30. Price, *Coinage in the Name of Alexander*, 206.

or stylized images, but on the testimony of those who claimed to have seen, touched, and eaten with Jesus after His death.[31]

Even coins from a ruler's own lifetime can mislead. Roman emperors struck coins proclaiming themselves "Restorer of Freedom" while actively crushing dissent. Cities issued coins bearing the likeness of gods and heroes no one believed to have walked the earth—Athena, Heracles, and mythic kings—yet no one claims those coins are proof of their historical existence. A coin proves that a mint was active and a design selected. It proves an image was circulated. But it cannot tell us what truly happened, who a man truly was, or whether the story stamped on the metal matched the world outside it. The ancients immortalized rulers, myths, monsters, and ideals alike, and the coin press made no distinction between them. The New Testament writers, by contrast, made sharp distinctions between myth and history, grounding their message in named witnesses and public events open to scrutiny.[32]

This is why comparing Alexander's coins to George Washington's face on the one-dollar bill is misleading. Of course, I am not suggesting Washington is a myth simply because his portrait appears on our currency. The difference is that, in his case, we have battlefield orders in his own hand, personal correspondence, hostile accounts from enemies, and preserved family records, evidence that strikes each note of the Five Pillars of Historical Confidence I outlined at the beginning of this book. Washington is not known by an image; he is known by a chorus of living voices preserved in ink and record. The same pillars stand beneath the life of Jesus, and in His case, the surviving evidence is both earlier and more abundant than for most ancient figures, including Alexander.[33]

The Scrolls and the Silence

Let's weigh their legacies, not merely in number, but in proximity, preservation, and credibility. For Alexander, our three most substantial narrative sources, Arrian, Plutarch, and Quintus Curtius Rufus, stand centuries removed from the man himself. Arrian and Plutarch were writing more than four hundred years after his death; Curtius Rufus, whose exact date is uncertain, is generally placed in the first century AD, still three centuries

---

31. John 1:1–3; Luke 24:36–43; Bauckham, *Jesus and the Eyewitnesses*, 7–11.

32. 2 Pet 1:16; Acts 26:26; Bruce, *New Testament Documents*, 31–33.

33. Blomberg, *Historical Reliability of the Gospels*, 41–42; Habermas and Licona, *Case for the Resurrection of Jesus*, 128–31.

after the events.[34] By contrast, the earliest Gospel was circulating within a single generation of Jesus's death, with multiple accounts emerging while hostile witnesses could still challenge them.[35]

The surviving manuscripts push the gap even further. For Arrian and Plutarch, the earliest complete copies do not appear until the tenth or eleventh century;[36] for Curtius Rufus, the earliest is from the ninth century.[37] Their own sources, eyewitness accounts such as Ptolemy's and Aristobulus's histories, are gone. The chain of custody is thin, fragmented, and largely untraceable. What we hold today is a literary echo, passed hand to hand across centuries, untethered from the original voice. The New Testament writings, however, remain tethered to named apostles and early disciples, preserved in a manuscript tradition beginning within decades, not centuries, of the events.[38]

If we were to truly consider the idea of "telephone" for any case, it would be for this one; truly, there is no confident preservation of Alexander, no consistent copying. We don't even have enemy testimony of him, but we do have some relics and artifacts, but as we discussed, that alone doesn't mean anything, unless you are willing to entertain Horus in a literal sense. Alexander existed, but probably not in the same sense that we know him or believe him to have. The case for Jesus is altogether different: it does not rest on relics or symbols, but on a preserved record of words and deeds, corroborated in part even by unfriendly sources.[39]

The Ghost of Echoes and the Man of Thorns

Alexander conquered the world, but left no voice. No letters. No journals. No final reflections.[40] Even the moment of his death is shrouded in mystery. Fever? Poison? Exhaustion? No one knows. The accounts are late, contradictory, and speculative, written by men centuries removed, filling the void with whatever ending suited their narrative. Alexander left no certainty, no closure.

---

34. Rufus, *Histories of Alexander* 1.1.

35. Blomberg, *Historical Reliability of the Gospels*, 41–42; Bauckham, *Jesus and the Eyewitnesses*, 124–47.

36. Arrian, *Anabasis* 1.1–2; Bosworth, *Commentary on Arrian* 1:29–30.

37. Rufus, *Histories of Alexander* 1.1; Hamilton, *Alexander the Great*, 24–26.

38. Metzger and Ehrman, *Text of the New Testament*, 51–53; Comfort and Barrett, *Text of the Earliest New Testament*, 17–19.

39. Josephus, *Antiquities* 18.3.3; Tacitus, *Annals* 15.44.

40. Arrian, *Anabasis* xv–xvi; Plutarch, *Alexander* 1.1.

Alexander the Great

In that silence, legend found its loudest echo. Only what others claimed he said, written centuries later, filtered through admiration, ambition, and the imperial pride of men who wanted to be gods. He became the prototype of divine kingship, the idol of those who crave power dressed as virtue.[41] But no god who became man ever looked like him. He scattered cities like stones behind a war chariot, building an empire of roads, statues, and fear. When the dust settled, there was no soul left, only silence, filled by those who needed him to be more than he was. His story grew louder only after he fell silent. Strip away the marble and the myth, and Alexander is armor without a man. This brings us to the comparison.

Alexander the Great cut the world with a sword, bent nations to his will, and left cities in his image. His armies carved borders into stone, his face stamped coins, his name claimed continents. Yet when death came, his empire splintered in his absence; his glory depended on those who could keep it breathing. Jesus Christ of Nazareth, by contrast, raised no sword, ruled no nation, and penned no manifesto. He died with no army, no coin bearing His name, and no borders drawn in His honor. His followers seized no thrones and carved no provinces.[42] They were hunted, scattered, and martyred, yet proclaimed His resurrection with a conviction that reshaped the conscience of the world.

Where Alexander's kingdom spread by conquest, Christ's spread by confession; where his edicts were enforced by spears, Christ's commands were sealed in wounds.[43] Alexander was shaped by the ambitions of others; Jesus still shapes the souls of others.[44] The words of the Macedonian are carved in stone; the words of the Nazarene are carved in conscience. It is not Alexander's name the broken cry in the dark, nor his decrees whispered at bedsides, shouted in foxholes, or wept in prison cells. His life did not fracture time in two. Alexander is the king of echoes, his glory loud, his truth faint. Christ is the voice behind the veil, quiet, piercing, eternal.

From a historian's perspective, the gap is striking. The Gospel of Mark was composed within thirty to forty years of Jesus's death.[45] Luke and John followed within the same generation. We possess P52, a fragment of John's

---

41. Suetonius, *Divus Julius* 88–89; *Augustus* 52; *Tiberius* 26.

42. Eusebius, *Church History* 37–39, 93–95; Pliny, *Letters* 10.96–97.

43. Habermas and Licona, *Case for the Resurrection of Jesus*, 128–31; Wright, *Resurrection of the Son of God*, 33–34.

44. Blomberg, *Historical Reliability of the Gospels*, 41–42.

45. Blomberg, *Historical Reliability of the Gospels*, 41–42.

PART I. LEGENDS WITHOUT WITNESSES

Gospel dated to around AD 125, barely one lifetime removed from the events themselves.[46] Complete codices such as Vaticanus and Sinaiticus, produced in the fourth century, still stand hundreds of years closer to their subject than anything written about Alexander.[47] The scale is equally unmatched: over five thousand surviving Greek manuscripts of the New Testament, copied across centuries and continents, with remarkable textual stability.[48] This is not merely a difference in quantity; it is a difference in historical integrity.

One legacy is a whisper, stitched together long after the dust had settled. The other is a witness preserved while the blood of the eyewitnesses was still warm. Critics often object that the Gospels are "biased" because they were written by believers. True. Yet nearly every ancient biography was written by admirers, disciples, descendants, or political successors. Imagine defending Luke with the same logic often used for Arrian: He claimed to use eyewitnesses; he was educated, careful, and detail-oriented; his tone was measured, not exaggerated.[49]

Would skeptics accept that? Hardly. They would demand original manuscripts, independent corroboration, hostile testimony, and Archeological support, and rightly so, because that is what historical integrity demands. Yet Arrian, writing four centuries after the events, quoting lost sources, and glorifying a warlord-turned-demigod, is rarely challenged. He is enshrined as "the most trustworthy source" without the same scrutiny reserved for the Gospels.[50] Arrian receives a free pass. Why? Because Alexander asks only for admiration, not surrender. His story ends on the battlefield, not at the cross.

---

46. P52 manuscript, ca. AD 125; Habermas and Licona, *Case for the Resurrection of Jesus*, 225.

47. Codex Vaticanus and Codex Sinaiticus (ca. AD 325–60); Bauckham, *Jesus and the Eyewitnesses*, 379–80.

48. Habermas and Licona, *Case for the Resurrection of Jesus*, 222; Wright, *Resurrection of the Son of God*, 33–34.

49. Blomberg, *Historical Reliability of the Gospels*, 155–60; Bauckham, *Jesus and the Eyewitnesses*, 93–132.

50. Arrian, *Anabasis* 1.1; Meier, *Marginal Jew* 1:167–71.

Hannibal Barca
Rome's Phantom Enemy

HANNIBAL BARCA WAS BORN in 247 BC and died sometime between 183 and 181 BC. He is remembered as the Carthaginian general who brought the Roman Republic to the brink of destruction during the Second Punic War. His campaigns, marked by bold strategy and relentless pursuit of advantage, reshaped the military and political landscape of the ancient Mediterranean.[1] He famously crossed the Alps with war elephants and dealt Rome crushing defeats at Trebia, Lake Trasimene, and Cannae, engagements that left the Republic reeling. His name has since become a symbol of defiance against imperial power, and his battlefield maneuvers remain case studies in modern military academies. The record reads like legend, even monumental. It is the kind of martial legacy often set alongside Alexander or Caesar. By contrast, the legacy of Jesus is not measured in battlefields taken or armies commanded, but in lives transformed, a legacy without a single military campaign, yet spread farther than any empire.[2] Here the historical image fractures: the Hannibal we know, the figure fixed in textbooks and documentaries, is a Roman construction. In the case of Jesus, the earliest accounts are not written by His enemies, but by those who claimed to have known Jesus, though His enemies left their own unwilling acknowledgments.[3] Every surviving account is drawn from his enemies. Not a single work from Hannibal's own hand remains, and no Carthaginian state archives have

---

1. Polybius, *Histories* 3.5; Livy, *Ab Urbe Condita* 21.1.1–21.1.4; Hoyos, *Hannibal*, 3.
2. Acts 1:8; Wright, *Resurrection of the Son of God*, 33–34.
3. Josephus, *Antiquities* 18.3.3; Tacitus, *Annals* 15.44.

PART I. LEGENDS WITHOUT WITNESSES

survived. The man who nearly brought the Republic to collapse endures only through the voices of those who labored to destroy him.[4]

The Silence of the Burned Library

The loss of Hannibal's own voice is inseparable from the fate of his city. Carthage did not merely lose a war; it was expunged from existence. In 146 BC, at the conclusion of the Third Punic War, Rome did not settle for victory but demanded eradication.[5] When the city fell, Roman forces razed it to its foundations, burning buildings, toppling monuments, and slaughtering inhabitants. Survivors were sold into slavery. What could not be seized was buried or destroyed. Ancient tradition holds that the soil was salted, a symbolic act to ensure the city would never rise again,[6] though this detail remains debated among historians. This was not ordinary conquest. It was an attempt at sterilization, a cultural erasure. Now, again, if we look at Jesus, attempts to erase His name in the first century, from suppressing His followers to forbidding their teaching, only seemed to amplify the spread of His message.[7]

Among the ruins perished Carthage's intellectual life. Its libraries, reputed to rival those of Alexandria, were plundered or reduced to ash. Scrolls vanished; archives disappeared; the language, laws, and literature of a civilization were consumed in flame. Now, the earliest Christian writings, however, began circulating within decades of the events, copied and carried across languages and borders faster than any empire could stamp them out.[8] The Carthaginian voice was not merely lost, it was deliberately silenced. What survived was filtered through Roman hands, selected to serve Roman purposes. A handful of agricultural treatises, most notably the work of Mago, were reportedly preserved and passed to Numidian allies,[9] but nothing substantial on Carthaginian religion, philosophy, or history remained.

---

4. Polybius, *Histories* 3.8; Livy, *Ab Urbe Condita* 21.5–6, 21.11.

5. Polybius, *Histories* 3.5–6; Livy, *Ab Urbe Condita* 21.1.1–5.

6. Polybius, *Histories* 3.5–6; Livy, *Ab Urbe Condita* 21.1.1–5; Appian, *Punic Wars*, 130–35.

7. Acts 4:17–20; Acts 8:1–4; Tertullian, *Apology*, 50.

8. Metzger and Ehrman, *Text of the New Testament*, 51–53; Comfort and Barrett, *Text of the Earliest New Testament*, 17–19.

9. Columella, *De Re Rustica* 1. Refers to Mago's agricultural treatise as preserved in Roman knowledge; no Punic originals survive.

In the historical record, this is the equivalent of executing a man and forbidding any eulogy, even from his family. The absence of Hannibal's own writings is not a mystery but a consequence of deliberate policy. Rome controlled the ashes and authored the aftermath. It is no surprise, then, that Hannibal's legacy is preserved in Latin rather than Punic, that he is remembered not as a son of Carthage, but as a figure conjured in the words of his adversaries. His voice did not survive. Only his shadow did. A final contrast here is that Jesus is remembered in the words of His followers, yet His life and death are also attested, however grudgingly, by the records of His adversaries.[10]

Polybius: A Captive Historian

Let's begin with Polybius. Born around 200 BC and dying in 118 BC, he was a Greek historian, politician, and most significantly a hostage-turned-ally of Rome.[11] The principal ancient voice we rely on for Hannibal's life once belonged to a man held captive by the very empire Hannibal sought to destroy.[12] From a bibliographical perspective, this alone should give the reader pause. When the principal witness for a subject is both temporally removed and politically aligned with the subject's enemies, the evidentiary ground becomes uneven. The earliest accounts of Jesus, however, come from within His own movement, with their claims preserved alongside the reluctant acknowledgments of hostile sources, giving us both sides of the field.[13] For Polybius, it does not automatically disqualify the account, but it demands a cautious reading, one that distinguishes between what Polybius reports, what his Roman patrons might have wanted preserved, and what has been irretrievably lost in the absence of a Carthaginian counter-voice.[14]

Polybius was taken to Rome in 167 BC as one of a thousand Achaean hostages following Rome's victory in the Third Macedonian War.[15] Accused

---

10. Josephus, *Antiquities* 18.3.3; Tacitus, *Annals* 15.44.

11. Polybius, *Histories* 1.1.

12. Polybius, *Histories* 3.1–2.

13. Josephus, *Antiquities* 18.3.3; Tacitus, *Annals* 15.44; Bauckham, *Jesus and the Eyewitnesses*, 7–11.

14. For a similar discussion of authorial bias and the politics of historiography, see Polybius, *Histories* 12.25; cf. Marincola, *Authority and Tradition in Ancient Historiography*, 112–18.

15. Polybius, *Histories* 30.13; Livy, *Periochae* 46.

of opposing Roman interests, he was deported from Greece along with other prominent statesmen and intellectuals. The hostages were dispersed among Italian towns under mild but indefinite confinement. After seventeen years, he secured release through the influence of Scipio Aemilianus, with whom he formed a close friendship that granted him intimate access to Rome's political and military elite.[16] After his capture, Polybius was brought into the orbit of the Roman elite, eventually becoming a trusted adviser to leading statesmen. Through his pen, Hannibal first takes shape in the historical record.

The chronology is notable. Hannibal died around 183–181 BC. Polybius wrote between roughly 146 and 120 BC, which is a gap of forty to sixty years, close enough to place him within living memory. His sources were not Carthaginian but Roman: the official annals, senatorial records, and the oral testimony of statesmen and soldiers who had fought in the war, many of them his own patrons.[17] Like Arrian on Alexander, he may have drawn on documents and eyewitness accounts now lost to us. Yet all of these were shaped by the same cultural perspective, that is, the victor's. In contrast, the Gospel writers were not patrons of empire but subjects under it, recording their testimony in defiance of both political and religious authorities.[18]

This single lens carries inherent risks. Without a surviving Punic narrative, there is no way to weigh Roman recollections against the testimony of Hannibal's own commanders, allies, or citizens. Such voices could have preserved his motives, clarified his strategies, or defended his reputation against Roman political spin. Instead, what we inherit is a portrait composed entirely from across the battlefield. Even Polybius's account is incomplete. Much of his treatment of Hannibal in *Histories* books 1–3 survives intact, but later coverage, especially his reflections on the war's aftermath in the lost portions of books 9 and 11, must be reconstructed from fragments or later epitomes.[19] Polybius admired Hannibal's genius, but he could not transmit Hannibal's voice. The general's own account has vanished; what remains is the empire's version of its most dangerous foe.[20] With Jesus, the

---

16. Polybius, *Histories* 31.23; Plutarch, *Life of Aemilius Paulus*, 28.
17. Polybius, *Histories* 3.6, 3.9; cf. Walbank, *Polybius*, 38–40.
18. Acts 4:17–20; Habermas and Licona, *Case for the Resurrection of Jesus*, 54–56.
19. Polybius, *Histories* 9.1 (fragments), 11.19 (fragments); see Walbank, *Historical Commentary on Polybius* 2:96–101.
20. Polybius, *Histories* 3.6. Modern analogy: Imagine if the only surviving account of Colonel Richard Winters of World War II came from a German officer, one who admired his skill but nonetheless wrote from the perspective of the enemy. Even an honest

preservation is the inverse: the empire could not erase His name, and the record we have is one His followers chose to proclaim openly, even under threat of death.[21]

Polybius leaves us with a disciplined but incomplete record, precise in strategy, silent on the man. When we turn to Livy, our next witness for Hannibal, we leave the careful analyst behind and enter the realm of the Roman storyteller. His pages are rich, patriotic, and unabashedly moralizing. If Polybius offers us Hannibal through the eyes of Rome's political elite, Livy gives us Hannibal as the Republic wanted him remembered: a cautionary figure in the drama of Rome's inevitable rise.

Livy: Rome's Storyteller

Titus Livius, born in 59 BC and dying in AD 17, was a historian of Rome, but more than that, a patriot and moralist, writing under the long shadow of Augustus and the emerging imperial order.[22] His life's work, *Ab Urbe Condita* (*From the Founding of the City*), was not merely a chronicle but a monument. Across its 142 books (of which only thirty-five survive in full), Livy sculpted Rome's past into a moral epic, equal parts history and civic instruction.[23] In that narrative, Hannibal is not presented as a man of flesh and contradiction, but as a crucible through which Rome's virtues are tested, a necessary villain whose defeat affirms the inevitability of Roman greatness. The Gospels do not cast Jesus as a prop in someone else's triumph, but as the center of the story; even in accounts written by those who rejected Him, He remains the disruptive figure, not the defeated foil.[24]

The chronological distance is immense. Livy wrote about Hannibal a century and a half to two centuries after the general's death.[25] By that time, Carthage had been rubble for generations. There were no survivors to interview, no living memory to consult. Livy never set foot in Carthage or met a single Carthaginian. His sources were exclusively Roman, earlier historians such as Fabius Pictor and Lucius Cincius Alimentus, senatorial

---

portrayal would be shaped by that vantage, because Winters was an American, and his enemy was Nazi Germany.

21. Acts 5:27–32; Wright, *Resurrection of the Son of God*, 33–34.
22. Suetonius, *Lives of the Caesars* 1; Livy, *Ab Urbe Condita* 1–3 (preface).
23. Livy, *Ab Urbe Condita* 1–30.
24. John 18:33–38; Josephus, *Antiquities* 18.3.3; Tacitus, *Annals* 15.44.
25. Livy, *Ab Urbe Condita* 23–25, 10–15, 174–79, 21–30.

records, family archives, and oral traditions preserved by the descendants of Rome's military elite. Every strand of his narrative was spun from the victor's loom. The accounts of Jesus were woven by those who followed Him, yet their central claim, His resurrection, was proclaimed in the very city and generation most able to disprove it.[26]

Livy admits his craft. He invents speeches, dramatizes councils, and shapes scenes for moral effect.[27] His aim is not forensic reconstruction but ethical theater. The central question is rarely "What happened?" and more often "What should the reader learn?" Hannibal becomes a pliable instrument: sometimes a foil to Roman virtue, sometimes a mirror for Roman vice, depending on the moral point to be made. Would Hannibal have truly spoken the lofty exhortations Livy puts into his mouth before battle, or delivered stoic monologues under siege?[28] Such moments echo the rhetorical speeches in other ancient histories: Curtius Rufus's Darius before Issus, Thucydides's Pericles, or Tacitus's Calgacus, crafted as much for the audience as for the record.

In Livy's hands, Hannibal becomes a character in Rome's self-portrait: a dangerous adversary who nonetheless serves the Republic's moral narrative. This is not history as modern historiography understands it. It is a national epic, crafted for Roman memory and Roman morality. And yet centuries later, we still quote Livy's Hannibal as though his words were authentic, rarely pausing to recall that they were scripted in Latin, on Roman terms, for Roman ears. The testimony about Jesus, however, was spoken first in the language and setting of His own people, preserved in Greek for a world audience, and copied across regions beyond the reach of any single empire's narrative control.[29] For Livy, the trail of witnesses from here on out only carries us further from the battlefield and deeper into the realm of literary construction. By the time we reach Plutarch, we are no longer dealing with near contemporaries or national historians, but with a biographer writing in the High Imperial period, shaping the lives of great men for moral instruction, not archival preservation.

---

26. Acts 2:32–36; Bauckham, *Jesus and the Eyewitnesses*, 124–47.

27. Livy, *Ab Urbe Condita* 21–30; cf. Woodman, *Rhetoric in Classical Historiography*, 63–72.

28. Rufus, *Histories of Alexander* 3.10–12; Livy, *Ab Urbe Condita* 21–30.

29. Metzger and Ehrman, *Text of the New Testament*, 51–53; Comfort and Barrett, *Text of the Earliest New Testament*, 17–19.

Hannibal Barca

Plutarch: The Philosopher's Glance

Plutarch of Chaeronea (AD 46–120) was a moralist, philosopher, and biographer best known for *Parallel Lives*, in which he paired Greeks and Romans to illustrate virtues and vices.[30] Yet Hannibal never received a biography of his own, no counterpart in Plutarch's gallery of remembered greatness.[31] Instead, he appears only in passing, most notably in *The Life of Fabius Maximus*, Rome's "Cunctator"[32] and the general who opposed him.[33] Even here, Hannibal is refracted through Roman eyes: Livy, Polybius, and the well-polished myths of empire.

Plutarch's method is as revealing as his omissions. He freely inserts fictional speeches, moral dilemmas, and dramatic scenes, not to preserve the historical record, but to illustrate philosophical points or civic ideals.[34] His craft belongs to the tradition of rhetorical biography, where the historical figure becomes an instrument for teaching, not a subject of forensic inquiry. Hannibal is never the focus; he is a foil in someone else's story.

The chronological gap is stark. Hannibal died around 183 BC. Plutarch wrote between AD 90 and AD 120, nearly three centuries later.[35] His sources were entirely Roman, drawn from authors who wrote centuries later, their accounts already distant—by time and ideology—from the events they claimed to record. By Plutarch's time, Hannibal was less a man than a figure of inherited legend, his image shaped by centuries of retelling. Plutarch's Hannibal, then, is not the commander as he was, but the commander as moral philosophy required him to be. He exists in Plutarch's pages to sharpen the virtues of others, to play his part in an ethical theater whose audience is Rome and its heirs.

---

30. Plutarch, *Parallel Lives* 350–81.

31. Plutarch, *Parallel Lives* 224–29.

32. Plutarch, *Fabius Maximus* 1. "Cunctator" (Latin for "the Delayer") was the cognomen given to Quintus Fabius Maximus Verrucosus for his strategy of avoiding pitched battle with Hannibal during the Second Punic War, instead wearing him down through attrition and harassment.

33. Plutarch, *Fabius Maximus* 350–81.

34. Plutarch, *Parallel Lives* 224–29.

35. Pelling, *Plutarch and History*, 243–45; Livy, *Ab Urbe Condita* 23–25; Polybius, *Histories* 4–9; Plutarch, *Life of Antony* 2–7.

PART I. LEGENDS WITHOUT WITNESSES

Appian: The Imperial Compiler

Appian of Alexandria (AD 95-165) was a Greek historian and imperial insider. Before turning to history, he worked as a legal advocate in Alexandria, representing the city's interests before Roman authorities, and later moved to Rome, where he argued cases involving provincial administration and taxation.[36] His success brought him Roman citizenship and a procuratorship[37] under Antoninus Pius, an imperial appointment that bound him to the ruling system he would later glorify in his histories.[38] For a man writing the story of Rome's enemies, this career path matters: his livelihood depended on imperial favor, and his narrative voice reflects the worldview of those he served.

His *Roman History* is arranged thematically, not chronologically, grouping conflicts by region or enemy.[39] This structure allowed Appian to craft each war as a self-contained arc of peril and triumph, ideal for moral and political messaging. But the method came at a cost: chronology was often compressed or distorted, with cause and effect sharpened for dramatic impact.[40] In *The Punic Wars*, this arrangement lets Hannibal's campaigns unfold without distraction from other Mediterranean events, heightening both the threat he posed and the inevitability of his defeat.

Appian drew on a blend of Greek and Latin authors, official records, and perhaps oral traditions still circulating in scholarly or aristocratic circles. Some of these sources no longer survive, meaning Appian occasionally preserves unique details. Yet, like Plutarch, his use of fictional speeches, moral framing, and thematic compression shapes Hannibal into a literary figure rather than a strictly historical one.[41] Appian's position was doubly

---

36. Appian, *Roman History*, preface, 12-14; Syme, *Roman Papers* 4:173-75. Appian describes his legal career and service as an advocate in Alexandria before moving to Rome.

37. "Procuratorship"—In the Roman imperial system, a procurator was an official appointed by the emperor to manage financial, administrative, or judicial duties in a province or imperial domain. The role varied widely in scope but often involved tax collection, oversight of imperial estates, and representation of the emperor's interests.

38. Appian, *Roman History*, Preface 12-14; White, *Appian's Roman History*, 1-3. His procuratorship under Antoninus Pius is noted in the preface, reflecting imperial patronage.

39. Appian, *Punic Wars*, 1-2. The thematic arrangement, by war and region rather than strict chronology, frames each conflict as a distinct narrative arc.

40. Marincola, *Authority and Tradition in Ancient Historiography*, 187-92. This method aids moral and political clarity but can distort sequence and causation.

41. Appian, *Punic Wars*, 1-135; cf. Marincola, *Authority and Tradition in Ancient Historiography*, 187-92.

removed: he wrote as a provincial Greek integrated into Rome's imperial elite, presenting the empire's conquests as part of an overarching, inevitable historical arc. Hannibal appears as a formidable enemy, but always in service to Rome's ultimate triumph, a narrative designed to affirm imperial order to both Roman and non-Roman readers. In Appian, Hannibal is part memory, part reconstruction, part imperial propaganda. His account is valuable for preserving fragments lost in other traditions, but his Hannibal is the product of late imperial historiography, filtered, distilled, and placed in a structure meant to celebrate Roman destiny.

Appian, Polybius, Livy, and Plutarch: Messengers of Rome

If Polybius was the strategist, Livy the dramatist, and Plutarch the moralist, then Appian was the imperial compiler. Writing in the High Roman Empire, Appian stood furthest from the Punic Wars in time, yet his *Punic Wars* gathers fragments from sources now lost, arranging them not chronologically but thematically, each war a self-contained arc of peril and triumph.[42] This structure was ideal for moral and political messaging, but it sharpened cause and effect for dramatic effect and often blurred the order of events.[43] His Hannibal is filtered through Polybius, Livy, and others, with speeches, moral framing, and imperial inevitability woven in for a Greek-speaking audience under Rome's rule.[44]

Polybius, by contrast, was closer in time and military mind. A hostage-turned-confidant of Scipio Aemilianus, he wrote within a generation of Hannibal's death.[45] His account is disciplined, analytical, and tactically precise, but still Roman in lens. His sources were the official annals, senatorial records, and veterans' recollections, many from the very class that destroyed Carthage.[46] Polybius could admire Hannibal's genius, but he could not give him a voice.

Writing under Augustus around 25 BC, Titus Livius was not a historian in the modern sense: he was a patriot with a pen soaked in purpose. *Ab Urbe Condita* was not just history; it was national mythology.[47] In that legend,

42. Appian, *Punic Wars*, 1–2.
43. Marincola, *Authority and Tradition in Ancient Historiography*, 187–92.
44. Appian, *Punic Wars*, 1–135.
45. Polybius, *Histories* 1.1; 3.6.
46. Polybius, *Histories* 3.6; cf. Walbank, *Polybius*, 38–40.
47. Livy, *Ab Urbe Condita*, preface, 1–10; Suetonius, *Lives of the Caesars* 1.

PART I. LEGENDS WITHOUT WITNESSES

Hannibal was not a man but a shadow, a monster at the gate, a crucible for Roman virtue. Livy invents speeches, staging Hannibal as a Stoic orator before battle.[48] Whether Hannibal spoke those words was irrelevant; the point was spectacle. The more eloquent the enemy, the more exalted the victor.[49]

Then came Plutarch, a philosopher, moralist, and biographer. Writing over three centuries after Hannibal's death, he pursued virtue, not facts. *Parallel Lives* was about lessons, not biography, and Hannibal received no dedicated life, only passing mentions in *The Life of Fabius Maximus*, the Roman "Cunctator" who opposed him.[50] Even there, Plutarch draws on the same Roman reservoir, Polybius, Livy, and now Appian's imperialized narrative, turning Hannibal into a moral example Rome could live with.[51]

Between these four, Hannibal is not preserved; he is performed. Their goal was not to know him, but to cast him, to fit him into a Roman morality play. Polybius gives us the strategist as seen from the enemy's camp; Livy, the dramatist; Plutarch, the moralist; and Appian, the imperial archivist. Together, they produce a Hannibal that ennobles the empire by giving its enemies tragic poise. Now flip this quad and apply it to Jesus. Pretend these four are Mark, Matthew, Luke, and John, only they are Romans. No Gospels. No disciples. No eyewitness voices. Just stylized accounts, edited for message, shaped for politics, polished for Caesar. Would we believe it? Would it pass the test? Only if He demanded nothing. Only if He asked for no repentance. Only if He were Hannibal. Then, perhaps, we would let Him linger, untouched, nonthreatening. Not with thorns, but with laurels. Not on a donkey, but riding through the Alps, carried on the back of empire.[52]

Believing the Conquered: The Consequence of Telephone?

Hannibal is universally accepted as a real historical figure. His battles are taught in military academies. His tactics are studied, his strategies admired, and his legacy appears in textbooks, documentaries, and historical

---

48. Livy, *Ab Urbe Condita* 21.1–4; 22.39–51.

49. Rufus, *Histories of Alexander* 3.10–12.

50. Plutarch, *Fabius Maximus* 1. "Cunctator" (Latin for "the Delayer") was the cognomen given to Quintus Fabius Maximus Verrucosus for his strategy of avoiding pitched battle with Hannibal during the Second Punic War, instead wearing him down through attrition and harassment.

51. Plutarch, *Parallel Lives*, introduction, ix–xxiii.

52. Matt 21:5.

compendiums as Rome's greatest adversary.[53] And yet, every surviving account of him comes from Rome. Not just any Rome, but victorious Rome. Storytelling Rome. Empire-building Rome. The same Rome that annihilated Hannibal's homeland, erased his culture, and burned the voices of his people into silence.[54] Carthage didn't just fall; it was buried, salted, and forgotten.[55] So how do we know about the Battle of Cannae? The crossing of the Alps? The flanking maneuvers, the speeches before battle, the vows of vengeance?[56] We know because Rome said so. Not a single Carthaginian account survives. Not a scroll. Not a letter. Not even a sentence in Hannibal's own words. His entire story is reconstructed by his enemies through hearsay, hindsight, and imperial narrative.[57] Even the most celebrated details, his war elephants, his cunning tactics, read more like epic poetry than verified reporting.[58] And still, we believe. Without resistance. Without demand for original sources. No one asks for a Punic gospel. No one questions why the man who nearly broke Rome is remembered only through Roman eyes.[59] Why? Because Hannibal doesn't threaten you. He doesn't call you to repentance. He doesn't confront your pride or demand your soul. He simply fought a war, lost it, and died. No one marches in the streets to resurrect Carthage. However, put Jesus in a history classroom, stripped of the pulpit, treated as fact, and in America, all hell breaks loose.

The Phantom and the Crown of Thorns

Hannibal's voice is gone. His breath was crushed beneath empire, his letters scorched with his homeland, his memories fed to the flame.[60] We quote his strategies but cannot hear his soul. His victories live on, but Carthage's memory has been reimagined through Roman eyes.[61] Not to honor him,

---

53. Polybius, *Histories* 3; Livy, *Ab Urbe Condita* 21; Plutarch, *Fabius Maximus*.
54. Polybius, *Histories* 3; Appian, *Punic Wars*, 132; Livy, *Ab Urbe Condita* 51.
55. Appian, *Punic Wars*, 132; Polybius, *Histories* 36.
56. Polybius, *Histories* 3; Livy, *Ab Urbe Condita* 21–23.
57. Miles, *Carthage Must Be Destroyed*, 3.
58. Livy, *Ab Urbe Condita* 21; Plutarch, *Fabius Maximus*.
59. Polybius, *Histories* 3; Livy, *Ab Urbe Condita* 21; Plutarch, *Fabius Maximus*.
60. Livy, *Ab Urbe Condita* 21; Polybius, *Histories* 3.
61. Polybius, *Histories* 3.

PART I. LEGENDS WITHOUT WITNESSES

but to use him. Rome preserved no "Gospel of Hannibal." They gave us the "Gospel of His Defeat."[62]

Now contrast that with Jesus. The Roman Empire killed Him too. But they failed to erase Him.[63] His followers preserved His words, spread them across continents, and died for them. His teachings endured, not because they flattered power, but because they defied it. Carried through fire. Kept alive by love. Jesus had friends. Hannibal had flames. Yet we question Christ and quote Hannibal as fact. Every quote, every tactic, every noble line before battle, these are not echoes of Hannibal. They are ventriloquism.[64] The voice of empire, wearing his skin like a trophy, its tongue dipped in victory. Rome didn't record him. Rome performed him. And we believed it. We etched their words into textbooks. We teach his moves at West Point, at Sandhurst, in military academies around the world.[65] We revere the shadow cast by the hand that destroyed him. We never asked for a Punic account. Never mourned the scrolls Rome fed to ash.[66]

Why? Because Hannibal leaves us undisturbed. He doesn't judge our sins. He doesn't stand at the door. He came with elephants, not crosses. He shattered empires, not hearts.[67] He bled for conquest, not redemption. And so the world accepts him, loud, legendary, nonthreatening. A war story retold by victors. A cautionary tale that asks nothing from the soul.

But Jesus speaks still. Through letters written in blood. Through witnesses who died before they denied Him. Through words no empire could erase. One man's voice was silenced and replaced with empire's memory. The other man's voice survived empire's fury.[68] We believe the ghost forged by fire, but we doubt the Word that walked through it. Jesus demands everything. He divides families. He unmasks hypocrisy. He claims authority not just over history, but over you. Over life. Over death.[69] He doesn't merely

---

62. Plutarch, *Fabius Maximus*; Livy, *Ab Urbe Condita* 21.

63. New Testament Gospels; Tacitus, *Annals* 15.44; Pliny, *Letters* 10.96–97; Josephus, *Antiquities* 18.3.3.

64. Livy, *Ab Urbe Condita* 21.

65. Gabriel and Metz, *From Sumer to Rome*, 75–79.

66. Polybius, *Histories* 3; Livy, *Ab Urbe Condita* 21.

67. Gabriel and Metz, *From Sumer to Rome*; Livy, *Ab Urbe Condita* 21.

68. Tacitus, *Annals* 15.44; Pliny, *Letters* 10.96; Josephus, *Antiquities* 18.3.3.

69. Luke 12:51–53; Matt 16:24–25; John 11:25.

enter the story, He rewrites it. And so we shift the standard. For Hannibal, hearsay is holy. For Jesus, even eyewitnesses aren't enough.[70]

Now pause, and perform the "Gospel Double Take." Take everything we've accepted about Hannibal: the silence, the enemy-written legacy, the posthumous myth. Now apply it to Jesus. Imagine a world where the Gospels never existed. No disciples. No Paul. No early oral tradition. Only accounts written 150 to 300 years later, by Roman historians.[71] Men who never met Him, never walked Galilee, never sat beneath the olive trees. Men who didn't know His voice, didn't speak His language, and served the empire that crucified Him.[72]

Now picture those same Roman writers putting long speeches in Jesus's mouth, deathbed proclamations, parables crafted for politics, sermons invented in hindsight.[73] No sources. No testimony. No names. Just story. Would you believe it? Would skeptics accept that version of Jesus as historical? Would professors teach it without footnotes of doubt?[74] Of course not. They'd cry bias. Propaganda. Imperial myth-making. And they'd be right. And yet, that's exactly what we accept with Hannibal. He left no writings. His allies left no scrolls. His voice is gone.[75] What survives comes only through Rome, the empire that burned his city, salted his earth, and then wrote his legend. Polybius, Livy, Plutarch, and Appian became his posthumous biographers, not as friends, not as witnesses, but as inheritors of his defeat. They sifted the ashes of Carthage and shaped what they found into a story Rome could tell.

In their hands, Hannibal's speeches swell with Roman pathos; his strategies march in Roman cadence; his image becomes the perfect foil to magnify Rome's glory. It is Polybius's cautionary tale, Livy's moral theater, Plutarch's character study, and Appian's imperial obituary, all harmonized to a single conclusion: Carthage's fall was inevitable, Rome's victory deserved. No defense. No disciples. No counter-voice from the Punic side. And still, we believe. No outrage. No debate. No skepticism. Why? Because

---

70. Bauckham, *Jesus and the Eyewitnesses*, 1–25; Ehrman, *Jesus*, chap. 3.
71. Tacitus, *Annals* 15.44; Pliny, *Letters* 10.96; Suetonius, *Lives of the Caesars*; Josephus, *Antiquities* 18.3.
72. Tacitus, *Annals* 15.44.
73. Livy, *Ab Urbe Condita* 21–30; Rufus, *Histories of Alexander* 3.11–12; 6.8–9; 8.1–14.
74. Ehrman, *Did Jesus Exist?*, 36–39; Crossan, *Jesus*, ix–xii.
75. Polybius, *Histories* 4.1–7; Livy, *Ab Urbe Condita* 6.9.

PART I. LEGENDS WITHOUT WITNESSES

Hannibal doesn't confront you. He doesn't ask you to repent. He doesn't say, "Take up your cross and follow Me."[76]

---

76. Matt 16:24.

Cleopatra VII
The Empire's Siren

CLEOPATRA VII PHILOPATOR, BORN in 69 BC and dying in 30 BC, was the last Pharaoh of Ptolemaic Egypt.[1] She ruled at a moment when her kingdom stood between the fading glory of the Hellenistic world and the rising dominance of Rome. Fluent in multiple languages, adept in diplomacy, and skilled in navigating the rivalries of empire, she was as much a political strategist as she was a monarch. Her alliances with Julius Caesar and Mark Antony, and her storied suicide, immortalized in the image of an asp pressed to her breast, secured her place in both academic history and cinematic myth.[2]

She is cast as brilliant yet dangerous, enchanting yet treacherous: a ruler whose wit matched her beauty, but whose ambition, Rome claimed, threatened the stability of the world. Yet the image we inherit is not the voice of Cleopatra herself. She left no memoirs, no diary, no royal decrees in her own hand.[3] No surviving Egyptian record speaks for her. The Cleopatra we know comes not from her people, but from the empire that conquered and erased them.[4]

What survives is a portrait painted almost entirely by her enemies, crafted first by Roman politicians as wartime propaganda, then reshaped by later historians, poets, and playwrights. Over centuries, this Cleopatra has been polished, exaggerated, and repackaged until the line between woman

---

1. Plutarch, *Antony* 85–86; Dio, *Roman History* 51.14.

2. Dio, *Roman History* 51.14; Suetonius, *Augustus*, 17.

3. Roller, *Cleopatra*, 198; Dio, *Roman History* 51; Goldsworthy, *Antony and Cleopatra*, 8–11, 80, 119, 123.

4. Grant, *Cleopatra*, 176; Dio, *Roman History* 51.

PART I. LEGENDS WITHOUT WITNESSES

and myth has all but vanished. As with Hannibal, the question demands to be asked: whose Cleopatra are we seeing?

History or Hostile Theater?

Before examining Rome's version of Cleopatra, we must ask whether the surviving accounts meet the basic criteria of reliable historical witness. As outlined in the introduction, sound history rests on five pillars:

1. Contemporaneity, proximity of the source to the events.
2. Multiplicity, multiple independent voices.
3. External corroboration, confirmation from neutral or hostile parties.
4. Archeological support, alignment between text and artifact.
5. Chain of custody, faithful preservation over time.

Applied to Cleopatra's principal Roman biographers, Plutarch, Cassius Dio, Suetonius, and Augustus himself, every pillar falters. None were contemporaries; all wrote more than a century after her death.[5] Multiplicity is absent; each drew from the same imperial tradition. External corroboration is nonexistent; no surviving Egyptian or neutral accounts remain to balance the Roman voice. Archeological evidence for her reign exists, but it is mute without written testimony to frame it. The chain of custody is broken, no original records in her hand, no archives from her court.

Even Augustus, the man who defeated her, omitted her name from his *Res Gestae*. This silence, far from accidental, served to erase her from Rome's official memory.[6] What survives is not historical preservation, but narrative control, a victory sealed in propaganda rather than truth.[7] Remove the imperial script, and Cleopatra's life all but vanishes from the record. And this is the paradox: the same empire that feared her voice now controls her story. We inherit not the testimony of a queen, but the verdict of her conquerors. Measured against the standards applied to other ancient lives, this is not history: it is the theater of victory, performed for eternity.

---

5. Plutarch, *Antony* 1.1; Dio, *Roman History* 50.1; Suetonius, *Augustus*, 17; Grant, *Cleopatra*, 176–78; Goldsworthy, *Antony and Cleopatra*, 356–61.

6. Augustus, *Res Gestae*, 25; Syme, *Roman Revolution*, 308–12.

7. Syme, *Roman Revolution*, 308–12; Pelling, *Plutarch and History*, 70–74; Grant, *Cleopatra*, 176–78.

CLEOPATRA VII

Plutarch's Queen: A Moral Tale

The most influential account of Cleopatra comes not from Egypt, but from Plutarch, a Greek moralist writing under the shadow of Rome. His *Life of Antony*, our primary window into her world, was composed in the early second century AD, roughly 100 to 130 years after her death.[8] Plutarch was no eyewitness. He never walked the halls of Alexandria, never consulted her court archives, never heard her speak. His sources were oral traditions and Roman histories already steeped in imperial bias.[9]

Plutarch did not pretend to be a historian in the modern sense. In his own preface to *Alexander*, he admits he is not recording "histories, but lives," concerned less with events as they happened than with the signs of character he believed revealed virtue, or its absence.[10] His aim was moral instruction, not historical recovery. Like a dramatist, he shaped his portraits to fit the moral arc, willing to bend fact to serve the lesson.

In *Life of Antony*, Cleopatra is not a sovereign navigating the collapse of a kingdom; she is a foreign enchantress, decadent and dangerous, the undoing of Roman virtue. Antony, once noble, is brought low by lust and pride. She becomes the embodiment of Eastern seduction, a threat not merely to a man but to the Roman ideal itself.[11] Plutarch stages their story with imagined speeches, poetic flourishes, and dramatic encounters, less a chronicle than a cautionary play, a queen reduced to a set piece for the empire's applause. This was his method elsewhere: Alexander the Great, too, was transformed into a philosophical archetype, scenes molded to fit a moral frame.[12] Cleopatra receives the same treatment. She is not preserved; she is performed.

The reach of this portrait is astonishing. When Shakespeare wrote *Antony and Cleopatra*, he relied not on Egyptian records or lost contemporary accounts, but on Plutarch.[13] The bard took the philosopher's fable and breathed it into tragedy, allegory became drama, suggestion became script, performance became memory. Thus, when we picture Cleopatra's golden barge, the asp at her breast, the silken voice, it is not her voice we hear. It

8. Plutarch, *Antony*.
9. Plutarch, *Antony* 85–86; Grant, *Cleopatra*, 176.
10. Plutarch, *Alexander* 1.
11. Grant, *Cleopatra*, 144–47.
12. Pelling, *Plutarch and History*, 70–74.
13. Shakespeare, *Antony and Cleopatra*; Plutarch, *Antony*.

is Plutarch's. And behind him, Rome's. Remove the moral fable, and the record collapses into rumor. Whether such a portrait could withstand the standards applied to other ancient lives is a question worth keeping.

Cassius Dio's Empire Lens

Cassius Dio was a Roman senator, historian, and consummate insider who wrote between AD 200 and 220, more than two centuries after Cleopatra's death.[14] By the time Dio set stylus to wax, Egypt was no longer a kingdom; it was a Roman province. Cleopatra was no longer a sovereign resisting conquest; she was myth, theater, and cautionary tale, buried beneath layers of imperial narrative. Her voice had long been drowned by the very world that silenced her.[15]

Dio's *Roman History* spans nearly a millennium, from Rome's legendary founding to his own day. He wrote not as a detached chronicler but as a senator steeped in the politics of the imperial court. His histories reflect both his insider's access and his elite perspective, shaped for an audience of Rome's ruling class. As with many ancient historians, moral judgments and political lessons are woven into the narrative. Foreign rulers in his work often serve as foils, their failures illuminating Roman virtue and the inevitability of empire. Cleopatra's place in this tradition was inevitable: she was the last great obstacle before Augustus's uncontested rule.[16]

In *Roman History*, Cleopatra is recast as temptation itself: ambition as corruption, charm as weapon, defeat as necessity. She is not portrayed as a monarch navigating geopolitical collapse, but as the final seduction before Augustus ascends to "cleanse" the world with empire.[17] Dio's sources were exclusively Roman. Many are now lost. None were Egyptian. He never questions their bias or seeks a counter-voice. For Dio, as for his audience, the Roman version was the only version.

His treatment of Cleopatra fits a broader pattern visible throughout his work. Consider Mithridates VI of Pontus, the so-called "poison king." Dio portrays him not as a strategist fighting for sovereignty against overwhelming Roman aggression, but as a paranoid, decadent monarch,

---

14. Goldsworthy, *Antony and Cleopatra*, 125.
15. Dio, *Roman History* 51.14.
16. Dio, *Roman History* 51.14.
17. Dio, *Roman History* 51.14.

defeated by the inevitable superiority of Rome.[18] Likewise, Jugurtha of Numidia appears in Roman accounts not as an independent African ruler, but as a moral foil whose cunning and treachery test Roman endurance before yielding to Roman discipline. In each case, foreign resistance is reframed not as legitimate defense of homeland but as arrogance before the destined world order. To resist Rome was to be already in the wrong. Cleopatra's story follows the same script. She is less queen than stage device, her downfall written to highlight Augustus's virtue and Rome's manifest right to rule.[19]

This pattern is not accidental; it is structural to Dio's history, which celebrates the consolidation of Roman order over "barbarian" or "exotic" resistance. Cleopatra's defeat thus becomes not just an episode, but a moral endpoint in the story of the Republic's transformation into empire. By absorbing her into this narrative arc, Dio ensured her survival only as a function of Rome's victory. And yet we call it history. The irony is sharp: critics often scoff at "using the Bible to prove the Bible," as though internal testimony is inherently suspect. Yet Dio's Cleopatra rests entirely on Roman voices to validate a Roman victory. He was a cultural outsider speculating on a queen from a dead civilization, with no writings from her court, no independent records, no eyewitnesses, only the whispers of the empire that erased her. His most famous image, the asp at her breast, the queen embracing noble suicide, has become cinematic canon. But it is a flourish, a symbol, a stroke of imperial theater, not verifiable history.[20] The evidentiary gap is unavoidable: remove the Roman chorus, and Cleopatra's voice vanishes. Whether such a record could withstand the standards applied to other ancient lives is a question history should not ignore.

Suetonius: Gossip as History

Suetonius was an imperial biographer writing in the early second century AD, about 140 to 150 years after Cleopatra's death.[21] His *Twelve Caesars* is not history in the modern sense; it is palace gossip bound in literary

---

18. Dio, *Roman History* 36.12–17.

19. Dio, *Roman History* 52.34; Sallust, *Jugurthine War*, 15–20 (for contrast in Roman moralizing patterns).

20. Dio, *Roman History* 51.14; Grant, *Cleopatra*, 190–92; Goldsworthy, *Antony and Cleopatra*, 383–86.

21. Suetonius, *Augustus*, 17.

form.²² Scandal was his currency, and he spent it lavishly. Unlike narrative historians, Suetonius arranged his biographies thematically rather than chronologically. Anecdotes were grouped by topic, family, public works, habits, and scandals regardless of sequence. The result was less a linear record than a mosaic of court whispers, where rumor and innuendo often outweighed sober testimony. In this framework, Cleopatra appears only in passing. There is no sustained account of her reign, no analysis of her diplomacy, intellect, or strategy. She is reduced to a fleeting spectacle: the lover of Julius Caesar, the exotic trophy Augustus nearly paraded in chains.²³ Even these glimpses are laced with insinuation rather than inquiry. Suetonius does not preserve Cleopatra; he accessorizes Rome's rulers with her image.

The queen who ruled fleets, studied astronomy, and spoke nine languages becomes a prop in another man's story.²⁴ Suetonius offers no attempt to verify sources, weigh slander against substance, or depict her as sovereign. His aim was entertainment, not preservation, tailored for a Roman audience eager to see foreign rulers mocked and diminished. And yet fragments like these are cited in textbooks, echoed in documentaries, and repeated as if they carried historical weight. A woman who once governed a civilization is remembered not for her mind or might, but as a rumor in another man's chamber. Remove the gossip, and nothing remains.

Augustus and the Making, and Unmaking, of a Queen

Long before the ink dried in Plutarch's *Life of Antony*, Cleopatra had already been conscripted into a far older and more dangerous narrative, one not penned by poets or philosophers, but by politicians.²⁵ In the final gasps of the Roman Republic, as civil war tore through the empire, Augustus, then Octavian, did not simply defeat Mark Antony; he defeated a myth. And to do so, he needed a villain. Cleopatra became the perfect foil.

Rome launched a full-scale propaganda campaign against her. Coins depicted her as a monstrous foreign queen, paired with images of Augustus as the embodiment of Roman virtue. Poems, plays, and murals recast her not as a sovereign ruler, but as a sorceress, an eastern temptress whose seduction unraveled Roman strength. She became the symbolic disease:

22. Grant, *Cleopatra*, 180; Goldsworthy, *Antony and Cleopatra*, 6, 8, 10.
23. Suetonius, *Julius Caesar* 1:52; *Augustus*, 17.
24. Grant, *Cleopatra*, 180; Goldsworthy, *Antony and Cleopatra*, 20, 350.
25. Grant, *Cleopatra*, 174–76.

exotic, indulgent, destabilizing.[26] Antony, once Rome's lion, was rewritten as her thrall, ensnared by perfume and whispers. This was not a record of events; it was a ritual of purification. Augustus cast himself as Rome's high priest, cleansing the Republic of foreign contamination.[27] He did not merely win a war; he restored moral order. Cleopatra's destruction was not incidental; it was sacramental. Her downfall became his coronation. Her ashes, the incense of empire. Her erasure, the price of his permanence.[28]

Yet perhaps the most chilling act in shaping her legacy came not from defamation, but from omission. In the *Res Gestae Divi Augusti*, his self-written eulogy carved into stone and displayed across the empire, Cleopatra is never mentioned.[29] Not her name, not her title, not even her death. Rome's greatest queen, its final adversary, vanished from the official record. This was no oversight; it was calculated erasure.[30] To name her would be to grant her weight. To speak of her would be to acknowledge her resistance. Augustus had no need to repeat the slanders; coins, murals, plays, and rumor had already done the work.[31] What he delivered was colder: silence. Mark Antony is condemned in the record, but Cleopatra is unspoken. She is unwritten. She is erased. Her final execution took place not on a battlefield, but in the ledger of empire.[32] This is how power rewrites history, not through debate, but deletion; not through rebuttal, but omission. When empires seek unchallenged victory, they do not merely destroy the body; they bury the past. Remove the propaganda and the silence, and Cleopatra's political reality is almost entirely lost.

No Egyptian Sources Survive—But Why?

We often hear the phrase, "No Egyptian records of Cleopatra survive." But few stop to ask the deeper question: why not? Was it simply the decay of time, or was it the deliberate erasure of a woman who stood too close to

---

26. Goldsworthy, *Antony and Cleopatra*, 356–59; Pelling, *Characterization and Individuality in Greek Literature*, 124–26, 213–16.
27. Grant, *Cleopatra*, 174–76; Syme, *Roman Revolution*, 308–10.
28. Syme, *Roman Revolution*, 308–10, 315.
29. Augustus, *Res Gestae*, 25–27.
30. Syme, *Roman Revolution*, 308–12.
31. Syme, *Roman Revolution*, 308–12; Pelling, *Characterization and Individuality in Greek Literature*, 213–16.
32. Syme, *Roman Revolution*, 315.

PART I. LEGENDS WITHOUT WITNESSES

the flame of empire? One answer begins in 48 BC, during Julius Caesar's siege of Alexandria. As Roman ships burned in the harbor, the fire spread. Some claim it reached the Library of Alexandria, the greatest repository of human knowledge the world had ever known.[33] Whether that blaze was the first spark or only one of many, the result was the same: scrolls turned to ash, voices were silenced, and a civilization's memory began to vanish.

Cleopatra ruled in the aftermath of that destruction. And while no letters, no speeches, no scrolls of hers survive, is it credible to believe she wrote nothing? Or is it more likely that what she did write was destroyed, buried, or left to rot by the very hands that conquered her? She did not simply lose a war; she lost the pen.[34] Egypt became Roman. The Nile flowed in Latin. Her memory, like her kingdom, passed into the custody of her enemies. Her silence was not an accident; it was curated. And curated silence is one of history's deadliest weapons.[35]

What survives today offers a glimpse of two Cleopatras. The first is Cleopatra the Myth: the decadent, manipulative, foreign temptress crafted by Augustus as the archetypal enemy, reinforced by poets and later reborn in Shakespeare and Hollywood.[36] The second is Cleopatra the Historical Administrator: a Greek-speaking Hellenistic monarch with a firm command of politics, economics, and diplomacy, documented in papyri, decrees, religious inscriptions, and coinage.[37] This Cleopatra was pragmatic, calculating, and politically astute, yet far less physically idealized than later depictions.[38] Remove the propaganda and the silence, and even these fragments reveal a sovereign whose reality is obscured behind the lens of her conquerors.[39]

---

33. Plutarch, *Caesar* 49.6–7.

34. Grant, *Cleopatra*, 176–78; Goldsworthy, *Antony and Cleopatra*, 356–61; Pelling, *Plutarch and History*, 70–74.

35. Syme, *Roman Revolution*, 308–12.

36. Syme, *Roman Revolution*, 308–12; Horace, *Odes* 1.37; Virgil, *Aeneid* 8.675–713; Propertius, *Elegies* 3.11; Shakespeare, *Antony and Cleopatra*.

37. Goldsworthy, *Antony and Cleopatra*, 296, 300; Grant, *Cleopatra*, 176–78; Pomeroy, *Women in Hellenistic Egypt*, 69–75; Chauveau, *Egypt in the Age of Cleopatra*, 112–14; Burnett, *Coinage in the Roman World*, 124–26.

38. Grant, *Cleopatra*, 176–78.

39. Syme, *Roman Revolution*, 308–12.

Cleopatra VII

Summing Up the Evidence: The Empire's Siren

Cleopatra died in 30 BC, defeated not only on the battlefield, but in the very fabric of memory.[40] She left behind no voice, no scroll, no decree. Not a single word of hers survives: no journals, no speeches, no records in her own hand.[41] No Egyptian archives remain to fill the silence.[42] The civilization that crowned her queen was swallowed by empire and left voiceless in the wake of Rome's victory. This is not a historical gap; it is the scar of conquest. Augustus, the architect of her downfall, never mentioned her name. Not in his letters, not in his memoirs, not even in his *Res Gestae*, his own stone-carved obituary.[43] Her erasure was deliberate. She was not condemned; she was unspoken. That is empire's highest victory: to erase without acknowledgment, to remove without rebuttal, to let silence write the ending.

Plutarch came more than a century later, writing not for recovery but for moral instruction.[44] His Cleopatra was a warning, not a woman. Cassius Dio followed two centuries after her death, recasting her as a temptress, merely a stepping stone on Augustus's divine ascent.[45] Suetonius mentioned her only in passing, a whisper in the scandal-laden margins of Rome's imperial gossip.[46] None of them preserved Cleopatra; they repurposed her, for drama, for legend, for Rome. The version sculpted by her enemies endures without question. She appears in textbooks, theater, museums, and cinema as though her image were forged from truth rather than propaganda.[47] But the woman we remember was never truly remembered. She was rewritten, redefined, reduced. Her voice did not echo through time; it was replaced. She is not preserved. She is not remembered. She is only repeated.

It would be one thing if Cleopatra's myth had died with the empire that birthed it. But the Roman script lives on, not in scrolls and ruins, but in studios and screens. From Elizabeth Taylor's lavish portrayal to Rome and Netflix's docudramas, Cleopatra remains trapped in the role Rome

---

40. Roller, *Cleopatra*, 3–4.
41. Roller, *Cleopatra*, 3–4.
42. Casson, *Libraries in the Ancient World*, 31–36.
43. Augustus, *Res Gestae*, 25–27.
44. Pelling, *Plutarch and History*, 70–74.
45. Dio, *Roman History* 51.14.
46. Suetonius, *Julius Caesar* 52; *Augustus*, 17.
47. Hughes-Hallett, *Cleopatra*, 3–5, 9–11, 278–80.

PART I. LEGENDS WITHOUT WITNESSES

assigned her: the seductress, the enchantress, the woman who brought down a man.[48] Rarely is she cast as a sovereign navigating the collapse of a civilization or a strategist resisting the weight of empire. Even in modern retellings, we follow Plutarch's lead.[49] Her story is not retold for clarity; it is repackaged for style. Why does this version endure? Because it flatters the empire. It keeps her consumable. The myth of Cleopatra as temptress allows the viewer to indulge rather than wrestle, to gaze upon her ruin without moral discomfort. Her downfall becomes aesthetic, not tragic.[50] It elevates the victor while romanticizing the vanquished. The conqueror remains noble; the queen remains beautiful. No questions asked.

She died, they say, with an asp at her breast. Draped in silk. Crowned in tragedy. A queen alone in a tomb of fading gold, the last breath of a vanishing empire. That image, iconic, intoxicating, has become eternal, painted on canvas, etched into celluloid, whispered through scripts and spectacles. But no eyewitness stood in that chamber. No Egyptian scroll preserved her final hour. The asp, the gown, the elegy, all come from Roman pens, stylized for drama, refined for empire.[51] Cleopatra ruled a civilization, spoke the tongues of diplomats and priests, commanded navies, and traced her lineage back to gods. But none of that survives. Not her words. Not her vision. Not her verdict. The real queen is gone. All that remains is her silhouette, drawn by her enemies, dressed by their agenda, crowned by their silence.[52] And so she drifts through history like smoke. Not preserved. Not remembered. Just repeated. She is the Queen of Smoke, visible, alluring, but never grasped. Her voice was not lost; it was taken, erased, replaced, rewritten by the very hand that crushed her. Rome told her story not to honor her, but to use her. And the world still recites it, not realizing the echo is imperial.

But now look to Christ. He left no palace, no statue, no marble epitaph etched by kings. He died not in silk, but in blood and thorn, lifted on a Roman cross, not a royal throne. His crown was ridicule. His robe, borrowed. His tomb, not sealed with legend, but opened by truth.[53] He had no warships, no scribes of empire, no empire at all. Just wounds. Just words. And still, His name cannot be erased. Cleopatra is remembered because Rome

48. Hughes-Hallett, *Cleopatra*, 278–80.
49. Pelling, *Characterization and Individuality in Greek Literature*, 213–17.
50. Roller, *Cleopatra*, 4–6.
51. Hughes-Hallett, *Cleopatra*, 32–36, 41.
52. Syme, *Roman Revolution*, 308–10, 315.
53. Bauckham, *Jesus and the Eyewitnesses*, 6–12.

needed a villain. Jesus is remembered because no empire could contain Him. Her story survives because it flatters the victor; His endures because it exposes them.[54] Her final breath was written by her enemies; His first whisper from the grave silenced them. One was turned into legend to veil defeat; the other became truth no myth could bury. She is remembered in smoke. He is remembered in fire.

---

54. Wright, *Resurrection of the Son of God*, 707–10, 726–32, 738.

Buddha (Siddhartha Gautama)
The Man Without a Manuscript

SIDDHARTHA GAUTAMA, THE BUDDHA, lived in the sixth century before Christ. Born a prince in northern India, he abandoned wealth and power in search of enlightenment. He taught of suffering, desire, and release. Yet, unlike other giants, he left no written word behind. No letters. No scrolls. No signature on papyrus.

No letters. No scrolls. No signature on papyrus. Siddhartha Gautama, the Enlightened One, who spoke of desire, suffering, and the cessation of self, left behind no written trace.[1] His disciples carried his words orally, passing down sermons and parables through memorized chants and communal recitation. The first written record of his teachings, the Pali Canon, emerged some four centuries after his death.[2] And even that came not from eyewitnesses, but from generations of monks echoing echoes before them.[3] The Pali Canon, the Mahayana sutras, and other Buddhist texts were not written in his lifetime, nor even in the century that followed.[4]

What we call "Buddhism" today is a compilation of traditions, philosophies, and practices that evolved and expanded over centuries, layered, reinterpreted, and regionalized. There is no singular Buddha to interrogate, only a voice carried through time, reshaped by the hands that held it. And yet, we do not doubt him. We do not demand forensic proximity. We do not ask for hostile witnesses. We do not scour the earth for signatures or sift papyrus fibers for proof. We accept the tradition, trust the transmission, and honor the wisdom that emerged.

1. Lopez, *Story of Buddhism*, 19.
2. Keown, *Buddhism*, 6.
3. Gethin, *Foundations of Buddhism*, 39.
4. Wynne, *Origin of Buddhist Meditation*, 5.

Buddha (Siddhartha Gautama)

Once more we see the pattern: a figure of immense influence whose record does not appear until centuries after his death. Alexander's surviving biographies, written three to four hundred years later. Buddha's canon, taking form after a similar span. And yet their distance from the man does not bar them from reverence. We accept them as history, however late the sources, however shaped by the hands of tradition. But when it comes to Jesus, the rules change. His record is not allowed the same span. His testimony is demanded at once, sifted, pressed, doubted. Because He does not leave room for abstraction. He does not invite admiration alone, but surrender. And so the silence of one becomes wisdom, while the witness of the other is called myth.

The Century Without a Name

For a century, Buddha's name lived only in memory. The earliest written accounts of his life and teaching, the Pali Canon, were compiled not in his lifetime, nor in the generation after, but centuries later.[5] The Buddhist councils, beginning with the First Council said to follow his death, did not preserve manuscripts. They preserved memories.[6] But whose memories? And how faithfully were they carried across four hundred years before ink touched parchment? Even the story that Ananda, his cousin and disciple, repeated the sermons word for word is treated with reverence, not scrutiny.[7] The reliability of oral tradition in an age of tribal war, displacement, and shifting kingdoms is rarely questioned in this case.[8] Instead, it is treated as sacred transmission, immune to the decay of time.

Now set that beside the transmission of the Gospels. The earliest layers of Christian tradition did not appear four centuries later, but within one. Paul's letters circulated by AD 40–50. The creed embedded in 1 Cor 15 was already formalized within five years of the crucifixion.[9] The Gospels were composed within a single generation, thirty to sixty years after the events, and they entered immediately into the arena of public testing.

---

5. Gethin, *Foundations of Buddhism*, 1–2.
6. Wynne, *Origin of Buddhist Meditation*, 6.
7. Lopez, *Story of Buddhism*, 19.
8. Keown, *Buddhism*, 7.
9. Bauckham, *Jesus and the Eyewitnesses*, 264.

Jewish leaders, Roman officials, and skeptical philosophers all had access to their claims, and ample opportunity to refute them.[10] Yet the accounts held.

With Buddha, there was no such trial. No cross. No empire trembling at his movement. His words were not indictments but reflections. Gentle. Abstract. Absorbed slowly. For such a message, memory could wander. But Christianity was born into fire. Its creeds were hammered on an anvil of blood. Its manuscripts were hidden, copied, smuggled. Its disciples stood trial in courts and perished in coliseums. Here lies the difference. One tradition could drift across centuries, unchallenged, and still be believed. The other was forced to stand at once in the blaze of history, and it endured. For the Buddha, silence was enough. For Christ, only truth would do.

The Peril of Memory

The Pali Canon, the first substantial record of the Buddha's teachings, was not written down until approximately 400 to 500 years after his death.[11] That is not a gap. That is a canyon. For half a millennium, everything attributed to the Buddha passed only through memory, mouth to mouth, decade after decade, across tribes, dialects, monasteries, and empires.[12] No scrolls. No parchments. No inscriptions in stone. Just whispers.

Some romanticize this as a triumph of sacred tradition. But any honest student of oral culture knows the truth: stories bend. Details drift. Transmission favors the memorable over the accurate, the useful over the faithful. What survives is not always what was said, but what served, ritual, reverence, or power.[13] Even sympathetic scholars admit it: what we possess is not the Buddha's transcript, but a tradition shaped by centuries of retelling.[14]

And when those words finally reached ink, they did not emerge as a single voice but as a chorus in conflict. The Pali Canon of Theravāda, the Sanskrit texts of the Mahāyāna, the Chinese Tripiṭaka, the Tibetan Kangyur, each diverges in language, content, and doctrine. In one stream, the Buddha appears as a historical teacher. In another, as a cosmic being radiating through infinite worlds. In early strata, his words are sober discourse. In later ones, miracles abound. No singular biography. No unified

10. Eusebius, *Church History* 1.3.
11. Gethin, *Foundations of Buddhism*, 43.
12. Keown, *Buddhism*, 6.
13. Lopez, *Story of Buddhism*, 21.
14. Gombrich, *What the Buddha Thought*, 5.

Buddha (Siddhartha Gautama)

witness. Just layers of memory turned into scripture, evolving as the centuries demanded.[15]

Now imagine if the Gospels of Christ had taken the same path. No Paul. No letters. No hostile references. No manuscripts for five hundred years. Only whispers, passed through broken languages and vanishing tribes. Would the world revere such a Jesus? Or would historians dismiss him outright as myth? But that is not what happened. Christ's life was recorded within a single generation. His words were quoted, disputed, copied, and preserved while hostile rulers and critics stood ready to refute them. His manuscripts multiplied across continents. His disciples bled and died rather than recant what they saw.[16]

A Fractured Voice

The deeper one wades into the ocean of Buddhist texts, the less one encounters a man and the more one encounters a prism. Siddhartha Gautama, who may have walked the earth as a teacher in ancient India, dissolves across centuries into a chorus of competing visions. What begins with a seeker beneath a tree ends as a cosmic presence scattered through cultures, philosophies, and metaphysical imagination. The Buddha's voice does not echo; it refracts.

In the Theravāda tradition, preserved in the Pali Canon, he is a mortal teacher who attained enlightenment, entered Nirvana, and pointed others toward liberation through discipline and detachment.[17] He dies. He is buried. Desire is extinguished. But in Mahāyāna, the Buddha ascends. He works miracles. He teaches from lotus thrones in celestial realms. He manifests in countless universes at once.[18] Here, he is no longer a teacher but a timeless principle. Sutras like the Lotus, the Heart, and the Avataṃsaka emerge centuries later, claiming to reveal "deeper truths" even when they contradict the earlier ones.[19] The fractures are not the scars of persecution but of evolution. Buddha becomes whatever the mirror of culture demands: monk, god, principle, void.

---

15. Lopez, *Story of Buddhism*, 23; Gethin, *Foundations of Buddhism*, 26.

16. Wright, *Resurrection of the Son of God*, 607–10; Tacitus, *Annals* 15.44; Josephus, *Antiquities* 18.3.3; Pilate Stone (archaeological evidence).

17. Gethin, *Foundations of Buddhism*, 26.

18. Keown, *Buddhism*, 33.

19. Lopez, *Story of Buddhism*, 25.

And the refraction only intensifies. In Tibet, the Buddha is transfigured through Vajrayāna esotericism and tantric ritual.[20] In China, he is braided into Confucian ethics and Daoist cosmology.[21] Each culture reshapes him, not maliciously but naturally. The result is not a single voice but a kaleidoscope: biography dissolving into abstraction, teachings diverging into contradiction. The Buddha becomes everything, and therefore nothing.

Now set this beside Christ. From the earliest Gospel manuscripts to the letters of Paul, from the martyrdom of Ignatius to the theology of Irenaeus, one voice resounds: Jesus Christ, the Son of God, crucified under Pontius Pilate, risen on the third day.[22] His message does not drift with empire; it collides with it. The manuscript tradition affirms this singularity. The creeds echo it. The fathers guard it, not as innovation but as preservation. Disagreements arose, but the foundation held. Christ is not remade by culture. He is revealed to it. The contrast is stark. The Buddha's identity scatters across centuries, refracted by imagination. Christ's identity stands, unbent, from the first generation onward. The one dissolves into interpretation. The other pierces history with testimony, blood, and resurrection.

China's Rewriting: Cultural Retrofits

When Buddhism entered China during the Han Dynasty, it did not arrive as a fixed creed. It arrived as clay. The Buddha was not merely translated; he was transformed. Teachings rooted in renunciation, detachment, and impermanence were reshaped to fit the architecture of Confucian duty and Daoist cosmology.[23] A message that once called a man to forsake family, caste, and nation was softened into one of filial piety, ancestral reverence, and cosmic balance. What began as disruption became digestion. Confucianism, the backbone of Chinese order, demanded loyalty to family, submission to elders, and reverence for ancestral lines.[24] Early Buddhism contradicted this. It told the seeker to let go: of possessions, of identity, even of kin. The monk who abandoned his house, his name, his father, was praised. Such teachings were intolerable in a culture built on duty to the father's will. Here the contrast with Christ is even starker. Confucianism

---

20. Wynne, *Buddhism*, 105.
21. Lopez, *Story of Buddhism*, 27.
22. Bauckham, *Jesus and the Eyewitnesses*, 10.
23. Zürcher, *Buddhist Conquest of China*, 24.
24. Keown, *Buddhism*, 32.

sanctified the earthly father; Christ declared, "Call no man your father on earth, for you have one Father, who is in heaven."[25] Where Chinese tradition enshrined ancestral lines, Christ severed them. Where Buddhism could be softened into filial piety, Christianity stood unyielding: faith in Him meant allegiance above clan, custom, and blood.

So the Buddha was retrofitted. His abandonment of wife and child, central to his Indian narrative, was muted or recast.[26] His detachment was reframed as temporary, his rejection of ties reinterpreted as harmony with tradition. Chinese translations of the sutras bore not only scribal fingerprints but also the sculpting of political hands and cultural lenses.[27] By the time Buddhism gained a foothold in China, the man beneath the bodhi tree was gone. In his place stood a figure polished smooth by Confucian hands.

Now imagine the same with Christ. What if the first records of Jesus surfaced eight centuries after His death, not in Aramaic or Greek, but in Mandarin? What if the Sermon on the Mount had been rewritten to exalt ancestral rituals instead of surrender to the Father in heaven? What if He blessed the dutiful son over the repentant sinner, praised harmony over repentance, and taught that righteousness came through tradition rather than faith? Would we still call Him Jesus, or would we recognize a cultural silhouette, safe for society, but no longer the man of Galilee?

Here lies the double standard. With the Buddha, such evolution is hailed as wisdom. With Christ, even a comma stirs controversy. Scholars scrutinize manuscripts written mere decades after His death,[28] while texts compiled centuries after the Buddha are canonized as scripture. Why? Because Christ does not bend to culture; He demands it bow to Him. He does not conform; He confronts. The Buddha may be reshaped because his silence permits it. Christ is feared because His voice still speaks, and it speaks the same, across tongues, across time.

Slim Stones and Empty Scrolls: The Archeological Void

What do we physically possess for the Buddha? Shrines, pillars, dedications. But no scrolls. No personal writings. No tomb. No artifact from his

---

25. Matt 23:9.
26. Gethin, *Foundations of Buddhism*, 31.
27. Wynne, *Buddhism*, 111.
28. Bauckham, *Jesus and the Eyewitnesses*, 6.

PART I. LEGENDS WITHOUT WITNESSES

lifetime that bears the name "Siddhartha Gautama."[29] The earliest references come centuries later. The Ashokan Pillars, erected by Emperor Ashoka two hundred years after the Buddha's supposed death, mention Lumbini as his birthplace.[30] But these are not witnesses of his day. They are monuments of devotion, not documents of history. Royal endorsements, not contemporary testimony.

Excavations at Lumbini and Piprahwa reveal early Buddhist reliquaries and communities, but they testify to belief, not biography.[31] They show where rituals were performed, where memory was preserved. But they do not verify the man. They confirm the spread of a movement, not the existence of its founder. The record is real, but it is retrospective, footprints of interpretation, not the figure himself. Now contrast this with Jesus Christ. We have cities He walked: Nazareth, Capernaum, Jerusalem. We have names of men who judged Him: Caiaphas and Pontius Pilate, carved into ossuary and stone. The Caiaphas ossuary, dated to His generation, names the high priest who presided at His trial.[32] The Pilate stone, unearthed in Caesarea, preserves the title of the prefect who condemned Him.[33] The terrain, the customs, the politics, the legal titles all match. The Gospel accounts are tethered to verifiable earth and ink.

For the Buddha, we are left with sacred architecture and retrospective homage. No contemporary inscription. No grave. No personal relic. No document from friend or foe in the centuries where he should have stood. What we possess is reverent echo, not original voice. Faith built on devotion, not evidence. His trail begins in silence, and centuries later, the stones still speak only in metaphor. This is not history in the forensic sense. It is legend memorialized by those who believed. For Buddha, we find shrines. For Christ, we find names. One is carved into temple dedications. The other into history itself.

Monuments to Myth: Why Is Buddha Treated Differently?

Across the ancient world, civilizations raised stones to their gods. The pyramids of Egypt rose to enshrine deified pharaohs. The ziggurats of

29. Keown, *Buddhism*, 8.
30. Wynne, *Buddhism*, 14.
31. Lopez, *Story of Buddhism*, 20.
32. Evans, *Jesus and the Manuscripts*, 59.
33. McDowell, *New Evidence That Demands a Verdict*, 310.

Buddha (Siddhartha Gautama)

Mesopotamia honored Marduk, Enlil, and Ishtar. The marble temples of Greece echoed with hymns to Zeus, Athena, and Apollo. The stepped pyramids of Mesoamerica bore the names of Quetzalcoatl and Tezcatlipoca, carved in stone and myth alike. These monuments endure as relics of worship, cultural memory encased in stone.[34]

But no scholar today mistakes them for biography. No one insists Apollo must have lived because Delphi stands. No one claims Quetzalcoatl walked the earth because a pyramid bears his name. The monuments testify to belief, not to a man.[35] So why is Buddha treated differently? The monuments to Siddhartha Gautama emerge not in his lifetime, but centuries after. Ashokan pillars, stupas, reliquaries—each marks the reverence of a later age, not the memory of an eyewitness. And yet his historicity is rarely challenged. He is spoken of with scholarly deference, not suspicion. No hostile cross-examination. No demand for contemporaneous records. No academic disdain for oral tradition spanning half a millennium.[36]

Why? Because Buddha is safe. He asks for reflection, not repentance. He offers introspection, not surrender. He speaks of suffering, not of sin. He does not claim to be the Son of God. He does not rise from the dead. His message is philosophical, not confrontational. It does not divide households, topple temples, or declare that every man stands condemned without grace. Christ does.[37]

Jesus of Nazareth is not safe. He is not a sage cloaked in parable and mystery. He is the Judge who comes with a sword. He does not flatter your pride; He crucifies it. He does not offer private enlightenment; He demands public allegiance. And that is why the world scours every Gospel line, interrogates every manuscript, mocks every miracle, and demands evidence beyond what it asks of any other ancient figure. Because if Christ is true, then the world is wrong. And if the world is wrong, the stakes are not philosophical. They are eternal.[38]

---

34. Scarre, *Chronicle of the Pharaohs*, 12; Kramer, *History Begins at Sumer*, 82; Boardman and Coe, *Oxford History of Classical Art*, 106; Coe and Houston, *Maya*, 88.

35. Lopez, *Buddhism and Science*, 4; Keown, *Buddhism*, 8.

36. Bechert and Gombrich, *World of Buddhism*, 71; Strong, *Buddha*, 2; Gombrich, *What the Buddha Thought*, 5; Wynne, *Origin of Buddhist Meditation*, 6; Gethin, *Foundations of Buddhism*, 43.

37. Wright, *Resurrection of the Son of God*, 28; McDowell, *New Evidence That Demands a Verdict*, 164; Bauckham, *Jesus and the Eyewitnesses*, 10.

38. Lewis, *Mere Christianity*, 52; Keller, *Reason for God*, 211; Wright, *Jesus and the Victory of God*, 36.

PART I. LEGENDS WITHOUT WITNESSES

Cutting Off the Skeptic's Response

A skeptic might object: "Ra and Zeus never claimed my soul either, and we still dismiss them despite their temples and myths." Fair enough. But here is the decisive difference: Ra, Zeus, Marduk, these were never presented as flesh-and-blood men in time and space. They were abstractions, mythic constructs born in ritual and legend, gods whose existence never demanded documentary proof or eyewitness defense. No historian expects a birth certificate for Apollo[39] either.

But the Buddha is different. He is said to have walked real ground, taught in real cities, died in a real grove. He is presented not as myth, but as man, a sage with dates, deeds, and disciples.[40] Yet the record is fractured, written centuries later, shaped by culture and devotion, rarely pressed under the historian's cross-examination. And still, he is granted credibility without confrontation.[41]

Jesus, too, is presented as historical. But unlike the Buddha, His story doesn't soothe; it strikes. He does not simply invite reflection; He calls for repentance. He doesn't just point to the path; He declares Himself the Way. His claim is not wisdom, but authority. Not perspective, but lordship. And that is why the scrutiny is relentless.[42] Buddha offers peace without judgment. Jesus demands allegiance through a cross. One is accepted. The other resisted. One offers calm. The other exposes the conscience. That is why the Buddha gets a podium. And Jesus gets the blade.[43]

The Safe Messiah

Let us be honest about why Buddha's story escapes the blade. It is spiritual softness, palatable to a world that flees pain and craves comfort. Buddha offers serenity. Christ demands surrender.[44] One whispers, "Detach." The

---

39. Scarre, *Chronicle of the Pharaohs*, 10; Boardman and Coe, *Oxford History of Classical Art*, 35; Kramer, *History Begins at Sumer*, 86.

40. Strong, *Buddha*, 3.

41. Gethin, *Foundations of Buddhism*, 43; Wynne, *Origin of Buddhist Meditation*, 6; Keown, *Buddhism*, 8.

42. Wright, *Resurrection of the Son of God*, 28; Keller, *Reason for God*, 33; McDowell, *New Evidence That Demands a Verdict*, 164.

43. Lewis, *Mere Christianity*, 52; Wright, *Jesus and the Victory of God*, 36.

44. Strong, *Buddha*, 7.

Buddha (Siddhartha Gautama)

other commands, "Repent."[45] One invites transcendence above suffering. The other requires you to shoulder it, with a cross on your back and your ego on the altar. Which message would a restless world prefer to enshrine? The one that demands nothing, or the One that demands everything?

And yet for all the reverence, the Buddha left no writings. No letters. No scrolls.[46] His words, if they were ever his, survived only by breath, echoes passed from mouth to mouth until they dissolved into memory and myth. The Pali Canon, revered as earliest, was not written until four to five centuries after his death.[47] Not by eyewitnesses. Not by disciples. But by distant communities, shaping oral tradition into doctrine long after the man was gone.[48] No manuscript. No hostile testimony. No tomb to examine. Only legend hardened into scripture.

The archeological record deepens the silence. Shrines, stupas, royal dedications, but nothing from his lifetime that names him.[49] The Ashokan Pillars, carved two centuries after his death, canonize belief, not biography.[50] And as Buddhism spread, the man dissolved further. In China, overlaid with Confucian ethics and Daoist metaphysics. In Tibet, retooled into ritual and mysticism. Buddha became whatever empire required. The man was swallowed by the myth. And yet, no one objects. No one demands a manuscript. No one interrogates the fractures between Theravāda, Mahāyāna, and Vajrayāna traditions.[51] The contradictions are forgiven. The absence is sanctified. Silence becomes sacred.

Now imagine the same for Jesus Christ. No Gospels. No Paul. No contemporaneous letters. Only scattered traditions emerging five centuries later, stitched together in foreign tongues. Would it pass muster? Would any historian hesitate before tearing it to shreds? Not a chance. It would be laughed out of the academy.[52] But Jesus is not permitted to be vague. He cannot be reduced to myth, cultural symbol, or spiritual ornament. He is not safe, because He does not soothe; He summons. Where Buddha whispers peace, Christ commands repentance. Where Buddha offers detachment,

---

45. Strong, *Buddha*, 2; Matt 16:24.
46. Strong, *Buddha*, 2.
47. Strong, *Buddha*, 27; Gethin, *Foundations of Buddhism*, 114; Keown, *Buddhism*, 55.
48. Wynne, *Origin of Buddhist Meditation*, 6.
49. Thapar, *Aśoka and the Decline*.
50. Ashoka Inscriptions, third century BCE.
51. Strong, *Buddha*, 3.
52. Evans, *Jesus and the Manuscripts*, 59.

Christ demands the death of self. And that is the double standard: history shows mercy to those who ask nothing of the soul, but Christ is crucified again and again, not because He is unclear, but because He is unmistakably clear. He does not ask for contemplation. He asks for everything.

Verdict: The Unsafe Christ

By every measure, the Buddha is treated gently. His silence is called serenity. His absence, sacred. His contradictions, forgiven. No one demands proof. No one raises a cross-examination. He is left untouched, because he asks nothing of the soul. But Jesus Christ? He is never left alone. His words are dissected, His Gospels pored over, His resurrection mocked and resisted.[53] He is not dismissed as myth but attacked as if He were dangerous history. And He is. Because if it is true, if the Gospels are eyewitness, if the tomb was empty, if the voice that spoke is the Word of God, then no man stands neutral. Every soul is summoned to bow.

That is why He is hated. That is why His record is pressed harder than any prophet or sage. Not because He is vague, but because He is clear. Not because He hides, but because He reveals. He does not soothe the conscience; He pierces it. He does not offer escape from suffering; He takes you through it, with a cross on your back. He does not whisper calm; He commands kings and beggars alike to repent, believe, follow. And so history bends. Buddha is crowned with incense. Christ with thorns.[54] Buddha's voice drifts into silence. Christ's still thunders across centuries. One fades into empire's myth. The other stands resurrected, demanding allegiance. And that is the judgment: the world loves its safe messiahs. But the unsafe One, the crucified and risen Christ, remains, unavoidable, inescapable, and undefeated.

---

53. Wright, *Resurrection of the Son of God*, 28; Ehrman, *Did Jesus Exist?*, 4.
54. Matt 27:29.

Confucius (Kong Fuzi)
The Ghost of Virtue

CONFUCIUS (KONG FUZI), BORN in 551 BC and dying in 479 BC,[1] is revered across the ages as philosopher, teacher, and moral architect of Chinese civilization. Born in the state of Lu to a family of diminished nobility,[2] he never ruled, never conquered, and never wrote. He sought office, advising rulers and serving briefly in minor posts, yet his counsel was largely ignored by the powers of his day.[3] Only later, under the Han Dynasty, was he raised to near-sacred stature, his memory pressed into service as the foundation of state orthodoxy.[4] He is credited with shaping what would become Confucianism, a framework of ethics and governance that ordered China's political institutions, family hierarchies, and societal norms for more than two thousand years.[5]

His teaching emphasized filial piety (*xiao*), the sacred duty of honoring parents and ancestors; ritual propriety (*li*), the disciplined observance of social custom; and moral uprightness (*ren*), the cultivation of virtue through fairness, justice, and empathy.[6] For these ideals, Confucius deserves recognition as one of history's towering intellectual influences. But now, as we have done with other giants of antiquity, we must look beyond the cultural halo and confront the question beneath the legacy: what do we actually know about the man behind the sayings? And what have we merely inherited without scrutiny—rituals, citations, and reverence handed down

1. Scarre, *Human Past*, 536.
2. Qian, *Shiji* 47.1–3; Creel, *Confucius and the Chinese Way*, 67–69.
3. Confucius, *Analects* 18.3–7; Brooks and Brooks, *Original Analects*, 44–47.
4. Nylan, *Confucian Tradition*, 21–24.
5. Creel, *Confucius*, 3.
6. Confucius, *Analects* 1.2; 2.4; 6.22.

like sacred furniture, accepted without ever testing if the hands that carved them were real?[7]

Echoes, Not Ink: The Problem with the *Analects*

The legacy of Confucius rests almost entirely on the *Analects*, a collection of sayings and reflections attributed to him by later followers.[8] But here is the problem: Confucius never wrote a single line. No scroll. No signed doctrine. No preserved teaching in his own hand.[9] Everything we know of him comes secondhand, compiled decades, even centuries after his death, passed through oral tradition, fractured by interpretation, and filtered through evolving schools of thought.[10] The *Analects* do not give us biography. No birth. No narrative arc. No death.[11] What they give is a patchwork of aphorisms, sometimes profound, sometimes contradictory, often reshaped to fit the political and moral needs of a later age.[12]

This is not the voice of a man; it is a cultural collage, assembled long after he was gone, shaped more by what Confucius was needed to say than what he actually said.[13] The further one peers into the text, the less certain the voice becomes. Even the solemn formula, "Confucius said . . .," is not quotation but invocation, an echo reverberating through layers of memory, myth, and ideological retouching.[14] Picture this: if we discovered a set of brief sayings attributed to Jesus, written centuries later, with no eyewitnesses, no named authors, no timeline, riddled with contradictions, would scholars defend its credibility? Would skeptics revere it? Not a chance. But with Confucius, the absence is ignored. The silence is sanctified. And the man is enshrined, because culture has chosen preservation over proof.[15]

---

7. Confucius, *Analects*, introduction; Brooks and Brooks, *Original Analects*, 4–5.
8. Confucius, *Analects*, introduction.
9. Creel, *Confucius*, 7.
10. Brooks and Brooks, *Original Analects*, 4–5.
11. Confucius, *Analects*, introduction.
12. Confucius, *Analects* 10–11; Creel, *Confucius*, 8–9.
13. Creel, *Confucius*, 7–9.
14. Brooks and Brooks, *Original Analects*, 44–47.
15. Evans, *Jesus and the Manuscripts*, 59; Wright, *Resurrection of the Son of God*, 606–10.

Confucius (Kong Fuzi)

A Voice That Never Spoke: The Myth of a Unified Confucius

To call the *Analects* a historical source is already a stretch. To treat it as the unbroken voice of Confucius himself is a greater leap.[16] This is no chronological account, no unified philosophy, no record of teachings delivered in time and place.[17] It is a mosaic, compiled across generations, edited through dynasties, shaped not only by memory but by political intent.[18] Scholars widely agree that the *Analects* as we have them today contain multiple layers, some tracing to early disciples, others redacted or inserted by Han scholars eager to align Confucianism with the imperial state.[19]

Contradictions abound. In one passage, Confucius appears as relativist; in another, as absolutist. One verse subordinates virtue to ritual; the next elevates virtue above form. These are not tensions within a single thinker but fractures within a tradition compiled for reverence, not rigor.[20] No manuscript survives from Confucius's lifetime. No original document. No firsthand account. Only fragments, evolving, unstable, reframed across the centuries.[21] As Bruce and Taeko Brooks conclude, "Many of the sayings attributed to Confucius were in fact developed long after his death, shaped by the ideological needs of later schools."[22] That is not authorship. That is curation, myth-making in slow motion. A voice formed not by breath, but by consensus.

And let us be honest: if the Gospels had followed that path, if the Sermon on the Mount had been rewritten by Roman magistrates, revised under Constantine, redacted for Tang sensibilities, reshaped for harmony with Confucian ideals, would the world still call it Scripture? Would skeptics treat it as the words of Christ? Not a chance. They would dismiss it as fabrication: political, compromised, void.[23] Yet with the *Analects*, there is no outcry. We nod. We quote. We revere. Why? Because Confucius offers

---

16. Confucius, *Analects*, introduction; Creel, *Confucius*, 7–9, 12–13.
17. Brooks and Brooks, *Original Analects*, 4–6, 15–16, 22.
18. Creel, *Confucius*, 12–13; Brooks and Brooks, *Original Analects*, 15–16, 22.
19. Brooks and Brooks, *Original Analects*, 4–6, 15–16.
20. Confucius, *Analects*, introduction; Brooks and Brooks, *Original Analects*, 4–6, 22, 31–33.
21. Creel, *Confucius*, 7–9; Brooks and Brooks, *Original Analects*, 4–6.
22. Brooks and Brooks, *Original Analects*, 268.
23. Evans, *Jesus and the Manuscripts*, 59; Wright, *Resurrection of the Son of God*, 607–10.

instruction, not incarnation. Ethics, not resurrection. Order, not obedience. And advice, no matter how inconsistent, never gets nailed to a cross.

Confucius as a Tool of the State

Confucius was not preserved because his teachings were revolutionary. He was preserved because they were useful.[24] From the Han Dynasty onward, rulers found in Confucianism the perfect scaffolding for empire.[25] The values attributed to him, filial piety, loyalty to authority, ritual propriety, social hierarchy,[26] did not threaten power. They stabilized it. Confucius became the philosopher-king's prophet, a sage whose words could be selectively quoted to justify obedience, submission, and imperial control.

Already in Sima Qian's *Shiji*, the first extended biography of Confucius, the sage appears not as a marginal thinker of Lu but as a timeless sage, a prophet of heaven whose mission was to restore order.[27] This is less biography than hagiography, a portrait written under Han patronage to sanctify Confucius as the archetype of loyalty, hierarchy, and cosmic legitimacy. In the very act of remembering him, the state remade him.

During the reign of Emperor Wu of Han (141–87 BC), Confucianism was formally adopted as state ideology.[28] Not for its transcendent truths, but for its political convenience. The court did not canonize Confucius out of reverence. They canonized him because his attributed teachings promoted hierarchy, justified bureaucracy, and reinforced the emperor's divine role as the "Son of Heaven."[29] Confucius was no threat to the state; he was a servant of it, posthumously drafted into the service of order.

This was not organic preservation. It was strategic assimilation. The *Analects* were filtered, edited, and standardized not for philosophical clarity but for political utility.[30] Dissenting interpretations were sidelined. Mystical or individualistic strains of early Confucian thought were trimmed away.[31]

24. Brooks and Brooks, *Original Analects*, 10–12.
25. Zürcher, *Buddhist Conquest of China*, 8–9; Creel, *Confucius*, 13–14.
26. Confucius, *Analects* 1.2, 2.4; Brooks and Brooks, *Original Analects*, 4–6, 15–16, 22.
27. Qian, *Shiji* 47.1–15.
28. Zürcher, *Buddhist Conquest of China*, 20–22; Creel, *Confucius*, 13–14.
29. Brooks and Brooks, *Original Analects*, 10–14; Zürcher, *Buddhist Conquest of China*, 20.
30. Brooks and Brooks, *Original Analects*, 1–6, 15–18.
31. Brooks and Brooks, *Original Analects*, 17–20.

Confucius (Kong Fuzi)

What remained was a version of Confucius molded for imperial exams and public conformity: a sage who questioned nothing, disrupted nothing, and sanctified everything.[32]

And what if Jesus had been handled the same way? Imagine Rome rewriting the Beatitudes to glorify the Senate. Imagine Christ's parables edited to extol Caesar's virtue.[33] You would not have the Son of God. You would have the Divine Bureaucrat. That is precisely what happened to Confucius. His legacy was not preserved to confront power. It was preserved to serve it. And that is why he was never crucified.

The Myth of Authorship: Echoes Without a Voice

Before we go further, we need to revisit the historical standard. What makes someone's words reliable? As laid out at the start of this book, the pillars are clear: contemporaneity (Was it written close to the time?), multiplicity (independent voices), external corroboration (even from enemies), archeological support, and a chain of custody from original to manuscript.[34] Without these, we don't have history: we have rumor, legacy, or propaganda. So let us apply the standard to Confucius. There is no signed doctrine. No autobiography. Not a single line written by his hand. Not even a confirmed eyewitness quotation.[35] "Confucius said . . ." is one of the most repeated phrases in global thought, and yet we have no historical confirmation that Confucius actually said any of it.[36] The *Analects* are a posthumous echo, a collaborative memory stitched together by unknown hands, shaped by political contexts, Confucian schools, and generations of evolving thought.[37]

Confucius is praised as sage, system-builder, voice of eternal wisdom. But what if the voice we hear isn't his at all? What if it is the voice of disciples' disciples, tradition speaking in his name to preserve authority that may never have been his? Scholars themselves acknowledge that the

---

32. Zürcher, *Buddhist Conquest of China*, 20–22; Brooks and Brooks, *Original Analects*, 20–25.

33. Wright, *Resurrection of the Son of God*, 28–31, 50; Evans, *Jesus and the Manuscripts*, 58–60.

34. LaBarbera, *Truth at the Gate*, x–xx.

35. Creel, *Confucius*, 7–9.

36. Confucius, *Analects*, introduction, ix–xiii; Brooks and Brooks, *Original Analects*, 268.

37. Brooks and Brooks, *Original Analects*, 10–20.

PART I. LEGENDS WITHOUT WITNESSES

Analects were compiled in layers, edited and reedited to reflect shifting values and dynastic agendas.[38] What we have is not biography. It is projection, an image of Confucius molded by those who needed his moral authority.[39]

Picture another scenario. Suppose the Gospels had no names. No Matthew. No John. No Paul. No Luke interviewing eyewitnesses. Suppose they were anonymous compilations, assembled centuries later from fragmented hearsay, with no timeline, no corroborating names, no firsthand anchors.[40] Would modern scholars quietly accept them? Would skeptics nod and say, "That seems reasonable?" Or would they tear them apart, branding them folklore wrapped in fiction? Confucius does not threaten. He does not proclaim divinity or demand repentance. He does not call hearts to be pierced or egos to be broken. He asks only for civility. And so no one asks for a signature. No one demands authentication. The burden of proof disappears when truth does not cut, but comforts.

Anchored in Memory, Drifting in Time, and Empty Trails

The skeptic might say, "Jesus didn't write anything either!" True, aside from that moment in the sand,[41] Jesus left no written scroll. But here is the difference: the Gospels were written within living memory of His death, not centuries later.[42] They were penned by eyewitnesses or by those who walked with them.[43] Luke opens with methodical clarity: he investigated, interviewed, and compiled the testimony of those who had seen and heard it firsthand.[44] Jesus was proclaimed publicly while His enemies were still alive to refute it, and they did not.[45] That is not drifting tradition. That is anchored testimony.

Confucius? His words passed through generations of memory, not mouths that heard him. Shaped by disciples of disciples. Filtered through

---

38. Brooks and Brooks, *Original Analects*, 17–25.
39. Brooks and Brooks, *Original Analects*, 1–6, 15–18.
40. Evans, *Jesus and the Manuscripts*, 22–50; Wright, *Resurrection of the Son of God*, 607–10.
41. John 8:6.
42. Blomberg, *Historical Reliability of the Gospels*, 41–70; Bauckham, *Jesus and the Eyewitnesses*, 1–38.
43. Bauckham, *Jesus and the Eyewitnesses*, 16–18, 38–42.
44. Luke 1:1–4.
45. Acts 2:22–32; Bauckham, *Jesus and the Eyewitnesses*, 51–54.

dynasties. Repeated not as history, but as ritual.[46] Confucius is honored across China in shrines, statues, and ceremonial halls, but the archeological trail beneath that reverence is thin, and disturbingly ceremonial.[47] What we have are tokens of veneration, not verification. No scrolls in his hand. No epitaph carved by disciples.[48] No object from his own lifetime bearing his voice, his thought, or even his name. The most-often-cited discoveries, like the bamboo slips found in the tomb of Prince Liu Xiu in 1973, date nearly four centuries after his death.[49] They contain paraphrased sayings attributed to him, but they are anonymous, secondhand, and deeply shaped by the politics of their era.[50] Others, such as the Guodian tomb strips, reference teachings from his supposed disciples, like Zisi, his grandson, but again, these are echoes, not evidence.[51]

Even the most iconic artifact, a bronze mirror from the tomb of Liu He bearing Confucius's image,[52] is not a historical receipt but a symbolic reflection. It tells us not what he said or did, but how he was later imagined. And the tomb at Qufu? Revered, visited, ornately preserved, but without original markers from his time.[53] No inscription. No engraving. Just ritual memory cloaked in stone. By contrast, pagan emperors and warlords left deeper trails: names carved in stone, laws etched in rock, cities raised to their glory.[54] With Confucius, the trail grows softer the closer you approach. Not a voice, but a vacuum, filled by the institutions that needed him.[55] With Christ, the words come while the wounds are still visible. With Confucius, the voice arrives only once empire is ready to use it.

If Jesus had left behind only paraphrased sayings written centuries later, no named disciples, no public ministry, no tomb, no terrain, would we call that reliable? Of course not. Scholars would tear it apart.[56] But Con-

---

46. Brooks and Brooks, *Original Analects*, 10–25.
47. Zürcher, *Buddhist Conquest of China*, 14–16.
48. Creel, *Confucius*, 6–8; Brooks and Brooks, *Original Analects*, 10–20.
49. Loewe, *Chinese Ideas of Life and Death*, 33–36.
50. Brooks and Brooks, *Original Analects*, 17–25.
51. Wynne, *Origin of Buddhist Meditation*, 1–30; *Guodian Bamboo Texts*.
52. Katz, "Oldest-Known Image"; Ziliang, "Excavating the Marquis of Haihun's Tomb."
53. Creel, *Confucius*, 21–25.
54. Scarre, *Human Past*, 62–91, 112–37.
55. Brooks and Brooks, *Original Analects*, 268.
56. Bauckham, *Jesus and the Eyewitnesses*, 1–58; Evans, *Jesus and the Manuscripts*, 40–60.

fucius gets a pass. His voice is easier, more palatable, asking little. It does not cut, it does not crucify. It comforts. No one's soul is on the line. No kingdoms threatened. No cross at the end.

One Man, a Hundred Masks: Confucius Reimagined

As Confucianism evolved, so did Confucius, fractured, repainted, reassembled by every dynasty, every doctrine, every regime that claimed him.[57] He became less a voice than a mirror, reflecting whatever the age demanded. This was not continuity. It was reinvention. In the Han Dynasty, he was recast as the ideal civil servant, a sage of submission and structure.[58] His sayings were fused with Legalism to forge a bureaucratic machine: the Legalist-Confucian hybrid, where ritual justified hierarchy and the emperor stood as axis between heaven and earth.[59] The goal was not truth. It was order.

Centuries later, the Song Dynasty gave rise to Neo-Confucianism. Suddenly, Confucius was a metaphysician. Thinkers like Zhu Xi grafted Buddhist and Daoist concepts onto his scaffolding, turning practical wisdom into celestial philosophy.[60] The man who once taught virtue in the marketplace became a mystic of cosmic principle.[61] The simplicity was gone. In its place: abstraction and incense. Other ages dressed him differently still. Some cast him as a dispassionate moral template, virtue without tears, ethics without empathy. Others styled him as a proto-scientist, a rationalist centuries ahead of the Enlightenment.[62] Each mask bore the same name. None bore the man.

Now ask: if this had happened to Jesus, if some called Him "monk," others "philosopher," others "archetype," each shaped by centuries of political drift, would historians take it seriously? Or would they tear it apart as myth in motion? Confucius did not survive history unchanged. He survived because he changed.[63] Over and over, until the man disappeared, and

---

57. Creel, *Confucius*, 55–70; Yao, *Introduction to Confucianism*, 146–65.

58. Makeham, *Lost Soul*, 45–48.

59. Yao, *Introduction to Confucianism*, 75–80; Schwartz, *World of Thought in Ancient China*, 302–20.

60. Yao, *Introduction to Confucianism*, 157–65; Angle, *Contemporary Confucian Political Philosophy*, 12–15.

61. Yao, *Introduction to Confucianism*, 157–65, 173–78.

62. Makeham, *Lost Soul*, 49–76, 77–102; Bell, *China's New Confucianism*, 22–26.

63. Bauckham, *Jesus and the Eyewitnesses*, 14–25.

only the myth remained. One man. A hundred masks. And no voice left to take them off.

When Philosophy Hides Behind Distance

Let's be brutally honest about the double standard. Why are men like Confucius, surrounded by ambiguity, absent of signatures, buried beneath centuries of political revision,[64] allowed to pass through the academic gates unchallenged? Why are philosophers spared the scrutiny that prophets endure? The answer is unsettlingly simple: because philosophy demands nothing from the soul. It requires no surrender. No obedience. No repentance. It speaks from a distance, principles, not presence. Insight, not incarnation.

Confucius spoke of ethics, ritual, and social harmony. His words, if they were ever truly his, have been reshaped, reinterpreted, filtered through dynasties and scholars who never heard his voice.[65] Yet the academic world does not tear down the *Analects*. No one demands hostile witnesses. No one applies the same forensic pressure they reserve for the Gospels.[66] Why? Because Confucius never claimed to be the truth. He pointed toward virtue, but never claimed to be its source.[67] Jesus did.

He did not say, "The way is good."
He said, "I am the Way."[68]
He did not offer abstraction.
He offered Himself.

That is not philosophy. That is collision. That is divine confrontation. His teachings were never meant to be detached aphorisms; they were extensions of His very identity. And that is why the Gospels are dissected line by line, century after century, manuscript after manuscript. Because if they hold, if He really said and did these things, then every life must answer. Every ego must yield.[69] The philosopher leaves you pondering. Christ

---

64. Brooks and Brooks, *Original Analects*, 268; Creel, *Confucius*, 7–13, 22–30; Yao, *Introduction to Confucianism*, 68–75.

65. Schwartz, *World of Thought in Ancient China*, 135–80; Makeham, *Lost Soul*, 1–10, 35–60.

66. Bauckham, *Jesus and the Eyewitnesses*, 1–17, 500–38; Blomberg, *Historical Reliability of the Gospels*, 23–52.

67. Lewis, *Mere Christianity*, 55–58; Keller, *Reason for God*, 132–48.

68. John 14:6.

69. Keller, *Reason for God*, 132–48; Lewis, *Mere Christianity*, 93–109.

leaves you exposed. And in a world terrified of truth with consequence, that makes all the difference.

The Standard Fails the Swap Test

Let's now apply the same historical standards skeptics use against Jesus to Confucius. Imagine if the teachings of Christ had survived only through secondhand recollections compiled four centuries after His death.[70] No Gospels. No named witnesses. No Paul, no Luke, no early church letters,[71] just disjointed fragments, passed through oral tradition, shaped by different schools of thought, and finally written down by anonymous compilers long after the Roman Empire had shifted its values. Would any serious skeptic accept that as a credible foundation for Christ's life and message? Not for a second. They would call it folklore, late-stage mythology, manipulated tradition.

Yet this is precisely the situation with Confucius.[72] He left no writings of his own. His wisdom, if it was his, was passed down through memory, sifted through disciples who disagreed with one another, then filtered through centuries of political editing.[73] What we have in the *Analects* is not a unified doctrine, but a mosaic, conflicted sayings, contradictory priorities, and evolving agendas, all shaped by the needs of emperors and institutions rather than the voice of the man himself.[74] And yet, this is accepted without protest. Why?

Because Confucius is seen as a philosopher. Jesus is seen as a threat.[75] One offers structure. The other offers surrender. One gives advice. The other demands repentance. And it is that demand, not the evidence, that invites scrutiny. When the standard is swapped, the inconsistency becomes

---

70. Bauckham, *Jesus and the Eyewitnesses*, 1–45; Blomberg, *Historical Reliability of the Gospels*, 23–44.

71. Blomberg, *Historical Reliability of the Gospels*, 23–44; Ehrman, *Did Jesus Exist?*, 78–116.

72. Creel, *Confucius*, 1–25; Brooks and Brooks, *Original Analects*, 268.

73. Schwartz, *World of Thought in Ancient China*, 137–72.

74. Brooks and Brooks, *Original Analects*, 268; Yao, *Introduction to Confucianism*, 81–98.

75. Keller, *Reason for God*, 166–80. On moral objections vs. evidential, see Lewis, *Mere Christianity*, 109–21. On pride and moral resistance, see Lewis, *Mere Christianity*, 120–21. Lewis argues that pride often prevents people from accepting the moral demands of Christianity, as they resist submission to a higher authority or moral law.

Confucius (Kong Fuzi)

blinding. The issue isn't credibility. It's consequence.[76] Confucius asks you to think. Christ asks you to kneel. And that, not manuscript gaps, is the real source of resistance.

The Ghost of Virtue

We do not know how he spoke, not his cadence, not his fury, not his laughter. We do not possess a single sentence in his own hand. No scroll. No dictated fragment. No authenticated word.[77] What survives are not his teachings, but his shadow, a silhouette shaped and reshaped by students, scribes, and statesmen. Not preserved for who he was, but molded for what society needed him to be. The *Analects* give us no birth, no death, no story.[78] Only disconnected sayings, stitched together across centuries, reverently passed down, but never verified. Even the phrase "Confucius said . . ." is speculation: a posthumous construction without source, without timestamp, without testimony.[79] There is no chain of custody. No hostile witnesses. No contemporaneous affirmation. No manuscript trail from man to page. No verified site. No adversarial corroboration. No preserved words written in his lifetime.

By the Five Pillars of Historical Confidence, multiplicity, corroboration, hostile sources, contemporaneity, archaeology, and chain of custody, Confucius fails them all.[80] And yet, we trust him. We quote him. We canonize him. Why? Because he does not claim to be the Truth. He does not demand repentance. He does not suffer. He does not rise. He offers virtue, not verdict. He is safe to believe in because he asks for little. Indeed, the ambiguity may be his greatest strength: each generation can reshape him without resistance. His silence is pliable. His absence makes him agreeable.

The Nazarene bleeds in the open. He walks in datable towns, speaks in attested dialects, is tried by known officials, and executed under recorded rulers.[81] His death is documented by friend and foe alike. His words come

---

76. Bauckham, *Jesus and the Eyewitnesses*, 1–15, 497–508.

77. Creel, *Confucius*, 27–38; Brooks and Brooks, *Original Analects*, 268.

78. Confucius, *Analects*, introduction, 9–11; Makeham, *Lost Soul*, 12–18.

79. Yao, *Introduction to Confucianism*, 91–98; Schwartz, *World of Thought in Ancient China*, 145–60.

80. LaBarbera, *Truth at the Gate*, x–xx; Bauckham, *Jesus and the Eyewitnesses*, 1–16, 493–538; Blomberg, *Historical Reliability of the Gospels*, 17–52.

81. Keller, *Reason for God*, 210–27; Lewis, *Mere Christianity*, 31–60; Blomberg,

PART I. LEGENDS WITHOUT WITNESSES

from named hands, from authors who lived among eyewitnesses, from disciples who died to preserve what they saw. No one is jailed for quoting Confucius. No empire ever banned his name. But men were torn apart in arenas for bearing witness to Christ.[82] And still, we call Him legend. Confucius is a ghost of virtue. Jesus is a man of wounds. And somehow, the ghost remains more believable, because the man speaks too clearly.

Safety in Virtue

Confucius left no wounds, only whispers. No blood, only sayings. His legacy floats like incense, fragrant, shapeless, reshaped by every hand that waved it through the air. He became a mirror, not a man; a sage remade for order, not truth. The empire preserved him because he could be bent, because he asked nothing that pierced, because his silence was useful. He is remembered as wisdom without witness, virtue without voice, a ghost of harmony drifting through history. But Christ cannot be remade. His story is anchored in time, His words sealed by suffering, His truth verified in blood. He is not pliable; He is present. Not a ghost, but God in flesh. Not whispers, but wounds. And while the world finds comfort in Confucius, it finds confrontation in Christ. For the sage can be quoted without consequence, but the Son demands surrender. One offers the safety of virtue. The other, the scandal of truth. And history still trembles where the Nazarene speaks.

Historical Reliability of the Gospels, 79–121; Josephus, *Antiquities* 18.3.3; Tacitus, *Annals* 15.44.

   82. Eusebius, *Church History* 437–83; Tacitus, *Annals* 15.44; Keller, *Reason for God*, 210–27.

PART II

Echoes Without a Voice

SOME FIGURES LEAVE NO writings behind—no signature, no scroll, no words in their own hand.[83] They live on not through direct testimony, but through the memory of their followers. In this section, we examine such a man: Socrates. A titan of Western thought, credited with shaping philosophy itself, yet he wrote nothing. Everything we know of him comes from others. His image is fractured, reconstructed through the dialogues of Plato, the memoirs of Xenophon, and the satire of Aristophanes.[84] Which Socrates is real? The relentless questioner of truth? The dutiful soldier? The mocking fool?[85] We do not know him as he was.[86] We know him only as others claimed he was. And yet, no skeptic dares to deny his existence. No academic dismantles his legacy.[87] In this chapter, we weigh the strange leniency given to secondhand legends, how history accepts what faith is so often asked to reject.[88]

---

83. Waterfield, *Why Socrates Died*, 10–11.
84. Johnson, *Socrates*, 19–25.
85. Stone, *Trial of Socrates*, 24–30.
86. Vlastos, *Socrates*, 45–50.
87. Plato, *Plato*, introduction, x–xii.
88. Evans, *Jesus and His World*, 8–10.

PART II

Voices without a Voice

Socrates
The Man of Many Voices

SOCRATES, THE SO-CALLED FATHER of Western philosophy, or so the story goes.[1] A name carved into the bedrock of reason itself. He lived in fifth-century Athens,[2] walking the same sun-soaked streets that would later produce Plato and Aristotle, together the so-called trinity of ancient thought. Yet unlike his successors, Socrates left behind no writings. No scrolls. No doctrine. Not a single sentence in his own hand.[3] Let us not brush past this: Socrates is the most quoted philosopher in Western history, and yet he never wrote a single word.[4] Not a scroll. Not a sentence. Not a signature. No diary, no dictated record, no letter preserved in the dust of time. And still, entire worldviews are built on the voice of a man who left behind no voice at all.[5] By the Five Pillars of Historical Confidence, contemporaneity, multiplicity, external corroboration, archaeology, and Chain of Custody, Socrates fails them all. No firsthand timeline. No hostile confirmation. No tomb. No chain of written legacy.

What we have instead is Plato's philosophical theater, Xenophon's loyal memoir, and Aristophanes's comedic smear—three masks, no man.[6] His image is refracted through disciples and dramatists, reconstructed by admirers and mockers alike. In this, Socrates stands beside Confucius:

---

1. Waterfield, *Why Socrates Died*, 241–45; Nails, *People of Plato*, 241–45.

2. Brickhouse and Smith, *Plato's Socrates*, 11–14; Waterfield, *Why Socrates Died*, 11–14.

3. Reeve, *Socrates in the Apology*, 1–10; Brickhouse and Smith, *Trial and Execution of Socrates*, 25–30.

4. Vlastos, *Socrates*, 3–4; Reeve, *Socrates in the Apology*, ix–x.

5. Brickhouse and Smith, *Trial and Execution of Socrates*, 7–10; Nails, *People of Plato*, 3–30.

6. Plato, *Apology*, 23; Xenophon, *Memorabilia* 1.1–2; Aristophanes, *Clouds*, 120–50.

neither left a word of his own, both remembered through later hands. Where Sima Qian gave us the hallowed Confucius, Plato and Xenophon give us the immortal Socrates, a man framed by interpreters as much as by life. Yet his shadow looms so large that everything before him is labeled "pre-Socratic," as if philosophy itself began when he began to speak.[7] But is this legacy anchored in the man, or in a myth? To answer that, we must turn to the portraits themselves: Plato's philosopher, Xenophon's gentleman, and Aristophanes's fool.

The Three Masks: Plato, Xenophon, and Aristophanes

To see Socrates, we must look through the eyes of others, but those eyes never agree. Instead of one consistent portrait, we're handed three masks, each crafted by a different voice, each bending the man to serve a different purpose.

Plato's Socrates

Plato (427–347 BC), Socrates's most famous student and later founder of the Academy, left behind more writings than any other disciple. Yet those writings blur the line between memory and invention. Why? Because Plato was never interested in chronicling a man: he was interested in teaching a truth. His dialogues are not transcripts of conversations; they are philosophical dramas where Socrates becomes the central actor.

In the early works, like the *Apology* or *Crito*, we glimpse a Socrates who still feels tethered to the streets of Athens, a gadfly confronting courts and citizens alike. But as Plato matures, so does his "Socrates." In the *Symposium*, he becomes a mystic mouthpiece for Diotima's doctrine of love.[8] A priestess who likely never existed outside Plato's imagination lends Socrates divine authority.[9] In the *Republic*, he outlines the blueprint of a utopia where philosopher-kings govern by reason.[10] By this stage, Socrates is no longer a man under trial but a prophet of Plato's own metaphysical system.

---

7. Guthrie, *History of Greek Philosophy* 1:7; Waterfield, *Why Socrates Died*, 1–20.
8. Plato, *Symposium* 201d–212c.
9. Plato, *Symposium* 201d–212c.
10. Plato, *Republic* 473c–540c.

Why write this way? Because Plato needed a vessel. Socrates, already condemned and martyred by Athens, was the perfect mask: he carried moral weight, cultural notoriety, and philosophical credibility. To put new, daring ideas into the mouth of a dead man gave them legitimacy, and immunity. What ruler or rival could argue with a philosopher already judged by the city itself? Plato found in Socrates a shield, a puppet who could speak radical truth without Plato himself standing trial.[11] Thus, the Socrates of Plato is never pure biography. He is a construct: the teacher refashioned as a timeless sage. Not the gadfly of Athens, but the oracle of Plato's Academy. Not a man with flesh and history, but a voice made to carry someone else's vision across centuries.

Xenophon's Socrates

Xenophon (c. 430–354 BC), soldier, historian, and student of Socrates, presents us with the most down-to-earth version of his teacher. Unlike Plato, Xenophon was not a philosopher of abstraction but a man of action: a mercenary, a general, and later a writer of histories. His *Memorabilia* and *Apology* give us a Socrates less concerned with cosmic truth than with practical living.[12] Here, Socrates is not the mystic dreamer of Plato, but a moral coach, concerned with moderation, civic duty, friendship, and self-discipline. Gone are the dialogues of metaphysical ascent. Instead, Xenophon's Socrates praises temperance, teaches obedience to the gods, and defends his life as one of public service.[13] It is a Socrates one might imagine as a sensible neighbor rather than a revolutionary.

Why does Xenophon write him this way? Because Xenophon himself was no revolutionary. A conservative admirer of Sparta, a commander in Persia, and a man who valued order over speculation, Xenophon needed a Socrates who fit his world: disciplined, pious, and safe. His teacher is reshaped to echo Xenophon's own ideals. Some have argued Xenophon misunderstood Socrates's depth. Others contend he deliberately stripped away the radical edge to preserve a more palatable image.[14] Either way, what survives is not the gadfly of Athens but a domesticated sage, less prophet than polite gentleman, framed to serve Xenophon's vision of virtue.

11. Vlastos, *Socrates*, 3–5.
12. Xenophon, *Memorabilia* 1.2, 4.4.
13. Xenophon, *Apology*, 1–2.
14. Dorion, "Rise and Fall," 5–7.

PART II. ECHOES WITHOUT A VOICE

Aristophanes's Socrates

And then comes Aristophanes, the comic playwright, who offers us the earliest portrait of Socrates, written not after his death, but while he was still alive. In *The Clouds*, Socrates is lampooned as a babbling sophist, his head literally "in the clouds," arguing over insects, measurements, and verbal tricks.[15] He is cast as a corrupter of youth, a ridiculous street preacher of nonsense. A clown. A fraud. A punch line. Imagine if the first public depiction of Jesus came from a Roman satire that painted Him as a delusional vagrant, would that be treated as reliable historical testimony?

Why did Aristophanes write him this way? Because Socrates was useful to lampoon. Athens in the late fifth century BC was in crisis, its democracy strained by war, its traditions threatened by new thinkers, its youth drawn to unorthodox teachers. Aristophanes needed a scapegoat, and Socrates, with his unsettling questions, shabby cloak, and crowd of followers, was an easy stand-in for everything destabilizing old Athens. His Socrates is less a man than a caricature of cultural anxiety.

And yet, contrast this with Socrates's contemporaries who actually wrote history. Thucydides, a generation's peer, anchored his *Peloponnesian War* with dates, battles, speeches, and cause-and-effect analysis.[16] Herodotus, though more prone to myth, still documented lineages, customs, and wars with scaffolding rooted in geography and names.[17] These men recorded history. Aristophanes wrote theater. And for Socrates, the so-called cornerstone of Western thought, we possess no historical chronicle at all. Only dialogues, apologias, and a comedy. Thus what survives of him is not a man, but three masks: Plato's mystic, Xenophon's gentleman, Aristophanes's fool.[18] No eyewitness record. No dateline. No chain of custody. Just voices bending him to their own ends.

If another teacher, one remembered in Gospels, not dialogues, had only three clashing portraits, none firsthand, scholars would tear Him apart. Yet this figure escapes such scrutiny, because he left only questions, never answers. What survives is not a man, but theater.

---

15. Aristophanes, *Clouds*, 94–145, 225–50.
16. Thucydides, *History of the Peloponnesian War* 1.22.
17. Herodotus, *Histories*, 1.
18. Dorion, "Rise and Fall," 1–23.

SOCRATES

The Trial: The Theater of Philosophy

Plato's *Apology* is one of the crown jewels of Western literature, a soaring defense of wisdom, virtue, and intellectual defiance. In it, Socrates stands before the Athenian court: serene, unflinching, delivering a master class in integrity before calmly drinking the hemlock. It is moving. It is majestic. It is also, almost certainly, fiction. There are no court records.[19] No transcripts. No jurors, prosecutors, or witnesses preserved. No independent historian verifies the proceedings. Not even the charges are clearly documented outside Plato's stylized account. Everything rests on the pen of a disciple writing decades later, elevating his teacher into a martyr for reason. The speech is too polished. The arc too precise. The ending too poetic. This is not legal history—it is philosophical theater.[20]

And consider the setting: democratic Athens, a city obsessed with civic recordkeeping. Thucydides, a contemporary of Socrates, catalogued tribunals, uprisings, and decrees with ruthless detail, naming individuals, motives, and outcomes.[21] Yet the most iconic trial in Athenian memory leaves no inscription, no court tablet, no trace in stone or scroll? Nothing? Now reverse the thought. Imagine if the trial of the Nazarene came to us only through one follower, without corroborating Gospels, without Pilate or Caiaphas, without the scaffolding of Passover or Roman law, without hostile witnesses or cultural frame, only a single, poetic retelling written decades later. Would scholars nod solemnly and call it philosophy? Or would they cry myth, fabrication, propaganda? They would tear it to shreds. But Plato's *Apology*? That is canon. It is taught in classrooms. Quoted in commencement halls. Framed as reason's triumph over ignorance.[22]

Why? Because Socrates flatters the mind. He makes no demand on the soul. His death requires no repentance, no rebirth, no cross. Christ does. He does not merely defend truth: He embodies it. His trial ends not with a clever speech but with a silence that thunders through history. His death is not philosophy but prophecy fulfilled, sin confronted, judgment borne. Socrates dies to console the thinker. Christ dies to convict the world. One is staged. The other struck, like lightning, tearing heaven from earth.

19. Brickhouse and Smith, *Trial and Execution of Socrates*, 7–10; Taylor, *Socrates*, 1–20.

20. Plato, *Apology*; Wilson, *Death of Socrates*, 63–67.

21. Thucydides, *History* 1.22.

22. Nails, *People of Plato*, xii–xiii; Blomberg, *Historical Reliability of the Gospels*, 215–20.

PART II. ECHOES WITHOUT A VOICE

Absence of External Confirmation

For a man hailed as the cornerstone of Western thought, Socrates leaves behind nothing but echoes. No Athenian record inscribes his speeches or trial. No decree carries his name. No foreign envoy, Babylonian, Persian, or Roman, bothers to note him. No grave. No stone. No dust-marked tomb. His existence survives only through Plato's reverent dialogues, Xenophon's moral essays, and Aristophanes's satire.[23] Not a mosaic of corroboration, but a fan club, a eulogy, and a cartoon.

Now imagine the same for the Nazarene. No Gospels. No Epistles (New Testament letters). No Tacitus. No Josephus. No Pilate on record. No crucifixion under empire. Only three conflicting essays, written decades later by loyal followers, and a Roman comedy lampooning Him as a fool. Would historians build their careers on such sand? Would scholars hold colloquia to parse His "wisdom?" Not a chance. They would shred it, myth, legend, propaganda.

Yet that evidentiary void is precisely the standard Socrates enjoys, unquestioned and unchallenged. Christ is different. His memory is not propped up by silence but hammered out in conflict. Caiaphas condemned Him. Pilate hesitated, then consented. Tacitus recorded His death.[24] Suetonius noted His following.[25] Pliny the Younger described His worship.[26] Even the Talmud, hostile as it is, preserves His name and crucifixion.[27] These are not endorsements. They are reluctant admissions. Friction, not flattery. Jesus's story was not coddled into existence; it was carved into the bedrock of history. We do not stand on rumor. We hold hostile receipts. A movement that bled its way through persecution, not privilege. A message that endured through blood, not bias.

Philosophical Immunity: The Idol of Academia

Why is Socrates untouchable? Because he asks nothing of you. He invites questions, but never verdicts. He makes you think, but never act. He never

---

23. Plato, *Apology* 17a–42a; Xenophon, *Memorabilia* 1.1–5.4, 3.7–4.2; Aristophanes, *Clouds*, 8–35.
24. Tacitus, *Annals* 15.44.
25. Suetonius, *Lives of the Twelve Caesars*, "Claudius" 25.
26. Pliny, *Letters* 10.96.
27. Babylonian Talmud, *Sanhedrin* 43a.

says, "Repent." Never says, "Follow me." Never demands allegiance, transformation, surrender. He is the perfect idol for academia: all abstraction, no accountability. A shrine to inquiry without conviction.

Academia calls him the "wisest man who ever lived,"[28] yet rarely pauses to ask how a man with no writings, no confirmed biography, no timeline, no hostile witnesses, and no grave has been canonized beyond critique.[29] No manuscript trail. No inscription. No anchor in history. And yet he stands, immune to cross-examination. Why? Because Socrates is harmless. He sharpens the mind but leaves the soul untouched. His ambiguity is his armor. He can be sculpted into whatever the age requires: skeptic, sage, secular saint. In that way, he is useful.

Jesus is not. He does not separate message from messenger. He does not say, "Here is the way." He says, "*I am the Way.*"[30] He does not point to truth; He embodies it. And that kind of clarity is intolerable to a world that prizes nuance over kneeling. Christ cannot be turned into a concept. He cannot be reduced to a mascot. He is either Lord, or liar.[31] That is why one is quoted in lectures, and the other is crucified in hearts.

Summing Up the Evidence: The Inherited Mind

Let us weigh him now, Socrates, against the very standards we've used for every giant. Unlike Plato, Aristotle, or even Confucius, whose words were either written or carefully transmitted, we have no direct trace of Socrates's mind. His absence is so profound that the very category of "pre-Socratic" philosophy exists as if he alone were the dividing line, a phantom turned into a milestone.

Contemporaneity? None. No record from his own lifetime. No writings. No inscriptions. Not a single speech recorded by someone who heard it.[32] Not one verified word in his own voice. Multiplicity of sources? Barely. Just three portrayals, Plato, Xenophon, Aristophanes, and they don't harmonize—they collide. One casts him as a mystic of eternal forms. Scholars call this tension the "Socratic problem": was Plato reporting the man, or inventing a mouthpiece for his own metaphysics? The problem itself is

28. Plato, *Apology* 21a–23b.
29. Bett, "Socrates," sec. 2.
30. John 14:6.
31. Lewis, *Mere Christianity*, 40–41.
32. Bett, "Socrates"; Nails, *People of Plato*.

PART II. ECHOES WITHOUT A VOICE

proof of the mask, that even in antiquity, Socrates's true voice was already obscured by another's agenda. One as a sober ethicist preaching moderation. One as a bug-eyed clown. And in Athens, comedy was not harmless. The stage was political weaponry. Aristophanes's lampoon was not just entertainment but persuasion, shaping public suspicion of Socrates long before the jury condemned him.[33]

These aren't perspectives; they're agendas.[34] External corroboration? Absent. No Babylonian envoy. No Persian chronicler. No Roman historian. Not a whisper beyond the Greek world.[35] Archeological support? Nothing. No grave. No household. No inscription. No artifact to tether him to the soil of time.[36] Chain of custody? Irrelevant. There is no original testimony to preserve. No firsthand record to trace. His entire memory is built on recollection, reinterpretation, reverence, passed like an heirloom, not preserved like history. And yet, he is canonized. Socrates is father of philosophy, enshrined in lecture halls, sheltered from critique. No historian demands contemporary confirmation. No scholar balks at the silence of hostile sources. No archeologist cries foul at the missing tomb. His emptiness is excused because he flatters the mind, never threatens the soul.

But Jesus of Nazareth? His words were written within living memory.[37] His life intersects with known officials. His crucifixion is recorded by both friend and foe.[38] His tomb was declared empty. His followers endured torture rather than recant.[39] And yet He is relentlessly questioned, dissected, dismissed. Why? Because Socrates asks nothing. He offers questions without consequence. Jesus does not. He claims not only to know the way, He claims to be it. He offers no detachable wisdom, only Himself. And that is the scandal. That is the offense. One is safe to quote. The other is dangerous to believe.

Socrates is safe. He remains in the mind, untouchable, unthreatening. Christ enters the will. He lays claim to the self. He overturns the altar, flips

---

33. Dover, *Aristophanic Comedy*, 67–72; Waterfield, *Why Socrates Died*, 52–60.

34. Bett, "Socrates"; Nails, *People of Plato*; Waterfield, *Why Socrates Died*, 52–60.

35. Bett, "Socrates"; Nails, *People of Plato*; Meier, *In the Fullness of Time*.

36. Brickhouse and Smith, *Trial and Execution of Socrates*, 7–10; Taylor, *Socrates*, 1–20.

37. Bauckham, *Jesus and the Eyewitnesses*, 7–17, 34–38.

38. Tacitus, *Annals* 15.44; Josephus, *Antiquities* 18.3.3; Pliny, *Letters* 10.96; Babylonian Talmud, *Sanhedrin* 43a.

39. Wright, *Resurrection of the Son of God*, 32–34, 607–10, 718–20.

the tables, demands the throne of the heart. That is why Socrates is admired, and Christ is crucified in every age. One is a mirror, reflecting the self. The other is a sword, dividing soul from flesh. One leaves you intact. The other requires you to die. For a man hailed as the cornerstone of Western thought, Socrates left behind no body, only shadows.[40] Aristophanes mocked him as absurd; later sculptors carved his features as caricature. Not a portrait, but a parody. His image was never fixed. His figure, never anchored. His life, never secured in stone. He is not a man of history, but of hindsight.

But Jesus? The earliest accounts we possess, letters and Gospels, aren't satire or stylized theater; they are urgent testimony.[41] No one paused to sketch His face because they were busy preserving His wounds. The emphasis was not His features but His impact: His words, His resurrection. The absence of His body is not oversight; it is ignition.[42] With Socrates, the missing body gathers dust. With Jesus, the missing body split history in two. One absence lies forgotten. The other demands an answer. We do not have His face. We have something far heavier. We have history bent around His absence. That tells us everything: Socrates disappears the deeper you dig. His birth year is debated, his life events vague, his death told only by loyalists, his tomb unknown. No epitaph, no inscription, no trace carved by contemporaries. His biography is a literary echo, not a historical bedrock. His voice is ventriloquism. His figure, a silhouette.

Christ stands opposite. His birth, His family, His enemies, His trial, His execution, anchored to names, places, and rulers still remembered.[43] Manuscripts multiplied within a generation. Cities and tombs remain. Testimony endured through blood. We do not just know His face; we know His fingerprints. Socrates is chalk on a wall, easily erased, easily redrawn. Jesus is a chisel in stone, impossible to ignore, dangerous to confront. And here is the truth: a silhouette can be admired without consequence. But a man with scars cannot. Once you see the wounds, you must ask why they're there, and who drove the nail. That is the question the world still runs from.

---

40. Zanker, *Mask of Socrates*, 3–5; Aristophanes, *Clouds* 8–35.

41. Bauckham, *Jesus and the Eyewitnesses*, 5–9.

42. Wright, *Resurrection of the Son of God*, 687–706.

43. Ehrman, *Did Jesus Exist?*, 174–80; Blomberg, *Historical Reliability of the Gospels*, 24–28.

PART II. ECHOES WITHOUT A VOICE

Three Masks and a King

So what do we have? A man without writings. Without records. Without a grave. Remembered only through masks and echoes. Socrates is not history's bedrock; he is its phantom. A ghost crowned by admirers, enshrined in syllabi, immune to scrutiny because he asks nothing of the soul. He is safe because he is silence. But silence does not satisfy. For a man hailed as the father of philosophy, should there not be a tomb? A marker? Some trace to anchor him in the earth he walked? He was only a man, and men leave remains. His missing body is not a mystery that stirred movements; it is an indifference that left none. His absence whispers doubt, not conviction.[44]

Christ is different. His missing body does not fade into silence; it erupts into history. The absence was noticed. Contested. Proclaimed. His tomb was remembered precisely because it was empty.[45] His followers did not craft masks in His place, they carried scars in His name. The body of Socrates is forgotten because it never mattered. The body of Jesus is absent because it mattered too much to ignore. And here lies the difference: philosophy gave us Socrates, but history bent around Jesus. One leaves us with questions. The other forces an answer. One is admired from a distance. The other is crucified when He draws near.

> *Socrates remains a mask, shaped by others, fading the deeper you dig.*
> *Christ remains a King, wounded yet risen, impossible to erase.*
> *The world still prefers the mask.*
> *But only the King can save.*

---

44. Brickhouse and Smith, *Trial and Execution of Socrates*, 7–10; Zanker, *Mask of Socrates*, 3–5.

45. Wright, *Resurrection of the Son of God*, 687–706; Bauckham, *Jesus and the Eyewitnesses*, 5–9.

# PART III

Documented Bureaucrats and Emperors

IN THIS SECTION, WE confront the giants of governance, men remembered not for their virtue, but for their visibility. Their names are carved into marble, minted on coinage, preserved in edicts, and echoed through imperial archives.[1] They were not remembered by faith, but by form: stone, statute, conquest, and control. Their legacies were not carried by apostles, but by scribes of the state. They are not legends whispered from disciple to disciple: they are bureaucrats, emperors, governors. And yet, the question remains: how much of what we accept as history is truth? And how much is curated fiction, shaped by the politics of power, survival, and propaganda?

1. Pontius Pilate, the Roman administrator whose brief encounter with Christ echoes louder than his entire career.[2]

2. Tiberius Caesar, shrouded in contradiction,[3] wielding absolute power from the shadows of the imperial machine.

3. Julius Caesar, the dictator who shaped Rome's legacy—through his own pen and the pens of those who served it.[4]

---

1. Millar, *Emperor in the Roman World*, 15–28; Grant, *Twelve Caesars*, 4–12. These works broadly confirm the bureaucratic and material legacy of Roman rulers—inscriptions, coinage, legal records.

2. Bond, *Pontius Pilate in History and Interpretation*, 1–3. Bond's analysis confirms Pilate's minimal footprint outside the Gospels, reinforcing the irony in this claim.

3. Suetonius, *Twelve Caesars* 1.3–6, 6.50 on the contradictory portrayals of Tiberius as aloof, tyrannical, and bureaucratically distant.

4. Caesar, *Gallic War* on Caesar, who literally wrote his own legacy through his *Commentaries*.

PART III. DOCUMENTED BUREAUCRATS AND EMPERORS

These men were known through documents, decrees, and dominion. But the world believes their stories, without hesitation, without anguish, without doubt. Until those same records mention the Nazarene.[5] Then suddenly, the scroll is suspect. The ink is questioned. And gospel turns to myth, because the subject is no longer Caesar. It is Christ.

---

5. Tacitus, *Annals* 15.44; Josephus, *Antiquities* 18.3.3; Pliny, *Letters* 10.96. These Roman sources mention Jesus, yet are often questioned more severely than state records of emperors.

Julius Caesar
The Emperor's Illusion

JULIUS CAESAR: ROMAN GENERAL, statesman, self-made legend. Born in 100 BC, cut down in 44 BC.[1] He wrote his own record, the *Gallic War* and *Civil War*, not only conquering lands but narrating his own rise.[2] He crowned himself in prose before Rome crowned him in office. Proclaimed "dictator for life," he fell beneath the knives of senators.[3] His death signaled the end of the Republic and the birth of Empire.[4] He is remembered as military genius, political reformer, and architect of imperial Rome. But beneath the marble busts and gilded rhetoric, what does the evidence truly say? Before we weigh Caesar's legacy, we recall the Five Pillars of Historical Trust: contemporaneity, multiplicity, external corroboration, archeological support, and Chain of Custody.[5] These are not theology, but methodology.[6] If any figure cannot stand on them, they should not be spared scrutiny simply because tradition made them famous. So let us test the man who forged the myth of Rome: Julius Caesar.

---

1. Suetonius, *Julius Caesar* 7–10.
2. Caesar, *Gallic War* 1.1; Caesar, *Civil War* 1.1; Canfora, *Julius Caesar*, 87–95.
3. Plutarch, *Life of Caesar* 57.
4. Goldsworthy, *Caesar*, 581–96.
5. LaBarbera, *Truth at the Gate*, x–xx.
6. Bauckham, *Jesus and the Eyewitnesses*, 7–9.

PART III. DOCUMENTED BUREAUCRATS AND EMPERORS

The Third-Person Throne: Caesar's Self-Made Narrative

Julius Caesar is often praised as one of the best-documented figures of antiquity.[7] After all, we possess his own words, firsthand accounts of war and politics. But those "accounts" are not what they seem. They are not history in the modern sense. They are self-forged mythology, written by a man who knew that while the sword could conquer nations, the quill could conquer time.

His two most famous works, the *Gallic War* and the *Civil War*, are written entirely in the third person: "Caesar advanced," "Caesar commanded," "Caesar conquered."[8] This was not humility. It was theater. By casting himself as a detached character in a historical drama, Caesar created the illusion of objectivity.[9] Rhetorical sleight of hand, commentary disguised as record, ego dressed as narrative. Far from neutral, these texts are performances meant to immortalize the man behind the myth.

Modern scholars have long acknowledged this manipulation. Ronald Syme called it "political propaganda at its most polished," crafted to justify Caesar's campaigns to Senate and people.[10] These were not journals. They were press releases carved in stone. Caesar curated his image with precision, erasing defeats, minimizing civilian casualties, inflating the size and threat of his enemies.[11] Every line bent to one purpose: Caesar as inevitable, not only in victory, but in history itself.

Pause and consider: what if Jesus had done the same? What if the Gospels read, "And Jesus, the wisest of men, healed all, confounded every foe, and ascended in glory?" Always in the third person. Always victorious. No betrayal. No agony in Gethsemane. No cross. Only power. Would scholars accept it? Would skeptics cite it as history? Of course not—they would dismiss it as propaganda, self-authored mythology posing as truth.[12]

And yet Caesar's version of himself remains untouched. Quoted in classrooms. Treated as foundational history. His voice stands unchallenged because he wrote it before anyone else could. His sword won territory, but

---

7. Goldsworthy, *Caesar*, 2–5.
8. Caesar, *Gallic War* 1.1; Caesar, *Civil War* 1.1.
9. Pelling, "Caesar's Narrative," 186–202.
10. Syme, *Roman Revolution*, 11.
11. Canfora, *Julius Caesar*, 102–10.
12. Bauckham, *Jesus and the Eyewitnesses*, 5–9.

Julius Caesar

his ink won eternity.[13] The truth is this: Caesar's greatest weapon was not military genius. It was narrative control. He didn't just conquer Gaul. He conquered how Gaul would be remembered. That is the difference. One man let others tell the story, and chose to die rather than write it himself. The other crowned himself with his own pen. And somehow, only one is doubted.[14]

Propaganda for Rome, Not Posterity

Who was Caesar writing for? Not historians. Not scholars. Not posterity. His *Commentarii* were crafted for the Roman masses, the Senate, and, above all, his own legions.[15] These were not records. They were weapons.[16] Field reports forged into manifestos. Justifications dressed as journalism. Caesar wasn't documenting events. He was directing perception. And he succeeded. When Caesar narrates his wars in the third person, he is not aiming at objectivity—he is crafting myth. The voice may sound detached, but the intent is deeply personal: to seduce the reader into believing they witness impartial history when in fact they absorb a story engineered for dominance.[17] Victories are spotlighted. Failures reframed. Enemies reduced to caricature. Rebellions recast as just causes to suppress. These are not chronicles. They are theater, scripted to affirm his power, justify his actions, and crown him in the court of public opinion. Caesar knew what every empire knows: Rome loved a winner. So he became one, by sword, yes, but more lastingly, by pen.[18]

Modern scholars admit as much. While Caesar's *Commentarii* are praised for clarity and elegance, they are rarely scrutinized for what they truly are: propaganda, not autobiography.[19] Not private reflections. Not impartial records. They were campaigns of persuasion, crafted to sway Senate, masses, and legions. Every sentence was a weapon wrapped in the language of report. And in Rome's political machinery, persuasion was not only ef-

---

13. Goldsworthy, *Caesar*, 247–50.
14. Cf. John 19:35; Luke 1:1–4.
15. Goldsworthy, *Caesar*, 392–95.
16. Wiseman, *Invention of History in Ancient Rome*, 83–85.
17. Syme, *Roman Revolution*, 55.
18. Riggsby, *Caesar in Gaul and Rome*, 70–73.
19. Goldsworthy, *Caesar*, 392.

fective. It was lethal.[20] Now consider the contrast: what if Christ had written His own Gospel in the third person, glorifying His miracles, omitting the cross, exaggerating the crowds, presenting Himself as an unchallenged savior? Would scholars accept it? Would skeptics deem it reliable? Of course not. They would dismiss it as propaganda, a cult manifesto. And yet Caesar does exactly this. He curates his image, controls his narrative, glorifies his power, and the world calls it history.[21]

Even by the Five Pillars, Caesar's record falters under scrutiny. Contemporaneity? Yes, but the sole witness is Caesar himself. That is not testimony. That is theater. Multiplicity? None. No rival voice, no counterweight. External corroboration? Rome's echo chamber.[22] Archaeology? Yes, but bricks and coins prove only presence, not truth. Chain of Custody? Preserved, yet propaganda endures as easily as honesty.[23] What then? We acknowledge the flaw. The Pillars are not a checklist that grants automatic trust; they are a lens. A source may stand on four of five and still crumble if its purpose is conquest rather than clarity. And Caesar's purpose is unmistakable. He was not writing history. He was manufacturing victory.

Suetonius and the Tabloid Lens

By the time Suetonius wrote the *Twelve Caesars* in the early second century, Julius Caesar had long passed from man into myth.[24] Suetonius was no historian in the classical sense. He was a gossip curator, secretary to Emperor Hadrian, compiling tales laced with rumor, scandal, and aristocratic drama.[25] His tone was not analytical but voyeuristic. He did not sift for truth; he entertained power. His pages drip with absurd anecdotes: Caesar weeping at Alexander's statue, laughing at omens, seducing senators' wives, even allegedly submitting himself to King Nicomedes of Bithynia.[26] Suetonius does not weigh evidence. He parades spectacle.[27]

---

20. Wiseman, *History in Ancient Rome*, 82–85; Syme, *Roman Revolution*, 56.
21. Bauckham, *Jesus and the Eyewitnesses*, 5–9.
22. Riggsby, *Caesar in Gaul and Rome*, 92.
23. Bett, *Propaganda and the Roman Historian*, 14.
24. Suetonius, *Twelve Caesars*, "Julius" 1.
25. Bradley, *Suetonius' Caesars*, 23–27.
26. Suetonius, *Twelve Caesars*, "Julius" 7, 52.
27. Wallace-Hadrill, *Suetonius*, 45–48.

Julius Caesar

And yet, we still quote him. Suetonius's Caesar, embroidered with gossip and theatrical invention, is treated as plausible, even when it reads like tabloid absurdity. Why? Because we enjoy the legend. We let the timeline stretch, the gossip stand, the spectacle masquerade as biography. Why? Because Caesar does not threaten the soul. He is safe. Distant. Entertaining.

But imagine if Suetonius had written about Jesus. Imagine our earliest Gospel arriving like the *Twelve Caesars*: stuffed with scandal and innuendo, written a century and a half after the fact.[28] Would scholars call it credible? Would skeptics nod and footnote? Of course not. They would dismiss it as propaganda, myth, religious fiction. And yet with Caesar, they nod and cite.[29] Because Suetonius's Caesar makes no demands. He does not say, "Repent." He does not claim lordship. He only entertains. And in the modern world, we forgive anything that entertains, except the truth that convicts.

Plutarch and the Lens of Morality

Enter Plutarch: Greek philosopher, priest of Delphi, author of the *Parallel Lives*.[30] He did not write as a historian but as a sculptor of virtue. His aim was not to preserve events but to shape character. His *Life of Caesar*, written more than 150 years after Caesar's death, was not a chronicle but a meditation on ambition.[31] Caesar is paired with Alexander the Great not to measure history but to reflect on greatness. This is not biography. It is a moral mirror.

Plutarch admits as much. He acknowledges smoothing contradictions, omitting what he deems irrelevant, amplifying traits to serve his lesson.[32] He was not giving us the man. He was crafting a parable. His tools were not dates or documents but themes: ambition, fate, virtue, vice.[33] He did not write with the ink of a historian. He carved with the chisel of a moralist. And yet Plutarch's Caesar is still cited as "history."[34] Not because it meets rigorous standards but because it flatters the story of greatness we prefer. To doubt it costs nothing. To believe it carries no consequence. So

28. Grant, *Twelve Caesars*, x–xii.
29. Edwards, *Death in Ancient Rome*, 77–80.
30. Plutarch, *Caesar* 3–5.
31. Seager, *Julius Caesar*, 2–4.
32. Plutarch, *Alexander-Caesar* 1.2.
33. Pelling, "Plutarch and Roman Politics," 145–64.
34. Lintott, "Value of Plutarch's *Lives*," 1–14.

PART III. DOCUMENTED BUREAUCRATS AND EMPERORS

we nod and accept it. We forgive the reshaping because Caesar demands nothing of us. Plutarch moralizes, yes, but only in the abstract.[35] Caesar becomes a character.

Now imagine if Christ's story were told this way: a philosopher, writing 150 years after the fact, with no access to eyewitnesses, no preserved names, no political context, only a stylized parable about humility and obedience, loosely tethered to a legend. Would scholars nod? Would skeptics stay silent? Of course not. Caesar is safe because his story instructs. Jesus is dangerous because His story transforms.[36]

Cassius Dio and the Senatorial Script

Cassius Dio, Roman senator of the third century, wrote his *Roman History* more than two centuries after Caesar's death.[37] His vantage was not memory but hindsight. Born in Bithynia, writing in Greek, and serving the Senate under the Severan emperors, Dio was no impartial chronicler. He was steeped in the imperial system and wrote for its ruling class. His Caesar is not a man on trial. He is inevitability itself, the Republic's decline, the Empire's rise. His narrative breathes resignation: Rome was always destined for monarchy, and Caesar was its chosen vehicle.[38]

But this is not history. It is retroactive justification. Dio's Caesar is molded by the imperial order Dio himself served under. His voice is the Senate's echo, written in an age when emperors were the norm.[39] The Republic had long been ashes; of course Caesar looked inevitable. His pen did not preserve a life. It preserved an outcome, monarchy as destiny. And yet scholars still lean on Dio, though he wrote centuries too late, drawing from lost sources and smoothing them into the pattern of inevitability.[40] By the Five Pillars his work collapses: no contemporaneity, no multiplicity, only imperial hindsight bound in literary polish. What Dio offers is not testimony but obituary, the Republic buried, the Empire enthroned.

Now imagine if Christ's story first appeared two centuries later, crafted by a court philosopher, shaped to flatter the rulers of the day. Would any

---

35. Pelling, "Plutarch's Caesar," 147–54.
36. Bauckham, *Jesus and the Eyewitnesses*, 5–9.
37. Dio, *Roman History* 37.1–3.
38. Dio, *Roman History* 44.1.
39. Millar, *Study of Cassius Dio*, 25–27.
40. Gabba, *Dio's Caesar*, 63–67.

Julius Caesar

take it as reliable? Or would we laugh at it as propaganda for the regime it served? Caesar's Dio is footnoted as history. Christ's disciples, writing within decades, are doubted. The irony could not be sharper: the later the witness, the safer the story. Caesar's myth is preserved. Christ's truth is denied.

Appian and the Propagandist Lens

Appian of Alexandria, writing in the second century, gave his account of Caesar in the *Civil Wars*.[41] His stage was not the man but the blood-soaked theater of Rome's collapse. Families divided, senators cut down, streets red with vengeance, Appian painted Caesar less as a person and more as the hinge upon which the Republic shattered and the Empire was born.[42] But Appian was no witness. He wrote nearly two hundred years after the fact, long after the dust had settled. His sources are uncertain, his perspective Roman, his agenda clear: to show empire as the tragic but necessary fruit of civil war.[43] In his hands Caesar is not examined; he is absorbed into destiny. The Republic falls, and Caesar becomes its storm, its inevitability.

By the Five Pillars, Appian fares no better than Dio. No contemporaneity. Multiplicity reduced to recycled tradition. External voices absent. Archaeology mute on motive. What remains is literature, not testimony, a tragic script written with hindsight.[44] His pages are not the pulse of Caesar's age. They are the elegy of a Rome already resigned to empire. Now imagine if the passion of Christ reached us only through such a voice: a philosopher, writing two centuries later, weaving a stylized tale of suffering and transcendence, stripped of names, dates, and eyewitnesses. Would scholars call it reliable? Would skeptics let it stand? Of course not. They would call it legend. But Appian is footnoted. Caesar's myth endures. Christ's truth is dismissed. The pen of empire is excused; the pen of disciples is condemned.

The Roman Chorus of Voices

So what do we have? Four Roman narrators, none contemporary, each bending Caesar into their own design. Suetonius, the gossip curator, gave

---

41. Appian, *Civil Wars* 2.1–5.
42. Appian, *Civil Wars* 2.110–17.
43. Carter, *Appian and the Romans*, 82–85.
44. Richardson, *Appian in Context*, 102–6.

us scandal and spectacle. Plutarch, the moralist, carved parables from ambition. Dio, the senator, resigned himself to monarchy as destiny. Appian, the tragedian, folded Caesar into the inevitability of civil war. Not one was close to the man. Not one preserved an unvarnished witness. Together they form a chorus, entertaining, instructive, resigned, tragic, but not reliable. Their pages are mirrors of their own times, not windows into Caesar's. And yet these are the voices we cite, the testimony we elevate, the pillars we lean on as though they can bear the weight of history. By the standards we claim to value—contemporaneity, multiplicity, external corroboration, archeological support, manuscript preservation—the case is thin. If these same voices had been our only accounts of Christ, written centuries late, colored by rumor, moralizing, resignation, and tragedy, they would be scorned. But because they speak of Caesar, we accept them. In the trial of history, the conqueror's shadow is forgiven. The crucified man is not.

Lack of Eyewitness Correction

One of the most overlooked advantages Caesar had in crafting his legacy was silence, not the silence of peace, but the silence of conquest. His *Commentarii* were not reflections. They were proclamations.[45] Why uncontested? Because no one was left to contest them. His enemies were either dead, disgraced, or politically broken. Pompey was defeated and assassinated. Cato chose suicide over submission.[46]

Cicero, the greatest orator of the age, praised Caesar's clemency in public, even calling him "a man for all humanity."[47] But in his private letters, his tone trembles with unease, admiration laced with fear. He saw Caesar's mercy not as benevolence but as power sharpened to a finer edge. His voice, like so many others, bent beneath the weight of survival.

Cato would not bend. He chose death. His suicide became the last, desperate protest of Republican virtue, a gesture later hailed as noble.[48] Yet even in death, his witness failed. He left no rebuttal, no counter-history, only a silence Rome could glorify but never hear.

---

45. Goldsworthy, *Caesar*, 220–25.
46. Plutarch, *Pompey* 78.4; Plutarch, *Cato the Younger* 66.4.
47. Cicero, *Letters to Atticus* 13.28; Syme, *Roman Revolution*, 113–15.
48. Plutarch, *Cato the Younger* 66.4; Seager, *Julius Caesar*, 133–35.

JULIUS CAESAR

Brutus and the conspirators fared no better. They struck Caesar down, claiming to restore liberty.[49] But the dagger that killed the man could not kill his myth. Instead of freedom, their testimony collapsed into chaos; the Republic drowned in the very blood they spilled. Betrayal silenced itself. And the soldiers? Their loyalty was absolute. He bought them with land, gold, and victory. He fed them glory, and they fed him silence.[50] No memoirs, no challenges, no doubts. Only devotion, drilled and disciplined, shouting his name louder than any opponent could speak.

So where are the counter-memoirs? The rebuttals?[51] The corrections from rival generals or surviving senators? There were none. Those who might have objected were already erased.[52] Caesar's version survived not because it was unassailable, but because he silenced the alternatives. He became the last voice standing. And when only one voice remains, even propaganda becomes precedent. Even a lie becomes law.

Now contrast that with Jesus. His enemies lived. They plotted, arrested, interrogated, and crucified Him.[53] The Sanhedrin endured. Roman officials remained. Pagan philosophers wrote. Yet they could not stop the record. The Gospels spread. The letters multiplied.[54] The tomb stood empty. And His followers did not slaughter their critics. They died under them. They bled in arenas, not on Senate floors.[55] Caesar silenced opposition to preserve his myth. Jesus's opposition shouted, and still could not stop the truth. One used power to erase resistance. The other allowed resistance to reveal power. And that, again, is the difference: Caesar ended the voices. Christ ignited them.

The Chorus of the Silenced

So the voices gather, and yet none stand. Cicero spoke with eloquence, but his words bent in the winds of fear. Cato thundered against Caesar, but his protest ended in self-destruction. Brutus and the conspirators raised daggers in liberty's name, but their witness dissolved into civil war. And the

49. Plutarch, *Brutus*, 17-20; Appian, *Civil Wars* 2.113-17.
50. Goldsworthy, *Caesar*, 292-95.
51. Goldsworthy, *Caesar*, 5-6, 418-20.
52. Syme, *Roman Revolution*, 4-5, 15-18, 377-79.
53. Mark 14-15; Luke 22-23.
54. Bauckham, *Jesus and the Eyewitnesses*, 5-9.
55. Tacitus, *Annals* 15.44.

soldiers, loyal, devoted, unflinching, roared Caesar's name until every other voice was drowned. Together they do not correct him. They confirm him. Their silence, their compromise, their failure, their loyalty, all became mortar for Caesar's myth. Not one preserved a rival account. Not one penned a counter-history. Their words, when spoken, were swallowed by Caesar's victories. Their absence left him uncontested. And so the verdict of voices is the same as the verdict of conquest: Caesar alone was heard. His enemies ended themselves. His allies muted themselves. His soldiers deified him in life, and his successors immortalized him in death. The trial of testimony ends not with correction, but with capitulation.

The Empire of Caesar vs. The Kingdom of Christ

Let's talk about paper, or rather, parchment. Skeptics posture as champions of hard evidence: verified documents, preserved records, reliable manuscript trails. So weigh Caesar and Christ on that battlefield. We possess just ten primary manuscripts of Caesar's *Gallic Wars*. That's it. Ten. And the earliest full copy dates to the ninth century, almost nine hundred years after Caesar's death.[56] Transmitted, recopied, curated by medieval scribes, centuries removed from the man, with no way to verify authenticity or correct bias. And yet no one blinks. No one objects. The content is accepted. The story believed. Caesar's legacy stands unshaken. Now compare that to the New Testament.

We have over 5,800 Greek manuscripts, plus tens of thousands more in Latin, Syriac, Coptic, and other languages.[57] Among them is P52, a fragment of John's Gospel dated within decades of Jesus's crucifixion, not centuries.[58] Complete codices like Sinaiticus and Vaticanus, from the fourth century, bridge directly to the early church.[59] The chain of transmission is vast, transparent, and internally consistent. Early church fathers cite the Gospels. Roman officials acknowledge the movement. Jewish sources attack it.[60] It is not a manuscript tradition. It is a manuscript flood. And it dwarfs every other ancient figure, including Caesar.

So ask the question plainly:

56. Metzger and Ehrman, *Text of the New Testament*, 34–35.
57. Wallace, *Revisiting the Corruption of the New Testament*, 24.
58. Comfort, *Encountering the Manuscripts*, 56–59.
59. Ehrman and Holmes, *Text of the New Testament*, 45–46.
60. Bauckham, *Jesus and the Eyewitnesses*, 267–70.

Julius Caesar

Why is Caesar believed with ten manuscripts written nine centuries later, while Jesus is doubted with thousands within the first three?
Because Caesar offers conquest.
Jesus offers a cross.

And the skeptic will always prefer a king with a sword to a King who says, "Deny yourself."[61] The manuscript evidence isn't just compelling. It is devastating to the double standard.[62] Caesar crowned himself with ink. He crossed rivers, razed cities, and rewrote the reasons afterward.[63] He wielded sword in one hand, pen in the other, and with them conquered not just Gaul, but memory itself. His *Commentarii*, written in third person, were not accounts but advertisements, not history but campaigns.[64] And because no one lived to refute them, they remained. But by the standards of serious history, the Five Pillars, Caesar's legacy begins to crumble. Contemporaneity? His writings survive only in manuscripts copied centuries later.[65] Multiplicity? A handful of sources, none independent, all stylized, all politically charged.[66] External corroboration? Sparse. His enemies were killed, silenced, or absorbed into empire.[67] Archaeology? Coins and statues prove he ruled, not what he wrote.[68] Chain of Custody? A dozen ancient copies, none earlier than the ninth century.[69] By the scales we claim to use, Caesar fails the test.

Now turn to Christ. He is recorded by those who walked beside Him. His words echo in four distinct Gospels. His life is confirmed not only by friends but by Roman officials and Jewish adversaries alike. Cities, priests, governors, disciples, named, placed, anchored in real time. His manuscript tradition is unmatched in the ancient world: over 5,800 Greek copies, fragments dating within decades of His life.[70] And still, He is doubted. Why? Because Caesar exalted himself and demands nothing of your soul. Christ let others speak, and then called you to surrender yours. Caesar wrote

---

61. Luke 9:23.
62. Wallace, *Revisiting the Corruption*, 27.
63. Suetonius, *Julius Caesar* 30–33.
64. Wiseman, *Myths of Rome*, 60–63.
65. Reynolds and Wilson, *Scribes and Scholars*, 9–13.
66. Scullard, *From the Gracchi to Nero*, 157.
67. Goldsworthy, *Caesar*, 446–52.
68. Boatwright et al., *Romans*, 228–32.
69. Metzger and Ehrman, *Text of the New Testament*, 36–40.
70. Comfort and Barrett, *Text of the Earliest New Testament*, 13–17.

himself into history and died to preserve his name. Christ wrote nothing, and died to preserve your eternity. Caesar conquered nations. Christ conquered death. Caesar silenced opposition. Christ ignited witnesses. Caesar left monuments that crumbled. Christ left disciples whose witness endures. Caesar's empire fell to dust. Christ's kingdom cannot be shaken.

Tiberius Caesar
The Forgotten Emperor

TIBERIUS CAESAR, BORN IN 42 BC, died in 37 AD, was the second emperor of Rome, the adopted son of Augustus, and ruler from AD 14 to 37.[1] He held dominion over the known world during one of the most consequential decades in human history: the crucifixion of Jesus Christ.[2] Yet despite presiding over the age that altered eternity, Tiberius himself remains a footnote. Overshadowed by the glory of Augustus and the infamy of Caligula,[3] his reign is remembered less for its might than for its murk. That murk wasn't an accident. It was constructed. In his final years, Tiberius withdrew from Rome, retreating to Capri[4] while bureaucrats and Praetorians governed in his name. Silence hardened into legend. The gaps were not left empty; they were filled with rumor. And rumor, repeated without rebuttal, ossifies into myth, especially when power shields it from scrutiny.[5]

What survives of Tiberius is not preserved clarity, but refracted memory. No writings in his own hand. No speeches. No letters. No personal testimony.[6] To be fair, few emperors left volumes. But with Tiberius, the silence is louder.[7] Because at the moment history most needed a record, the reign under which the Son of God was condemned, the emperor at its center vanished behind the veil. He left behind no voice, only rumor, reflection,

---

1. Tacitus, *Annals* 1.3; Suetonius, *Twelve Caesars*, "Tiberius" 5.
2. Luke 3:1; Tacitus, *Annals* 15.44.
3. Suetonius, *Tiberius* 21–23; Scullard, *From the Gracchi to Nero*, 153–55.
4. Tacitus, *Annals* 4.57–8.1; Suetonius, *Tiberius* 39–41.
5. Pelling, *Plutarch and History*, 1–14.
6. Shotter, *Tiberius Caesar*, 5–7.
7. Levick, *Tiberius the Politician*, 1–2, 107–9.

PART III. DOCUMENTED BUREAUCRATS AND EMPERORS

and secondhand sketches written long after his death.[8] By the Five Pillars of Historical Credibility, contemporaneity, multiplicity, external confirmation, archaeology, and Chain of Custody, Tiberius is no titan. He is a shadow. A ruler reconstructed by others, never seen clearly in his own time. And yet, no one doubts him. So let us ask it plainly: why is the emperor who left no testimony, no trail, and no voice accepted without hesitation, while the crucified God, echoed in thousands of manuscripts, named by enemies, and preserved across centuries, is treated as fiction? Let's begin.

The Emperor No One Talks About

Tiberius Caesar reigned during one of the most pivotal moments in human history: the crucifixion of Jesus of Nazareth.[9] He held absolute power over the Roman world. And yet, despite all his authority, all his armies, titles, and control, he drifts through history like a rumor.[10] Let that sink in: the most powerful man alive during the most significant death the world has ever known, and his record is soft. Speculative. Hollow. Why? This was no minor provincial official. This was Caesar. Emperors crave legacy: they etch victories in stone, commission poets, and raise statues to themselves. Augustus filled the empire with monuments. Nero filled it with fire and verse. But Tiberius? He leaves almost nothing. No memoirs, no manifestos, no grand declarations.

Instead, he retreats, both physically and historically. In AD 26, he vanishes from Rome and never returns.[11] By AD 30, when Jesus stands before Pontius Pilate, Tiberius is isolated on the island of Capri, surrounded by whispers, paranoia, and silence.[12] The emperor of the known world... missing from the center of history. That should be an anomaly. It should raise alarms. Why did he disappear? Why does his narrative fade just as Christ's begins to rise? Is it coincidence, or consequence? How is it that the ruler of an empire escapes scrutiny, while the crucified carpenter bears the weight of every question? Historians rarely ask. Textbooks barely linger.[13] The silence is left unchallenged, becoming its own kind of story, a ghostly shrug across

8. Tacitus, *Annals* 6.6; Suetonius, *Twelve Caesars*, 145.
9. Tacitus, *Annals* 15.44; Eusebius, *Church History* 2.2.
10. Levick, *Tiberius the Politician*, 1–5.
11. Tacitus, *Annals* 6.50–51; Suetonius, *Twelve Caesars*, "Tiberius" 39.
12. Shotter, *Tiberius Caesar*, 63–67; Suetonius, *Twelve Caesars*, "Tiberius" 40–42.
13. Champlin, "Tiberius the Wise," 306–30.

the page. And maybe that's the answer. Maybe history, like power, abhors a rival. Because Jesus's emergence didn't just mark a new faith. It marked a disruption.[14] A fracture in the order. And so Tiberius is allowed to fade. He slips into the background because to ask where he was is to ask who Christ truly was.[15] And that is the question history dares not answer.

The Cynic with a Quill: Tacitus's Tiberius

Tacitus, Rome's sharpest pen and fiercest political skeptic, wrote the *Annals* between AD 110 and 120.[16] He was no apologist. No sentimental chronicler. He despised emperors, detested tyranny, and wielded language like a dagger. His sentences cut. His portraits bleed. And yet, even in his contempt, he could not erase the record. His portrayal of Tiberius is brutal: a man consumed by suspicion, withdrawn to Capri, twisted by fear, and surrounded by corruption.[17] Tacitus paints him as a decaying shell of a ruler, a man whose retreat mirrors the moral collapse of the empire itself. He does not soften. He does not glorify. He dissects. But—and here lies the irony—in all his cynicism, Tacitus still confirms the timeline. He verifies the structure. He names the names. His hatred could not hide the history.

> *Christus, from whom the name [Christian] had its origin, suffered the extreme penalty during the reign of Tiberius at the hands of one of our procurators, Pontius Pilate. (Annals 15.44)*[18]

Here it is. A hostile witness, writing eighty years after the fact, aiming to mock and marginalize a rising sect, yet instead, cementing the timeline. Tiberius reigned. Pilate governed. And Jesus was executed. Tacitus didn't set out to fan the flames of faith. He meant to douse them. But even his sneer becomes one of the strongest non-Christian confirmations of Jesus's death in all ancient history.[19] We've seen this pattern before: enemies affirm what friends preserve. Rome's cynic records what Rome's poets and priests could never silence. And though Tacitus's tone is cold, the facts are clear. He couldn't erase Christ, because history already held Him in its grip. Tiberius

---

14. Wright, *Jesus and the Victory of God*, 153–72.
15. Bauckham, *Jesus and the Eyewitnesses*, 15–30, 493–524.
16. Tacitus, *Annals* 1.1.
17. Tacitus, *Annals* 6.50–51.
18. Tacitus, *Annals* 6.50–51.
19. Tacitus, *Annals* 6.50–51.

ruled. Pilate judged. The Nazarene was crucified. The man who tried to undermine Christianity ended up testifying against his own intent. That is how history works, when truth refuses to die.

The Gossip Scribe: Suetonius's Tiberius

Suetonius, writing nearly two centuries after Tiberius's birth, gives us not history but scandal, a lurid anthology of rumor and rot.[20] His *Twelve Caesars* is part biographical sketch, part imperial roast, weaving court gossip, archival whispers, and salacious detail into what reads like a political soap opera.[21] It is as if TMZ rewrote the *Encyclopedia Britannica* with a grudge and a quill. He delights in the absurd. He leans into it. His Tiberius is no emperor but a degenerate recluse, lurking on Capri in a palace of vice, cruelty, and madness.[22] Sexual deviancy. Paranoia. Sadistic games. Suetonius pours it on because his audience, steeped in post-Neronian hunger for imperial scandal, demanded fire, not footnotes. Rome consumed these stories as civic entertainment, a kind of "safe rebellion," mocking the throne without burning it down.

On retiring to Capri he devised a pleasance for his secret orgies: teams of wantons of both sexes, selected as experts in deviant intercourse and dubbed "analists," copulated before him in triple unions to excite his flagging passions. He trained little boys (whom he termed "tiddlers") to crawl between his thighs when he went swimming and tease him with their licks and nibbles.[23]

Suetonius offers no citations, no cross-examination, only spectacle. Unlike Tacitus, who analyzes events, Suetonius stages them as if they were theater.[24] By the Five Pillars of Historical Scrutiny, he collapses beneath his own theatrics. And yet, even buried beneath vulgarity, Tiberius still stands. His reign is fixed. His rule overlaps precisely with the years the Gospels record. The scandal cannot touch the dates; the ridicule cannot erase the record. Even if the palace burned with vice, the calendar burned on. Tiberius, for all his grotesque excesses, is still confirmed as ruling from AD 14 to 37.[25]

20. Suetonius, *Tiberius*, 61–76.
21. Suetonius, *Tiberius*, 61–76.
22. Suetonius, *Tiberius*, 43–44.
23. Suetonius, *Tiberius*, 43.
24. Rose, *Dynastic Commemoration*, 86–87.
25. Barnes, *Sources of the Historia Augusta*, 124.

His name is stamped like a watermark across the crucifixion of Christ. And here lies the irony. Had Suetonius used the same tone against Jesus, mocking His miracles, branding His disciples as deluded, His teachings as madness, modern skeptics would dismiss the account as bias, forgery, or legend. But for Tiberius? The gossip is treated as gold. The later the source, the more decadent the tale, the more eagerly it is cited. Yet even in mockery, Suetonius cannot escape chronology. He may decorate the truth, but he cannot delete it. Capri becomes grotesque, but it is still Capri. The emperor becomes infamous, but he remains the emperor. And so Christ's death under Pilate, who governed under Tiberius, is secured in the very framework Suetonius despises.[26] The scandalous scribe becomes a reluctant witness, proving, despite himself, that even in filth, the calendar holds.[27] He offers no gospel, but he cannot escape its outline. He tried to bury truth in shame, yet all he did was chisel the stage. And standing on it, mocked, bloodied, unshaken, is the very figure his empire could not erase.

The Loyal Insider: Velleius Paterculus's Glowing Tiberius

Velleius Paterculus, soldier, senator, and historian, gives us Tiberius through the eyes of a loyal subordinate. He fought under him in Germany and Pannonia, and his *Roman History*, composed around AD 30, glows with admiration.[28] Unlike Tacitus or Suetonius, he did not write decades later, sharpened by cynicism or scandal. He wrote as an eyewitness, in the service of the man he praised.

> One finds it hard to decide whether to admire his limitless acceptance of toil and danger or his limited acceptance of honors.[29]

He crowns Tiberius: "Our greatest general." The language is hymn, not history. His portrait is duty, toil, and modesty. It reads like a soldier's anthem to his commander. But loyalty has its cost. Proximity gave Velleius access, but it also bound his pen. His bias bleeds through every line, even as his dates and details remain consistent with the harsher accounts that

---

26. Tacitus, *Annals* 15.44; Suetonius, *Twelve Caesars* 44.1.
27. Habermas, *Historical Jesus*, 192.
28. Paterculus, *Roman History* 2.94; Cadoux, "Introduction."
29. Paterculus, *Roman History* 2.122. Commentary on Tiberius' legacy from a loyalist perspective.

followed.[30] Where Tacitus dissects and Suetonius derides, Velleius sings. It is not analysis; it is liturgy. Yet still, it is evidence. For bias may color the paint, but it cannot erase the canvas. And here lies the irony: Rome allows loyalty when it flatters its Caesars. The soldier's hymn is received as history. But when the apostles raise their voices in loyalty to Christ, men who also walked with Him, served under Him, and saw Him face to face, it is dismissed as delusion.[31] Same proximity. Same devotion. Different verdict.

The Emperor in Three Mirrors

Three portraits. Three verdicts. Tacitus gives us Tiberius dissected, precise, suspicious, and cold. Suetonius gives us Tiberius mocked, grotesque, scandalous, and obscene. Velleius gives us Tiberius adored, loyal, dutiful, and almost sanctified. Strip away the tone, and one truth remains: Tiberius reigned. His dates stand. His presence frames the calendar of Christ's death. Each source bends under bias. Tacitus sharpens his cynicism. Suetonius feeds the mob with scandal. Velleius drowns the record in praise. Yet the facts they circle are immovable: Tiberius ruled from AD 14 to 37, Pilate governed Judea under his authority, and within that window Christ was crucified.[32]

None of them set out to defend the Gospels. Yet all three, critic, gossip, and loyalist, anchor the same chronology. And this is the paradox: for emperors, even slander and flattery are counted as history. For Christ, eyewitness loyalty is waved away as myth. Suetonius can mock Tiberius with orgies, and scholars still accept his testimony. Velleius can sing hymns of devotion, and his words are still catalogued as evidence. But when apostles record what they saw with Jesus, healing the blind, calming storms, rising from the grave, the verdict changes. Same bias. Same proximity. Different outcome.[33]

So the record stands in spite of itself. Rome tried to dissect, mock, or glorify its emperor, and accidentally preserved the frame around the cross. Whatever else they gave us, Tacitus, Suetonius, and Velleius all testify to the same backdrop: the reign of Tiberius, in whose shadow Christ was executed. The empire cannot erase Him. It can only set the stage.

30. Cornell, *Fragmentary Roman Historians* 2:786–94; Syme, *Roman Papers* 4:175–92.

31. Bauckham, *Jesus and the Eyewitnesses*, 5–9.

32. Tacitus, *Annals* 6.50–51; Suetonius, *Twelve Caesars*, 134; Paterculus, *Roman History* 2.94.

33. Bauckham, *Jesus and the Eyewitnesses*, 5–9; Habermas, *Historical Jesus*, 192.

Tiberius Caesar

Tiberius Left No Words—And That Speaks Volumes

Unlike Julius Caesar, who carved his own glory into the record with polished prose and theatrical self-commentary, Tiberius Caesar left behind nothing. No memoirs. No speeches. No private reflections. Silence itself became his legacy.[34] Silence in history is never neutral. It is strategy, or judgment. Perhaps strategy. Tiberius was notoriously private. He fled the Roman spotlight for the cliffs of Capri,[35] shunned ceremony, and recoiled from the vanity his predecessor indulged. Yet whether deliberate or not, this silence created a void, and that void was quickly filled by others. Tacitus smelled rot. Suetonius fed it to the mob.[36] By refusing the pen, Tiberius surrendered his legacy to cynics and chroniclers who saw what they wanted, not what he was.

Ironically, Jesus too wrote nothing. But His silence did not decay into rumor; it thundered into testimony. His absence of ink became a presence of witness; His silence became salvation. One ruler's retreat invited slander. The other's left behind resurrection.[37] Even the voices that praised Tiberius did not truly speak for him. Velleius Paterculus sang hymns of loyalty because he was a soldier; in Rome, morale was survival. Suetonius scandalized because post-Nero Rome craved imperial theater.[38] Tacitus sharpened suspicion into cynicism. None of them chronicled Tiberius; they performed him.

And what of Christ? He too left no scroll. Yet His words were spoken aloud, echoed in hostile courts, remembered by disciples, enemies, and martyrs alike. While Tiberius hid on a mountain, Christ walked into the city. While Tiberius ruled in silence, Christ stood before Pilate and declared: "I came to bear witness to the truth."[39] And the man above Pilate, the emperor who could have intervened, remained silent. The silence of Tiberius is not noble. It is hollow.[40] It is the silence of a man who watched history pivot under his rule and chose retreat. He offered no voice. No

---

34. Shotter, *Tiberius Caesar*, 8–12.

35. Suetonius, *Twelve Caesars*, "Tiberius" 39–43.

36. Tacitus, *Annals* 4.1–6.50; Suetonius, *Twelve Caesars*, "Tiberius" 65; Pelling, *Plutarch and History*, 235–45; Levick, *Tiberius the Politician*, 138.

37. Bauckham, *Jesus and the Eyewitnesses*, 15–22.

38. Paterculus, *Roman History* 2.94; Suetonius, *Twelve Caesars*, "Tiberius" 43–44; Tacitus, *Annals* 1.1–6.50.

39. John 18:37.

40. Shotter, *Tiberius Caesar*, 112–23; Levick, *Tiberius the Politician*, 165–75.

PART III. DOCUMENTED BUREAUCRATS AND EMPERORS

defense. No verdict. And that says more than any scroll ever could. He let others speak for him. And none of them whispered grace.

The Timeline Locks in Place—"When God Bled, the Emperor Slept"

No matter what anyone believes about miracles, the crucifixion of Jesus of Nazareth is locked into a Roman timeline. And that timeline bears the name of Tiberius Caesar. The Gospels place Jesus's death between AD 30 and 33.[41] Tiberius reigned from AD 14 to 37. Pontius Pilate, prefect of Judea, served from AD 26 to 36, appointed by Tiberius himself.[42] The census under Quirinius, the imperial taxations, the governors and prefects, all of it unfolds on Rome's clock.[43]

Even the hostile witnesses agree. Tacitus, dripping with cynicism, names Christ's execution under Pilate during Tiberius's reign.[44] Suetonius, buried in gossip, still anchors events in the same administration.[45] Velleius Paterculus, glowing with loyalty, confirms the emperor sat on the throne at the very hour the Gospels describe.[46] These are not Christian sources, they are Roman ones. And yet they confirm the time. When God bled in Jerusalem, Tiberius was on the throne.

The irony is inescapable: the emperor of the known world, ruler of armies, holder of law, the image of power, retreated into silence on the cliffs of Capri. While the most consequential execution in history unfolded in his domain, he left no comment. No decree. No judgment. Nothing. But the calendar did not forget. The crucifixion of Jesus is not just theology, it is stamped into Roman governance like a seal in wax.[47] You don't need to believe in angels to know He lived and died. You only need a Roman ledger. At the top of that ledger stands one name, written in imperial ink: Tiberius.[48]

---

41. Tacitus, *Annals* 6.19.
42. Josephus, *Antiquities* 18.35, 89.
43. Josephus, *Antiquities* 18.1–2; Luke 2:2.
44. Tacitus, *Annals* 6.19.
45. Suetonius, *Tiberius*, 43–44.
46. Paterculus, *Roman History* 2.94.
47. Tacitus, *Annals* 6.19.
48. Tacitus, *Annals* 6.19; Josephus, *Antiquities* 18.35, 89; Paterculus, *Roman History* 2.94.

Tiberius Caesar

The Forgotten Emperor Who Watched the Cross

Tiberius Caesar is not denied by history. He is merely forgotten by it. Three portraits remain: Tacitus, the cynic who painted rot in silk robes; Suetonius, the gossip who turned Capri into a theater of filth; Velleius, the loyal soldier who sang praises and skipped the shadows.[49] Together, they form not a man but a mosaic, cracked, partial, warped by motive. He left no writings. No defense. No reflection. And yet no one questions his existence. Because Tiberius makes no demands on the soul. He calls for no repentance. He offers no path, no cross, no mirror. He did not say, "I am the Way." He did not confront the heart. He merely ruled. And for that, he is left alone.

Jesus did not remain alone. He stood trial not only before Pilate but under the gaze of Rome's empire and the weight of history itself. His timeline is not carved by belief but confirmed by hostile witnesses.[50] His name echoes across governors, censuses, inscriptions, and coins.[51] You don't need Scripture to place Him in time. You only need the silence of an emperor whose title hung over the execution warrant.[52] Tiberius never saw Him. He never stood in that court. He sat on Capri while the veil tore in the temple.[53] He ruled the world, and missed its redemption. The eternal pierced the temporal. And the emperor did not flinch.

And what became of him? He faded. He retreated. He left no words. Buried with honor, but not awe. No gospel bears his name. No movement follows his virtue. No soul sings his praise at dawn. He wielded power, but he could not halt the blood that redefined history. Tiberius is remembered, but only as a date stamp.[54] For when God bled, the emperor slept. And history remembers which one of them rose.

Summing Up: The Emperor Who Slept Through God's Trial

So let the verdict be spoken.

---

49. Tacitus, *Annals* 4.1–6; Suetonius, *Tiberius*, 43–44; Paterculus, *Roman History* 2.94.

50. Tacitus, *Annals* 6.19; Suetonius, *Lives of the Caesars*, "Claudius" 25.4; Paterculus, *Roman History* 2.94.

51. Josephus, *Antiquities* 18.1–2; Luke 2:1–2; Pilate Inscription (Caesarea Maritima).

52. Tacitus, *Annals* 6.19; John 19:12–15.

53. Suetonius, *Tiberius*, 43–44; Matt 27:51.

54. Tacitus, *Annals* 6.19; Luke 3:1.

PART III. DOCUMENTED BUREAUCRATS AND EMPERORS

Tiberius Caesar, emperor of Rome, heir of Augustus, master of armies and law, took his throne, but not his stand. He left behind no words, no witness, no defense. He watched the world from Capri while the world's Redeemer was nailed to wood. History remembers him only as a date, a shadow over the page, a silent figure at the edge of the cross. He held the power to decree life or death, yet it was under his reign that Life Himself was sentenced. And when the blood fell, he did not stir. Augustus crowned the empire with marble, Tiberius retreated into silence, but Christ, condemned under both their shadows, rose from the grave. One emperor built monuments; the other hid on a cliff. Neither could stop the kingdom that came through a torn veil and an empty tomb. He passed away in silence. But the one condemned beneath his prefect rose in power. Tiberius ruled men for a season. Christ rules kingdoms for eternity. One was forgotten in the dust of Capri; the other is confessed on every continent, in every tongue. The court of history has reached its judgment: Tiberius bore the title of Caesar, but it was Jesus who bore the title "Son of God." And only one of those names still saves.

Pontius Pilate
The Man Who Stood Before Truth

PONTIUS PILATE, THE ROMAN governor who presided over the trial of Jesus, gave the order for His crucifixion, and then washed his hands before the crowd, declaring himself innocent of the blood he had condemned.[1] His birth and death remain uncertain, but his decade as prefect of Judea is clear:[2] AD 26 to 36. He is remembered not as a zealous persecutor but as a reluctant executioner, a political pragmatist balancing imperial demands with local unrest.[3] A man straining to preserve peace, yet standing before the Prince of Peace.

What strikes most is the silence: we possess no writings from Pilate himself. For centuries, critics claimed he was invention, a villain conjured by Gospel writers to serve a theological plot. They pointed to the absence of Roman records, inscriptions, or self-testimony. At best, only Christian texts dared to speak his name, with passing acknowledgment by Jewish voices like Josephus and Philo.[4] These too were dismissed as biased, untrustworthy, partisan. Pilate, they said, was legend, not flesh.[5]

But pause here. If the only witnesses to your existence are branded suspect, you are erased. This is the logic. The testimony itself may be sound, but if the voice carries faith, it is silenced. And yet, how many of history's "giants" are remembered on thinner grounds, their shadows accepted without question? Alexander? Hannibal? Socrates? Cleopatra? Pilate's life was doubted precisely because it brushed against Christ.

1. Matt 27:24.
2. Josephus, *Antiquities* 18.3.1.
3. Philo, *Embassy*, 299–305.
4. Josephus, *Antiquities* 18.55, 89; Philo, *Embassy*, 299–305.
5. Meier, *Marginal Jew* 1:56–71; Evans, *Jesus and the Manuscripts*, 15–20.

PART III. DOCUMENTED BUREAUCRATS AND EMPERORS

Another Erased Governor

For centuries, Pontius Pilate was dismissed as a Christian phantom, a theatrical villain conjured by Gospel writers to stage their cosmic drama. In the eighteenth and nineteenth centuries, especially under the sway of rationalist critics and German higher criticism, Pilate's existence was openly denied. Ferdinand Christian Baur and others dismantled the Passion narrative piece by piece, reducing its actors to symbols. Lacking any Roman inscription or independent testimony beyond Jewish or Christian sources, Pilate was among the first to be cast aside.[6] Academic journals of the era often treated him as a narrative device, a shadowy antagonist invented to place Jesus in opposition to Rome.[7] The reasoning was circular but seductive: if Pilate appears only in religious texts, and those texts are biased, then Pilate himself must be fictional.

The implications cut deep. If the man who sentenced Jesus never existed, then the Gospels were not memoir but myth, not testimony but theology dressed as history. Even well into the twentieth century, suspicion lingered. Pilate became not just a doubtful figure but a keystone in the skeptic's case against the historical credibility of Christ. But that is not how we treat anyone else. Alexander the Great has no birth certificate. Cleopatra left no diary. Hannibal has no statue confirmed to have been carved in his lifetime. Yet their names are spoken without hesitation, their legacies embraced as fact. Pilate alone was silenced, for he stood too close to the Christ. To admit Pilate was to admit the trial. And if the trial was real, then what transpired within it mattered.

So he was filtered from memory. Not for lack of evidence, but for fear of where evidence would lead. Pilate became the erased governor, the bureaucrat history refused to name. And then the earth spoke. In 1961, at Caesarea Maritima, a limestone slab broke the silence: "Pontius Pilatus, Prefect of Judea."[8] A voice not from Gospel, sermon, or parable, but from Roman stone. The kind of testimony the skeptic demands. And it spoke the same name the Gospels had spoken for two millennia.[9] Truth does not erase. It waits. Sometimes beneath soil. Sometimes beneath stone. But always it waits.

---

6. Evans, *Jesus and the Manuscripts*, 57–58.
7. Evans, *Jesus and the Manuscripts*, 57–58.
8. Zangenberg, "Archaeological Evidence of Pontius Pilate," 29–36.
9. Bruce, *Jesus and Christian Origins*, 56–57.

The Pilate Stone: Archaeology's Thunderclap

In 1961, among the windswept ruins of Caesarea Maritima, Italian archaeologist Antonio Frova unearthed a limestone block that would thunder through the halls of scholarship.[10] At first glance, it looked ordinary, just another fragment from Rome's imperial architecture. But within its weather-worn face lay a name buried under centuries of doubt. Damaged, yes. Partial, yes. But unmistakable. Pontius Pilate. Prefect of Judea. The so-called "Pilate stone" was no relic of Christian tradition, no verse of Scripture, no theological embroidery. It was Roman dedication. Roman title. Roman stone.[11] For generations skeptics had dismissed Pilate as fiction, a stage prop for Christian drama. But this was masonry, not manuscript. Cold, carved, and undeniable. With one strike of the spade, archaeology did what debate could not: it anchored Pilate in the dust of real history. The erasure failed. His name, once silenced, rose from ruin like buried truth gasping for air.

> Latin Inscription:
> [DIS AUGUSTI]S TIBERIÉUM
> [... PONTI]US PILATUS
> [... PRAEF]ECTUS IUDA[EA]E
> [... FECIT D]E[DICAVIT]
> Translation:
> "To the Divine Augusti [this] Tiberieum
> ... Pontius Pilate
> ... Prefect of Judea
> ... has dedicated [this]"[12]

Its significance was immense. First, it confirmed Pilate's historicity and title as prefect, precisely as recorded by Josephus, Philo, and the Gospels.[13] Second, it fixed him in place and time, ruling Judea under Tiberius, the very years when Christ stood before him. This was not vague rumor but hard inscription: name, title, location. Not ink. Stone. Before this discovery, skeptics leaned on absence: no Roman record, no contemporary inscription, no official trace. The Gospels were branded biased; Josephus and Philo, suspect.

---

10. Evans, *Jesus and His World*, 95–96.
11. Frova, "Caesarea Maritima: The Excavations," 256–59.
12. Evans, *Jesus and His World*, 100–1.
13. Evans, *Jesus and His World*, 100–1.

Pilate, therefore, was reduced to a literary construct.[14] But the Pilate stone shattered that construct. Doubt may be fashionable, but stone is stubborn. Even Bart Ehrman concedes: "We have some coins . . . and one, only one, fragmentary inscription discovered at Caesarea Maritima in 1961 that indicates that he was the Roman prefect. Nothing else. . . . Does that mean he didn't exist? No. . . . He certainly existed."[15] From the lips of a skeptic: absence of abundance is not absence of truth. The Pilate stone is convergence, archaeology meeting testimony, stone echoing Scripture. The ground itself bore witness. And in that witness, history bowed toward Christ.

The Gospels' Profile: Literary Convergence

For all the accusations that the Gospels are biased, embellished, or invented, there is a striking convergence: when it comes to Pontius Pilate, the portrait is consistent across all four. Matthew, Mark, Luke, and John, different regions, audiences, and emphases, yet the same man.[16] Pilate is cautious. Pilate is conflicted. Pilate is calculating. And in the end, Pilate capitulates. None portray him as bloodthirsty or monstrous. He is the governor caught between pressure and conscience, balancing imperial duty with an unsettling encounter with innocence. And history turned on a man who tried not to choose, but chose all the same.

In Mark, the earliest and most succinct, Pilate is almost mechanical, efficient, curt, pliable.[17] He finds no fault in Jesus, offers Barabbas, and yields with little resistance. In Matthew, hesitation grows. He listens to his wife's dream, washes his hands, and declares himself innocent of the blood he spills. In Luke, resistance sharpens. Pilate pronounces Jesus innocent three times, even deferring to Herod in an effort to escape judgment.[18] And then comes John. Pilate here is unraveling. He speaks with Jesus. He asks, "What is truth?" He vacillates between fear and pragmatism, between survival and clarity. In John, Pilate is no longer in control of the moment—the moment controls him. He sees truth but will not follow it.[19]

---

14. Bond, *Pontius Pilate in History and Interpretation*, 3–10.
15. Ehrman, *New Testament: A Historical Introduction*, 254.
16. Blomberg, *Historical Reliability of the Gospels*, 40–46.
17. Dunn, *Jesus Remembered*, 141.
18. Brown, *Death of the Messiah*, 732–36.
19. Carson, *Gospel According to John*, 591–99.

These are not carbon copies. No identical lines. Four witnesses describing the same storm from different windows.[20] And yet, their portraits converge: weak in spine, sharp in mind, torn between justice and politics, too cowardly to stop what he knows is wrong. Fiction diverges. Fabrication fractures. Lies spiral outward. But truth has a way of converging, especially when told by those who were there. Across the Gospels, Pilate is not hero or villain, but mirror. He sees innocence, but fears consequence. Four writers, decades apart, addressing different communities, all deliver the same man. That tells us something vital. Pilate was real, too real to ignore, too flawed to fabricate. He stands in all four Gospels as a man cracked open by history, frozen in one of the most consequential hours the world has ever known. We see the same man:

- A Roman governor reluctant to execute.
- A politician offering Barabbas as a scapegoat.
- A man who questions truth, then turns from it.
- One who washes not only his hands of guilt, but of responsibility.

The tones diverge, but the profile does not. Matthew shows cowardice. Mark shows capitulation. Luke shows hesitation. John shows philosophical distance. But all agree: this man condemned Jesus, reluctantly, politically, without clarity. The contrast with Socrates is instructive. Plato paints a metaphysical hero. Xenophon, a civic moralist. Aristophanes, a comic buffoon. The sources fracture, contradict, reshape.[21] But the Gospels? Different tones, audiences, aims, yet one Pilate emerges. That carries historical weight. For fiction diverges. Eyewitnesses converge. And the Pilate they preserve is not exaggerated. He is disturbingly plausible: the bureaucrat who bends, the official who deflects, the politician who stalls until justice suffocates behind him. A man who fears position more than the cost of condemning the innocent. Perhaps that is the final proof: no one invents weakness when narrating the death of their hero. Pilate is remembered for the scar he left on memory. And scars, unlike legends, are honest.[22]

---

20. Bauckham, *Jesus and the Eyewitnesses*, 112–36.
21. Vlastos, *Socrates*, 45–48.
22. Wright, *Jesus and the Victory of God*, 546–52.

PART III. DOCUMENTED BUREAUCRATS AND EMPERORS

Hostile Corroboration: Josephus & Tacitus

Two names dominate the secular confirmation of Pilate's existence, and neither had any reason to bolster the claims of Christianity. Flavius Josephus, a Jewish historian writing in the late first century,[23] and Tacitus, a Roman senator writing in the early second, stand as pillars of reluctant corroboration. They did not set out to validate the Gospels. But in their attempt to document political history, they nailed down a crucifixion.

Josephus on Pilate

In *Antiquities of the Jews* (book 18), Josephus recounts multiple clashes between Pilate and the Jewish people.[24] Pilate introduces Roman military standards into Jerusalem, emblems bearing the emperor's image. A riot breaks out. Pilate responds with threats of slaughter. Later, he seizes temple funds to build an aqueduct. Another riot follows. Again, bloodshed. Josephus doesn't glorify these events; he preserves them like civic scars. These weren't triumphs; they were grievances. That matters. Myths don't get preserved because they angered the populace. Inconvenient truths do. Then comes the *Testimonium Flavianum*, Josephus's brief but loaded mention of Jesus:[25]

> Pilate, at the suggestion of the principal men among us, had condemned Him to the cross.[26]

Scholars continue to debate potential embellishments in the *Testimonium Flavianum*, but virtually all agree that the mention of Pilate's role is original. Why? Because it aligns perfectly with everything else Josephus records. Pilate was a political problem, a name etched into the memory of a people not for glory, but for grief.

---

23. Josephus, *Antiquities* 18.63–64.
24. Josephus, *Antiquities* 18.55–62.
25. Josephus, *Antiquities* 18.62–64.
26. Josephus, *Antiquities* 18.3.3.

Tacitus on Pilate

Tacitus hated Christians. In *Annals* 15.44, he called their faith a "pernicious superstition"[27] and mocked its spread. And yet, even in his disdain, he confirms what believers had always claimed:

> *Christus, from whom the name had its origin, suffered the extreme penalty during the reign of Tiberius at the hands of one of our procurators, Pontius Pilatus.*[28]

That's it. Cold. Bureaucratic. No sympathy. No agenda to convert. Just a Roman historian referencing official archives, and in doing so, affirming the Gospel's political skeleton.

> *Pilate, at the suggestion of the principal men among us, had condemned him to the cross.*[29]

Josephus had no cause to exalt Christians. A Jewish priest and aristocrat writing under Roman patronage, his aim in *Antiquities* was to defend Judaism before a hostile empire.[30] To him, Christians were a disruptive sect with little honor. Yet even in that posture, he preserves Pilate's clashes with the Jews and names him as the one who condemned Jesus. He writes not to bolster faith but to catalog grievances, and in doing so, confirms the governor whose shadow fell across Christ.

Tacitus stands even further from sympathy. A Roman senator and governor, his histories dripped with contempt for those he deemed threats to Roman order. Christians, he sneered, were "hated for their abominations," a "pernicious superstition" that festered in the empire's cracks.[31] His reference to Christ's crucifixion is cold bureaucracy, not belief. Yet precisely because he despised them, his testimony bites deeper. Tacitus would never invent a detail that gave Christians credibility. He named Pilate because the archives forced him to.

---

27. Tacitus, *Annals* 15.44.
28. Tacitus, *Annals* 15.44.
29. Josephus, *Antiquities* 18.63.
30. Josephus, *Jewish War* 1.3; *Antiquities* 1.1–4.
31. Tacitus, *Annals* 15.44.

PART III. DOCUMENTED BUREAUCRATS AND EMPERORS

Why This Cuts Deep

Tacitus and Josephus didn't write to affirm faith. They wrote to record friction.[32] Neither praised Jesus. Neither promoted His followers. And yet, both planted Pilate firmly into the historical timeline. Skeptics may resist quoting Josephus on Jesus, but they cannot erase what he said about Pilate. Because the man who condemned Christ left ripples even enemies couldn't ignore. That's not propaganda. That's resonance.

The Irony of His Historical Weight

Pontius Pilate was a bureaucrat, one of dozens of Roman prefects scattered across the empire.[33] He was no king. He wrote no philosophy. He conquered no lands, led no legions, minted no coins, carved no marble, left no statues. He was not beloved by the Senate, nor praised in song. And yet two millennia later, the world still speaks his name. Why? Because heaven made sure the trial could not be forgotten.

Caesars wrote poems to themselves. Generals built triumphal arches. Conquerors stamped their glory into coin and stone.[34] But none of them, not one, has been as historically confirmed as the governor who tried to wash innocence from his hands.[35] Pilate sought plausible deniability. He gave in to the mob, surrendered justice, and vanished into the routines of empire. But history would not let him disappear. God would not let him.

That is the irony. Pilate, a minor official who satisfied no nation and served no god, is more firmly fixed in the record than many emperors. He is etched in stone, preserved in hostile pens, and carried in the most widely distributed documents of antiquity.[36] His weight comes not from who he was, but from whom he met. The crucifixion gave Pilate a permanence no biography could. He became absorbed into the greatest story ever told, not as hero, but as timestamp. He tried to flee history. Instead, he became its witness.

---

32. Josephus, *Antiquities* 18.63–64; Tacitus, *Annals* 15.44.
33. Bond, *Pontius Pilate in History and Interpretation*, 18–22.
34. Boatwright et al., *Romans*, 315.
35. Ehrman, *New Testament*, 289–90.
36. Bond, *Pontius Pilate in History and Interpretation*, 3–4, 29–30; Tacitus, *Annals* 15.44; Matt 27; Mark 15; Luke 23; John 18–19.

And yet, the double standard glares. Pilate is confirmed by multiple streams: the Gospels, Josephus, Tacitus.[37] Hostile witnesses verify him unintentionally.[38] Archaeology carved his name back into daylight in 1961.[39] And still, for centuries, critics denied him, not because evidence was absent, but because its implications were unbearable. To admit Pilate is to admit the trial. To admit the trial is to admit the crucifixion.[40] And the crucifixion demands not curiosity but accountability. No one questions Alexander. Hannibal is accepted without protest. Cleopatra is embraced without resistance.[41] Their sources are fragmentary, partisan, contradictory, and yet they are received as fact. But Pilate? Pilate is too close to the Christ. And for many, that is too dangerous.

The Governor Who Faced God

History did not want to remember Pilate. And for centuries, it pretended not to.[42] While emperors were carved in marble and philosophers etched in ink, Pilate, a minor prefect, was whispered as myth. Too many wanted him gone. Too many needed him forgotten. For to admit that Pilate stood before Jesus is to admit that Jesus stood before judgment. But then came the stone. Now his name is carved not only in Gospel ink, but in Roman limestone.[43] Confirmed by enemies. Preserved by accident.[44]

Pilate did not preach. He did not convert. He left no words of wisdom. All he did was flinch. All he did was fold. He tried to stay neutral while heaven's verdict walked into the room. And that is why we remember him, not for his title, but for his silence when God stood before him. We remember emperors in statues, philosophers in quotes. But Pilate? Pilate is remembered for trying to walk away, for washing his hands while eternity

---

37. Matt 27; Mark 15; Luke 23; John 18–19; Josephus, *Antiquities* 18.3.3; Tacitus, *Annals* 15.44.

38. Josephus, *Antiquities* 18.3.3; Tacitus, *Annals* 15.44.

39. Frova, "Caesarea Maritima: The Excavations," 256–59.

40. Matt 27; Mark 15; Luke 23; John 18–19.

41. Grant, *Twelve Caesars*, 18–21; Polybius, *Histories* 3.11–16; Livy, *History of Rome* V 21.1–30; Plutarch, *Life of Antony* 24–33; Dio, *Roman History* 51.1–17.

42. Bond, *Pontius Pilate in History and Interpretation*, 1–4.

43. Frova, "Caesarea Maritima," 256–59.

44. Tacitus, *Annals* 15.44; Josephus, *Antiquities* 18.3.3.

PART III. DOCUMENTED BUREAUCRATS AND EMPERORS

bled at his feet. And the water could not save him. Because no one stands beside the Nazarene and walks away clean.[45]

> *Not then.*
> *Not now.*
> *Not ever.*

When the cost of belief is high, history demands ironclad proof. But when the cost is low, when nothing is on the line, rumor will do. Legends are accepted without scrutiny. Myths are passed without footnotes. But not here. Not with Pilate.[46] Because to accept Pilate is to get dangerously close to Jesus.[47] And that nearness demands more than curiosity; it demands a verdict. Pilate's memory endured because truth leaves splinters no empire can erase. The world tried to forget him. But history, like heaven, remembered.

Pilate is unlike the others we have put on trial. Alexander marched with armies. Hannibal carved terror into Rome's soil. Cleopatra bent empires with her will. They shaped history by force of genius, ambition, or desire. Pilate did none of this. He left no speeches, no monuments, no victories. His legacy is one moment, one courtroom, one decision he tried not to make. And yet that moment weighed heavier than a thousand campaigns. For Pilate did what no conqueror ever did: he stood face to face with the Author of history. He washed his hands before the crowd, but history washed nothing away. He sought neutrality, but neutrality before Truth is itself a verdict. His silence condemned him louder than any sentence he pronounced.[48]

That is why Pilate endures. His name is etched in hostile pens, carved in Roman stone, whispered through Gospel witness,[49] not because he was great, but because he was weak. And weakness before Christ becomes immortal. Empire wanted to forget him. Heaven would not allow it. In Pilate we see the mirror of every man who encounters Jesus and hesitates. He tried to walk away clean, but no water could wash him. Not then. Not now. Not ever.[50] And so Pilate remains, standing forever before the Nazarene,

45. Matt 27:24.
46. Ehrman, *New Testament*, 254.
47. Evans, *Jesus and His World*, 49–50.
48. Matt 27:24.
49. Tacitus, *Annals* 15.44; Josephus, *Antiquities* 18.3.3; Frova, "Caesarea Maritima," 256–59.
50. Matt 27:24.

not as judge, but as the judged. For as Christ told him: "You would have no authority over Me at all unless it had been given you from above."[51] Pilate washed his hands and left the world stained with silence.

---

51. John 19:11.

PART IV

The Prophet and His Community

SOME MEN LEAVE BEHIND an empire. Others, a faith. But few leave behind a living community still echoing their words centuries later. In this section, we turn to Muhammad, the prophet of Islam, whose name commands reverence across nations.[1] He is the most documented man in Arab history, yet those documents were written by followers, decades after his death,[2] in a faith tradition that wove theology, politics, and conquest into one.[3] This section is not about dismissing the man. It is about measuring the method:

1. Who wrote what?
2. When did they write it?
3. How do we treat a man shielded from scrutiny, yet shaped by the same history others are doubted for?

We do not explore the doctrine of Islam, but rather the documentation of its founder,[4] placing Muhammad under the same standard of scrutiny applied to Jesus,[5] and asking why, in many circles, the rules seem to change.

---

1. Peters, *Muhammad and the Origins of Islam*, 3.
2. Donner, *Narratives of Islamic Origins*, 25–27.
3. Crone and Hinds, *God's Caliph*, 4–6.
4. Motzki, "Biography of Muhammad," in *Prophet Muhammad*, 68–70.
5. Reynolds, *Emergence of Islam*, 23–26.

PART IV

The Prophet and His Community

Muhammad
The Prophet and the Pen

MUHAMMAD IBN ABDULLAH IBN Abdul-Muttalib. The name itself is a lineage, a chain of inheritance:

- Muhammad, the given name, "praised" or "praiseworthy."
- ibn Abdullah, "son of Abdullah," his father.
- ibn Abdul-Muttalib, "son of Abdul-Muttalib," his grandfather, chief of Quraysh in Mecca.

The chain can be drawn further: ibn Hashim, founder of the Banu Hashim clan. Roots, branches, and bloodlines, a tree meant to anchor him in a people's memory. Born around AD 570 and dead by AD 632, Muhammad stands as the "Seal of the Prophets," the final messenger of Islam.[1] Around him now gathers nearly two billion souls worldwide, binding their identity to his word and example.[2] His life is carried not only as prophet, but as statesman, general, and legislator, a figure who fused faith with power, law with sword, revelation with rule.[3]

And yet, the claim of preservation hangs over him like a mantle: the Quran as the unbroken word, the Hadith as his remembered voice, the community as his lasting frame.[4] But how secure is that mantle when measured by the same scale that weighed Alexander, the Caesars, or Socrates? When preservation itself becomes the argument, the trial sharpens. Already, a whisper of contrast arises. Where Muhammad is remembered for preserving

---

1. Watt, *Muhammad at Mecca*, xv; Lings, *Muhammad*, 2–4.
2. Nasr, *Heart of Islam*, 28; Pew Research Center, "Future of World Religions."
3. Donner, *Muhammad and the Believers*, 56–65.
4. Brown, *Hadith*, 5–10.

the law and order of a people, Christ is remembered for embodying truth beyond people, law, or empire, a preservation not of custom, but of eternity.[5]

The Dating Problem: Too Much, Too Late

For a figure who reshaped half the globe, Muhammad's historical timeline begins startlingly late. The first full biography of his life comes from Ibn Ishaq, written not in his century, but more than a century after his death in AD 632.[6] Imagine if the first comprehensive account of Abraham Lincoln appeared in the year 2020, relying only on secondhand stories, with not a single surviving letter, speech, or document from those who actually knew him. That is the scale of delay we face.

And even Ibn Ishaq does not survive. His Sīra comes to us only through Ibn Hisham, a later editor who confessed he had excised what he deemed offensive. He omitted, in his own words, "things which it is disgraceful to discuss" and "matters which would distress certain people."[7] In modern terms: the first biography is lost, and the version we hold is the first censorship of the first biography. This raises a fundamental problem. If the earliest record of Muhammad's life is already a redacted version of a missing manuscript, what exactly are we trusting?

Now weigh this against Jesus of Nazareth. The earliest record of Him comes not a century later, but within twenty years of His crucifixion: letters of Paul, who claimed to encounter Him personally and bore chains for His name.[8] The Gospels followed soon after, within the lifetime of eyewitnesses, under public scrutiny, naming rulers and officials who could confirm, or refute, their claims.[9] For Muhammad, history waits more than a century, then enters through a filtered voice. For Jesus, testimony begins within one generation, carried by blood and by ink. If Christ's life had been recorded only after 130 years through a redacted scroll, it would be called legend. Yet for Muhammad, it is called history, and two billion have swallowed it whole, mistaking silence for certainty.

---

5. John 14:6.
6. Ishaq, *Life of Muhammad*, xiii–xiv.
7. Ibn Hisham, *Al-Sīrah al-Nabawiyyah*; Ishaq, *Life of Muhammad*, xiii.
8. Ehrman, *New Testament*, 85–88.
9. Bauckham, *Jesus and the Eyewitnesses*, 7–12, 14–18.

Muhammad

The Man and the Myth: Timeline Inconsistencies

We are told that Muhammad's life is meticulously preserved, that every saying, every battle, every marriage is cataloged with precision. But look closer, and the cracks appear.[10] The earliest Islamic sources, the Hadith and the Sīra, do not yield one portrait. They yield many. And those portraits often contradict.[11] How many wives did he take? Some traditions say eleven, others thirteen. Some claim nine at once, others fewer.[12] A hadith reports that Aisha was six at betrothal and nine at consummation.[13] Other sources omit the matter entirely. Which is true?

The battles tell the same story of fracture. Badr, Uhud, Khaybar, the Trench, accounts diverge on who struck first, how many fell, and what words were spoken before the clash.[14] Even the Night Journey, the Isra and Mi'raj, slips into haze. Was it literal or symbolic? Before or after the Hijra? The sources cannot agree.[15] This is not history. It is mythology with footnotes.[16] And this is why Ibn Hisham trimmed Ibn Ishaq's original: too many contradictions, too many wounds to the myth. He removed what was "disgraceful." He shaped the man to fit the memory.[17]

Now set this against the Gospels. Four witnesses. Four distinct voices. Yet the spine of history holds. The crucifixion week converges: Pilate, Caiaphas, Herod. The sequence aligns: arrest, trial, scourging, cross, tomb. The differences are of emphasis, not contradiction. When truth stands, testimony converges. When power curates, stories multiply, and integrity dissolves. For myths built too close to the sun always drip wax. For truth nailed to wood, the form endures.[18]

---

10. Reynolds, *Emergence of Islam*, 21–26.
11. Peters, *Muhammad and the Origins of Islam*, 19–22.
12. Watt, *Muhammad at Medina*, 274–75.
13. Bukhari, *Ṣaḥīḥ al-Bukhārī*, Hadith 5134.
14. Spencer, *Did Muhammad Exist?*, 73–76.
15. Khalidi, *Muslim Jesus*, 11–14.
16. Holland, *In the Shadow of the Sword*, xxv–xxvi.
17. Ishaq, *Life of Muhammad*, xiii.
18. Bauckham, *Jesus and the Eyewitnesses*, 5–12, 274–78, 482–84.

PART IV. THE PROPHET AND HIS COMMUNITY

The Quran: Revelation Without Biography

The Quran stands as Islam's sacred center: believed to be the very speech of God, given to Muhammad over twenty-three years between AD 610 and 632.[19] Preserved first on tongues and scraps, then gathered under Abu Bakr, and finally fixed under Uthman around AD 650, it is the book that defines a civilization.[20] And yet, for all its weight, it tells us almost nothing of Muhammad himself. It is not a life. It is not a story. It is a voice.[21] His name appears sparingly. There is no Bethlehem, no Golgotha, no birth, no death, no arc of years. What we receive are commands, visions, warnings, fragments of judgment and promise.[22] This raises the unavoidable question: if we did not already believe in Muhammad, would the Quran alone prove that he lived? The answer is no. The book escapes scrutiny because of its form. Its authority is theological, not historical. It gives us divine speech without human frame, revelation without biography.[23] And here the contrast sharpens. Where Muhammad is left as shadow behind a voice, Christ is proclaimed as the Word become flesh, history embodied, not merely spoken.[24]

Quran vs. Gospels: Divine Claim vs. Human Testimony

The Gospels, unlike the Quran, invite scrutiny. They are written in the voices of eyewitnesses or their close companions.[25] They tether their narratives to names that history cannot erase, Pilate, Herod, Tiberius, and set their events in public squares, in storm-tossed seas, in Roman courts.[26] Their pages pulse with chronology and geography, fixed in time and place. The Quran, by contrast, moves without anchor. It avoids sequence, resists narrative, leaves most names unspoken, and offers little geography to test its claims.[27] The Gospels embrace history. The Quran bypasses it. But the divide cuts deeper still. The Quran issues decrees. The Gospels deliver testimony. The Quran

---

19. Sinai, *Qur'an*, 1–4.
20. Burton, *Collection of the Qur'an*, 32–35, 115–21.
21. Wansbrough, *Quranic Studies*, 1–4, 79–84.
22. Neuwirth, *Scripture*, 15–19, 55–58.
23. Wansbrough, *Quranic Studies*, 79–84.
24. John 1:14.
25. Bauckham, *Jesus and the Eyewitnesses*, 6–12, 38–41, 601–7.
26. Blomberg, *Historical Reliability of the Gospels*, 41–45, 103–6, 198–203.
27. Neuwirth, *Scripture*, 11–17, 48–53, 82–85.

demands submission. The Gospels summon repentance. The Quran seeks to build a state. The Gospels center on a cross. One commands the law. The other commands the soul. And this is why one is revered without resistance, while the other is torn apart, again and again, yet endures. For truth does not hide behind command; it bleeds through witness.

Ibn Ishaq: The Lost Biographer

Ibn Ishaq (AD 707 to 767) produced the first known biography of Muhammad, the *Sīrat Rasūl Allāh*, more than a century after Muhammad's death in (AD 632).[28] The work itself is lost. What survives comes only through Ibn Hisham (AD 833), who confessed that he cut material he judged offensive or "disgraceful."[29] Thus, the earliest full account of Muhammad's life is not a record; it is a redaction. Built on oral traditions, layered with embellishment, and filtered through later political and theological agendas, it is history already shaped by myth.[30]

What if the path was the same for Jesus? A biography written more than a hundred years after His death. The original gone. The surviving text an edited version, stripped of "embarrassing" content, approved only through the lens of later authority. Would modern scholars accept such a source without question? Would skeptics bow to its authority? Of course not. And yet this is precisely what the world is asked to accept for Muhammad: a life preserved not in witness, but in revision, where the man is always one step removed, and the myth always one step closer.

The Hadith Crisis: Mountains of Sayings, Seas of Contradiction

If the Quran gives doctrine without biography, the Hadith tries to fill the void. But what it offers is not clarity; it is chaos. Imagine a sea of more than 600,000 alleged sayings, actions, and permissions attributed to Muhammad, carried by memory, traded across tribes, shaped by regions, sharpened by politics.[31] What began as remembrance became rumor. What began as reverence became rivalry.

---

28. Ishaq, *Life of Muhammad*, xiii–xiv.
29. Peters, *Muhammad and the Origins of Islam*, 242–44.
30. Donner, *Narratives of Islamic Origins*, 132–40.
31. Brown, *Hadith*, 5–7.

Into this storm stepped scholars like Bukhari and Muslim, centuries after Muhammad's death, tasked with sifting memory from myth. Their verdict? Rejection. Imam Bukhari, the most rigorous of all collectors, accepted only about 7,000 hadith out of 600,000, a rejection rate over 98 percent.[32] Even among those, many are duplicates. Muslim's *Sahih* was equally ruthless.[33] Why? Because contradictions were everywhere. One chain claimed Muhammad did one thing; another swore he did the opposite.[34] Some hadith flattered tribes, others shored up rulers, still others justified war. It became a marketplace of piety, each faction selling its own Muhammad.

And yet, despite this avalanche of contradiction, the Hadith stands as the second pillar of Islam, shaping law, ritual, morality, and daily life.[35] Think on that: an entire civilization structured on a foundation where 99 percent of the original material was deemed untrustworthy. Now turn the question. What if Christianity had walked the same path? Imagine the early church sifting through hundreds of thousands of sayings of Jesus, preserving only 1 percent. Imagine each sect producing its own "authentic" version, one keeping miracles, another discarding parables, another trimming the Beatitudes. Would skeptics accept that? Or would they dismantle it as incoherent, manipulated, mythologized?

But for Islam, complexity is treated as sophistication. Contradiction is baptized as diversity. Silence on rigor is reframed as piety. Yet confusion is not credibility, and contradiction is not canon. When a tradition admits it had to discard the overwhelming majority of its own voice, how strong is what remains? This is not about defaming a faith. It is about applying the same standard. If only 1 percent of Jesus's sayings had survived, He would be buried in legend. Instead, His words and deeds stand through converging witness, and for that, He is crucified again and again.[36]

Josephus vs. Hadith: The Double Standard Again

Skeptics love to pounce on Josephus. A single disputed line about Jesus in the *Antiquities of the Jews*? "Interpolated! Unreliable!" They treat one

32. Juynboll, *Authenticity of the Tradition Literature*, 20–25.
33. Azami, *Studies in Early Hadith Literature*, 98–102.
34. Motzki, "Musannaf of ʿAbd al-Razzāq al-Ṣanʿānī," 1–21.
35. Peters, *Islam*, 118–20.
36. Bauckham, *Jesus and the Eyewitnesses*, 274–78, 482–84.

contested passage as enough to dismiss an entire historian.[37] But turn to the Hadith, volumes compiled centuries after Muhammad, admitted to contain fabrication, contradiction, and political bias, and suddenly the same skepticism evaporates. Entire libraries of late, redacted tradition are granted foundational authority.[38] This is not skepticism. It is selective immunity. When the cost of belief is high, only perfection will do. When the cost is low, contradiction is excused as diversity, fabrication reframed as faith.

Consider the irony. Josephus names Jesus within a generation of His death. Tacitus corroborates the crucifixion under Pilate. Early Christian letters and Gospels multiply in the same century.[39] Yet critics dismiss these as too fragile, too compromised. Meanwhile, Hadith literature, shaped through centuries of oral rumor and rejected by its own collectors at a rate of 98 percent, remains unchallenged as the bedrock of Islamic practice. The standard is not consistent. It bends with convenience. And truth does not need convenience; it survives scrutiny. That is why the record of Christ endures every trial, while the record of Muhammad must be shielded by exemption.

The Militarization of Memory: A Sword-Shaped Story

History is never neutral. It is written by those who survive to wield the pen, and in early Islam, that pen was shaped like a sword. After Muhammad's death in AD 632, the Rashidun Caliphate expanded with startling speed. By AD 661, Persia had fallen, Byzantium was fractured, and the Levant lay in Arab hands.[40] This was not diffusion of belief. It was a military revolution. The men who claimed Muhammad's mantle wielded both scripture and steel, and memory was forced to bow before both.

Dissent was not debated. It was destroyed. From the beginning, apostasy in Islam carried the penalty of death, traced to Muhammad's own command: "Whoever changes his religion, kill him."[41] This was not mere theology. It was the policing of history. The message was clear: deviate from the canon, and your voice ends with you. In such an atmosphere, memory does not develop; it is enforced. The Hadith were compiled under caliphs

---

37. Josephus, *Antiquities* 18.63–64.
38. Peters, *Muhammad and the Origins of Islam*, 242–44.
39. Tacitus, *Annals* 15.44; Ehrman, *New Testament*, 85–88.
40. Kennedy, *Great Arab Conquests*, xiii–xvii, 3–6, 209–14.
41. Bukhari, *Ṣaḥīḥ al-Bukhārī*, Hadith 3017.

PART IV. THE PROPHET AND HIS COMMUNITY

who profited from doctrinal control.[42] Biographies were preserved by those closest to power. No dissenting eyewitness survived. Silence was not consensus; it was fear.

Now compare the cruciform rise of Christianity. The Gospels emerged not under empire's shield but empire's sword. Their authors were hunted, not hired. Their words endured not by decree but by blood. Martyrs carried the text, and their deaths confirmed it.[43] No empire backed them. No sword preserved them. And yet, their witness survived. That is the difference. A lie does not make martyrs; it makes victims of propaganda. Where truth stands, men die to testify. Where empire rules, men die to conform. Rome tried to bury the Christian word, and failed. The early caliphate killed the competition, and succeeded.[44] That is not preservation. That is propaganda in armor.

Hadith vs. Gospels: Two Testimonies

The Gospels were written within thirty to seventy years of Jesus's life, biographies anchored in real times, real places, real names, real geography, and public events.[45] Their authors do not hide; they invite scrutiny. They write in the open, naming rulers, citing witnesses, exposing themselves to contradiction if false.[46]

The Hadith collections, by contrast, Islam's primary record of Muhammad's sayings and actions, were compiled a century and a half to two centuries after his death.[47] By then, rumor had multiplied into thousands of chains. Fabrication was rampant, sects disagreed, and scholars themselves admitted that most was false.[48] Bukhari and Muslim rejected more than 98 percent of the material, preserving only fragments.[49]

What if Christians dismissed 98 percent of Jesus's words as fraudulent? Nothing would remain. The faith would collapse under the weight of

---

42. Brown, *Hadith*, 83–90, 129–33, 175–77.

43. Ehrman, *Triumph of Christianity*, 111–17, 137–41, 217–22.

44. Cook, *Muhammad*, 65–70, 74–77; Donner, *Narratives of Islamic Origins*, 28–35, 123–29, 145–49.

45. Blomberg, *Historical Reliability of the Gospels*, 41–68; Bruce, *New Testament Documents*, 7–15.

46. Bauckham, *Jesus and the Eyewitnesses*, 5–12.

47. Brown, *Hadith*, 18–31.

48. Juynboll, *Authenticity of the Tradition Literature*, 64–85; Brown, *Hadith*, 86–112.

49. Brown, *Hadith*, 97–99; Motzki, "Collection of the Qur'an," 60–77.

absence. But Muhammad's story persists, propped on a fractured frame, shielded by tradition rather than sustained by history. That is the measure of the two testimonies. One stands on converging witness, tested by time and persecution. The other survives by curation, trimmed to fit power and preserved by reverence. Which would you trust, the testimony that bleeds to survive, or the testimony that edits to endure?

Quran vs. Old Testament: A Misleading Parallel

Yes, the Old Testament contains laws, much like the Quran. But here is the crucial difference: the Torah weaves law into story. Genesis, Exodus, Judges, Kings, narrative and legislation intertwine. The commands are set in lineage, in conflict, in covenant, in the dealings of God with His people.[50] The Quran, by contrast, delivers law without story. No unfolding chronology. No biographical arc. No sweeping timeline. It governs without narrating.[51] The Old Testament breathes law into living history; the Quran suspends law above it. And here enters Christ. He did not discard the law but fulfilled it: "I have not come to abolish the Law but to fulfill it." His command was love, not governance.[52] His teaching was not detached decree but living word, embedded in birth, in miracles, in death, in resurrection, in trial before rulers and empire.[53] By contrast, Muhammad's words arrive filtered, distant, fragmented, detached from chronology, without a cross, without a resurrection, without a narrative bloodline that ties divine law to divine sacrifice.[54]

The Absence of Early External Sources: A Prophet Unmentioned

Apply the Five Pillars of Historical Credibility—contemporaneity, multiplicity, external confirmation, archaeology, chain of custody—and watch what happens.[55] In the earliest decades, Muhammad fails them, not because he was unknown, but because the world said nothing. No Roman dispatches warn of him. No Persian records track him. No Byzantine scribes react to

---

50. Alter, *Art of Biblical Narrative*, 33–36, 114–17.
51. Wansbrough, *Quranic Studies*, 79–84, 95–98.
52. Matt 5:17.
53. Wright, *Jesus and the Victory of God*, 387–91, 431–35, 615–19.
54. Donner, *Narratives of Islamic Origins*, 132–36, 145–49.
55. LaBarbera, *Truth at the Gate*, x–xx.

a prophet-turned-warlord said to be uniting tribes and redrawing Arabia's map. Nothing.⁵⁶ Coins bear no image. Inscriptions are silent.

Archaeology produces no contemporary trace of his life. Manuscripts come only much later. This is not omission; it is vacuum, silence too loud to ignore. If Muhammad truly reshaped the world in his own lifetime, politically, militarily, spiritually, why does no contemporary outside his movement record him? Not even as rumor? Not as rebel? Not as regional threat? Within the first generations after Jesus's crucifixion, His name surfaces in Roman history (Tacitus), Jewish history (Josephus), imperial chatter (Suetonius), and hostile rabbinic tradition (the Talmud).⁵⁷ He drew reaction, resistance, revision, because the world saw Him and tried to write Him off. But they had to write.

With Muhammad, external notice comes much later, well into the second century of Islam, and even then largely retrospective. By that time, the empire ascribed to his legacy had already redrawn borders and spanned continents. Yet while he lived, not a single contemporary rival wrote of the founder.⁵⁸ For a man said to wield sword and scripture, the absence is staggering, unless what we call "history" is backfilled theology, codified long after the fact. The first echoes of Jesus were enemies confirming what friends preserved.⁵⁹ The first echoes of Muhammad? Silence, until the scribes were safe and the system set.⁶⁰

The Name Appears in History—But with Ambiguity

We are told that Muhammad changed history, yet the first echoes of his name arrive strangely late, and strangely soft. The earliest inscription is not from Mecca. Not from Medina. But from Jerusalem, on the Dome of the Rock, around AD 691, nearly sixty years after his death.⁶¹ And even there, the name gives no story. No tribe. No birthplace. No deeds. Only

---

56. Hoyland, *Seeing Islam as Others Saw It*, 37–41, 51–55, 393–95.

57. Tacitus, *Annals* 15.44; Josephus, *Antiquities* 18.63–64, 20.200; Suetonius, *Claudius* 25.4; Babylonian Talmud, *Sanhedrin* 43a.

58. Hoyland, *Seeing Islam as Others Saw It*, 37–41, 51–55, 393–95.

59. Bruce, *Jesus and Christian Origins*, 29–36, 37–46, 52–55.

60. Holland, *In the Shadow of the Sword*, 45–52, 54–67.

61. Hoyland, *Seeing Islam as Others Saw It*, 17–20; Borrut, "Vanishing Scriptures," 1–30.

"Muhammad," "the praised one." Praised by whom? For what? The words proclaim theology, not biography. They read like doctrine, not history.[62]

The coins tell the same tale. Early Umayyad currency bears the name "Muhammad," but without context. Sometimes the title seems more honorific than personal, raising questions whether "the praised one" pointed to a prophet, or even to Christ Himself, invoked under that title by Syriac Christians.[63] Speculative, yes. But the ambiguity is undeniable. By the Five Pillars of Historical Evidence—contemporaneity, multiplicity, external confirmation, archaeology, chain of custody—these traces leave us wanting.[64] They mark a movement, not a man. A name, not a narrative.

With Christ, His name bursts into coins, graffiti, court records, and hostile writings within decades.[65] His teaching spread not on banners of conquest but through the wounds of martyrs. His followers did not mint slogans; they bore scars. They did not carve doctrine into domes; they carried crosses into prisons and arenas. Jesus did not need ambiguity. His history walks in daylight. With Muhammad, even archaeology whispers. The silence is loud. And where memory falters, power writes the script.

Summing Up the Evidence: The Prophet of Preservation

By the same standards applied to every figure in this book, contemporaneity, multiplicity, external corroboration, archaeology, and chain of custody, Muhammad's record fractures. The Quran is not biography. Compiled after his death, it gives commands but no story, declarations without life.[66] The Hadith, Islam's biographical backbone, was not written until 150 to 200 years later, and more than 98 percent of its material was judged unreliable even by Islamic scholars themselves.[67] Memory became rumor. Rumor became rivalry. Rivalry became redaction.

Ibn Ishaq, the first biographer, wrote more than a century after Muhammad's death. His work survives only through Ibn Hisham, who

---

62. Luxenberg, *Syro-Aramaic Reading of the Koran*, 19–24, 34–36; Puin, "Observations," 107–11.

63. Walker, *Catalogue*, 1–8, 34–36; Grierson, *Numismatics*, 45–48.

64. Shoemaker, *Death of a Prophet*, 18–23, 64–69; LaBarbera, *Truth at the Gate*, x–xx.

65. Tacitus, *Annals* 15.44; Josephus, *Antiquities* 18.63–64; Suetonius, *Claudius* 25.4; Bruce, *Jesus and Christian Origins*, 29–36, 37–46, 52–55.

66. Guillaume, *Life of Muhammad*, xxiv–xxv.

67. Brown, *Hadith*, 3–7.

PART IV. THE PROPHET AND HIS COMMUNITY

confessed to cutting "disgraceful" material and shaping the man to fit the myth.[68] External voices? Absent. For decades, no Roman, Persian, or Byzantine scribe so much as names him. Archaeology is sparse, inscriptions ambiguous. Early coins and monuments bear the word "Muhammad," but stripped of context. Some scholars argue these earliest references were not even to a man, but to Christ Himself as "the praised one."[69] The Dome of the Rock inscription, nearly seventy years after his death, affirms theology, but omits Mecca, tribe, and story.

What remains is not biography but preservation by power: fragmented memory, late embellishments, doctrinal censorship, and military dominance. Not one hostile voice from his lifetime. Not one independent confirmation. If we contrast this with Christ, who, within fifteen to thirty years of His crucifixion, His life is already written.[70] Multiple witnesses, friendly and hostile, fix Him under Pilate, in Judea, executed by Roman law. External sources confirm Him: Tacitus, Josephus, Suetonius, the Talmud.[71] Archaeology aligns with the Gospels: ossuaries, coins, inscriptions, the methods of crucifixion itself. Manuscripts of His words multiply across the Mediterranean within a generation, copied, guarded, proclaimed by men who sealed their witness in blood.[72]

And yet only one is denied. Only Christ is endlessly scrutinized. Not because of evidence, but because of implication. Muhammad asked for allegiance. Jesus demands the soul. One secured silence with empire. The other provoked witness through martyrdom. One built memory through fear. The other through blood. That is the difference. Myths drip like wax when held too close to the sun. Truth endures because it is nailed to wood. Empire can preserve silence. But only truth can raise martyrs. And history itself still bends to His cross.

---

68. Guillaume, *Life of Muhammad*, xxii–xxv.
69. Holland, *In the Shadow of the Sword*, 376–78.
70. Blomberg, *Historical Reliability of the Gospels*, 41–44.
71. Tacitus, *Annals* 15.44; Josephus, *Antiquities* 18.63–64; Babylonian Talmud, *Sanhedrin* 43a.
72. Bruce, *New Testament Documents*, 10–12.

PART V

Singular Among History

THE TRIAL NOW TURNS to the One at the center of time. The gates are opened. And standing there is not a conqueror, philosopher, prophet, or emperor, but a carpenter. A Nazarene.

1. He wrote no books.
2. He led no armies.
3. He never ruled an empire.

And yet His words turned the world upside down.[1] This section presents not just the evidence for His existence, but the inconvenient abundance of it. Manuscripts more numerous, earlier, and more geographically dispersed than any other figure examined.[2] Eyewitness accounts.[3] Martyrdoms.[4] Internal consistency. And bold claims unlike any made before or after. A man whose life fulfilled prophecy, confronted institutions, and offered salvation, then and now. Here, the standard changes. Because believing in Him changes the implication for all of us—he breaks the mold. There is no parallel. There is no second. The question is no longer "Did He exist?"; it is: "What will you do with Him once you find out He did?"

---

1. Acts 17:6 ("These that have turned the world upside down are come hither also").
2. Bruce, *New Testament Documents*, 10–14; Metzger and Ehrman, *Text of the New Testament*, 51–53; Blomberg, *Historical Reliability of the New Testament*, 25–30.
3. Bauckham, *Jesus and the Eyewitnesses*, 5–7, 34–38.
4. McDowell, *Fate of the Apostles*, 37–42.

Jesus of Nazareth
The Carpenter in the Records

WE HAVE ARRIVED AT the last name on history's docket: the Nazarene. But He is not simply another figure in the gallery of giants. He is the fork in the road, the point where all paths divide,[1] where evidence collides with eternity, and where history no longer whispers, but demands an answer. No name has shaped the world more. No life has divided time.[2] His story has been told in every tongue, on every continent, remembered in suffering, repeated in silence,[3] and still He remains the most doubted of them all.

Why? Because He does not ask for admiration. He demands surrender.

If you have not yet noticed, take it now: Alexander conquered kingdoms. Caesar forged empire. Muhammad carved law from conquest. But Jesus of Nazareth made a claim none of them dared: not that He spoke the truth, but that He was the Truth.[4] That kind of claim does not ask for applause; it demands a verdict.[5] He must be tried, not quoted. Weighed, not admired. He is not like the others. He never claimed to be.

He is the verdict.

---

1. Lewis, *Mere Christianity*, 40–41. Lewis describes Jesus as the "fork in the road," the decisive point where all choices diverge.

2. Wright, *Resurrection of the Son of God*, 690–91. Wright argues that the resurrection uniquely reshaped history and divided time itself.

3. Bauckham, *Jesus and the Eyewitnesses*, 34–40. Bauckham shows that the Gospel traditions were grounded in eyewitness memory, remembered in suffering, not mythologized in silence.

4. John 14:6.

5. McDowell, *New Evidence That Demands a Verdict*, xxi–xxiii. McDowell frames the claim of Christ as a demand for judgment rather than admiration.

PART V. SINGULAR AMONG HISTORY

The voice.
The gravity pulling all judgment into orbit.

And so we test Him, not with sentiment, but with the same standard used for every name before: contemporaneity, multiplicity, external confirmation, archaeology, chain of custody.[6] The Five Pillars of History. The same fire that melted every other figure. And when the test is finished, only One will still be standing. Let us walk the final trial. One last time.

The Gospel Writers

The Gospels, Matthew, Mark, Luke, and John, are not anonymous legends whispered through centuries of superstition. They are rooted testimonies, written within a generation of the events they record, forged in a world where liars were stoned and frauds were crucified, not celebrated.

Mark, written around AD 65 to 70, draws from the preaching of Peter, the disciple who walked beside Christ, denied Him, and died for Him. Early tradition calls Mark "Peter's interpreter."[7] This is not mythology; it is memory turned manuscript.

Matthew, dated AD 70 to 85, is attributed to the tax collector turned apostle. His Gospel drips with Jewish custom, Aramaic idioms, and detailed temple references, marks of a Jewish eyewitness writing to a Jewish world still intact before Jerusalem fell.[8]

Luke, the physician and companion of Paul, wrote between AD 80 to 90. He tells us plainly: "I investigated everything carefully from the beginning."[9] Luke does not spin tales; he cross-examines witnesses. His Gospel reads like it was prepared for court.

John, last to write (AD 90 to 100), was no distant observer. He stood at the foot of the cross. He outran Peter to the tomb. He testifies: "He who

---

6. Craig, *Reasonable Faith*, 163–69; Habermas, *Historical Jesus*, 152–62, 187–206; Habermas and Licona, *Case for the Resurrection of Jesus*, 128–31. Craig outlines the criteria of authenticity, contemporaneity, multiple attestation, coherence, dissimilarity, and external confirmation used in the historical method. Habermas surveys extrabiblical testimony (Josephus, Tacitus, Pliny, the Talmud) alongside early creedal material such as 1 Cor 15. Together with Licona, Habermas develops the "Minimal Facts" approach, testing the resurrection on data accepted across scholarship.

7. Eusebius, *Church History* 3.39.

8. Carson and Moo, *Introduction to the New Testament*, 144–52.

9. Luke 1:3.

saw it has borne witness... his testimony is true."[10] These were not scribes in caves weaving legend. These were men staring down death, writing because they remembered, and could not forget. And the world has never been the same.

The Gospels did not drift into authority; they were anchored there from the start. Early Christian voices, Papias, Irenaeus, Clement of Alexandria, Origen, all affirmed their authorship.[11] No rival claims emerged. No alternate names gained traction. Why? Because the early church knew who wrote them, and many bled to protect that truth.

By AD 125, fragments like P52[12] already contained the Gospel of John, decades after it was written.[13] This is not legend forming. This is memory still warm from the hands that lived it. And their preservation? Unmatched. Over 5,800 Greek manuscripts survive, more than any work of antiquity.[14] Early copies appear within a generation of the originals. Translations into Syriac, Coptic, and Latin carried them across continents.[15] The Gospels were not voted into power by councils or kings. They were recognized immediately, because those who read them still remembered the footsteps of the men who wrote them.

Critics object that manuscript counts are unfair, that Christian texts benefited from scribal networks and later institutional support.[16] Some of that is true. But even when all allowances are made, the Gospels still stand apart. They were not preserved in elite libraries. They were smuggled, copied, proclaimed under threat of death. Their survival is not the result of comfort. It is the result of conviction. And that changes everything.

The Manuscripts Bear Witness

Critics say the Gospels were passed like whispers in the dark, corrupted, legendary, untrustworthy. But the manuscript tradition behind the New Testament does not whisper. It thunders.[17] No ancient figure, not Caesar,

10. John 19:35.
11. Bruce, *New Testament Documents*, 22–23, 112–13.
12. P52 (ca. AD 125).
13. Comfort, *Complete Text*, 36–40.
14. Wallace, *Manuscript Evidence*, 29–30.
15. Metzger, *Early Versions of the New Testament*, 50–52, 70–75, 100–2.
16. Ehrman, *Misquoting Jesus*, 90–95.
17. Bruce, *New Testament Documents*, 15–17.

not Alexander, not Socrates, comes remotely close to the textual avalanche surrounding the life, death, and resurrection of Jesus Christ.

Consider P52, the Rylands Papyrus, dated around AD 125, found in Egypt. A fragment of John's Gospel, it was written barely thirty to forty years after the original.[18] Already copied, already carried across nations, without printing presses, without global networks. That is not how legends spread. That is how testimony survives.

And P52 is only the beginning. Plato's works survive in about 250 manuscripts. Aristotle in fewer than 50. Julius Caesar in barely a dozen. The New Testament? Over 5,800 Greek manuscripts, 10,000 Latin, and more than 20,000 in other ancient languages.[19] Many within a century or two of the originals. In ancient terms, that is lightning speed. Most texts survive only in copies nearly a thousand years later. Why this explosion? Because Christians weren't preserving folklore. They were preserving lifeblood. These weren't fireside stories. They were depositions, carried through war, copied under persecution, smuggled across empire. Not nostalgia. Necessity. They believed the world depended on it.

Even the Dead Sea Scrolls prove the tradition of precision. Among them lies a scroll of Isaiah, dated nearly a millennium earlier than any other copy, and virtually unchanged.[20] A few spelling differences. Nothing more. The Jewish scribes were guardians. And the early church, shaped by that discipline, treated the Gospels the same.[21] Does this prove divine inspiration? No. But it destroys the myth of corruption. What we hold in our hands today is what they held in theirs.[22] The real question is not whether Jesus existed; the manuscripts have already settled that. The question is: What will you do with what He said?

Too Early to Be Legend

Socrates left no writings.[23] What we know comes only through disciples like Plato and Xenophon, recorded long after his death. Alexander's story is worse still; his most influential biographies weren't written until nearly four

18. Comfort, *Complete Text*, 36–38.
19. Metzger, *Text of the New Testament*, 34–37.
20. Cross, *Ancient Library*, 152–56.
21. Emmanuel, *Textual Criticism of the Hebrew Bible*, 23–28.
22. Bruce, *New Testament Documents*, 17–18.
23. Plato, *Phaedo* 59b–60b; Waterfield, *Why Socrates Died*, 3–5.

centuries later by Plutarch and Arrian in the second century AD.[24] By the time the ink dried, memory had already hardened into myth.

The Gospels are different. They arrive within decades of the crucifixion: Mark around AD 65–70,[25] Matthew and Luke by 85, John by 100.[26] These are not echoes from the void. They are fresh imprints, close enough for memory still to burn and for critics still to bite.

And no one could stop them. Eyewitnesses were alive: Roman officials, Jewish leaders, soldiers, citizens, all capable of confirming or denying.[27] If the claims were false, backlash would have been instant. Instead, many enemies converted.[28] Why? Because what they saw broke them. The Gospels did not evolve into legend. They detonated into history, with names, rulers, dates, and geography tied to real time.[29] This is not mythology whispered in shadows. It is testimony shouted in daylight. And when history is allowed to speak, the Gospels do not whisper. They roar.

The Dust Still Speaks: Archaeology and the Nazarene

Skeptics echo the refrain: "There's no archeological evidence for Jesus."[30] It sounds damning, until you look closer. Because the dust does not lie. And the stones have begun to cry out.[31]

Nazareth: From Rumor to Rock

For decades, critics scoffed at Nazareth. Too small, too obscure, too perfectly placed. Some went further, claiming it was fiction, invented by Gospel writers to give Jesus a prophetic hometown that never was. Then came 2009. Archaeologists uncovered a first-century house buried beneath

---

24. Plutarch, *Life of Alexander*; Arrian, *Anabasis*; Fox, *Alexander the Great*, 4–5.

25. Bruce, *New Testament Documents*, 7–10.

26. Blomberg, *Historical Reliability of the Gospels*; Bauckham, *Jesus and the Eyewitnesses*, 192–200.

27. Bruce, *New Testament Documents*, 39–42.

28. Blomberg, *Historical Reliability of the Gospels*, 52–53.

29. Bauckham, *Jesus and the Eyewitnesses*, 93–122.

30. Price, *Christ-Myth Theory*, 61–64; Baras, "Archaeology and the Historical Jesus," 321–33; Crossan, *Jesus*, 199–201.

31. Evans, *Jesus and the Remains*, 3–5.

Byzantine and Crusader stone.[32] Hewn from limestone, framed by rough walls, strewn with Roman-era pottery, it stood as a silent witness. Nearby tombs, quarries, and agricultural installations sealed the case: Nazareth was no invention. It was a marginal village, inhabited in the time of Jesus, exactly as the Gospels describe.[33] And that is the point. Jesus was not born into Rome, or Alexandria, or Athens. He came from a village so dismissed that even His own people asked, "Can anything good come out of Nazareth?"[34] The evidence says yes. And it left a footprint in the dust.

Pilate's Inscription, Caiaphas's Ossuary, Crucifixion Nails

Nazareth is not the only stone that speaks. In 1961, excavators at Caesarea uncovered a limestone block inscribed with the name of Pontius Pilate, prefect of Judea, the very ruler who condemned Christ.[35] In 1990, a family tomb yielded an ossuary bearing the name "Joseph son of Caiaphas," high priest of the trial.[36] At Giv'at ha-Mivtar, skeletal remains revealed heel bones pierced by nails, physical testimony to the Roman practice of crucifixion in the very century Jesus died.[37] These are not legends. They are names carved in stone, bones sealed in earth, iron driven through flesh. Together they frame the Gospels not as myth, but as memory.

The Stones Cry Out

Archaeology will never produce a shard labeled "Jesus of Nazareth." That is not how history works. But it gives us the texture, the setting, the names, the rulers, the punishments, all aligning with the world of the Gospels. The dust bears witness. The stones answer skeptics. And that is the difference. Legends leave no footprints. Myths leave no nails. But the Nazarene has both. His life is etched into the ground of Galilee and Jerusalem, and His cross is carved into the bones of history itself.

---

32. Dark, *Archaeology of Nazareth*, 47–53; Dark, "Sisters of Nazareth Convent," 133–76.
33. Bagatti, *Excavations in Nazareth*; Strange, "Nazareth," 1050–51; Pfann, *Nazareth Village Farm Report*; Taylor, *Essenes*, 115–17.
34. John 1:46.
35. Frova, "Caesarea Maritima," 256–59.
36. Greenhut, "Burial Cave of the Caiaphas Family," 230–57.
37. Haas, "Anthropological Observations," 38–59.

Stone Synagogues: The Framework of a Ministry

The Gospels say Jesus taught in synagogues across Galilee, in places like Capernaum, Chorazin, and Magdala. Critics once scoffed, arguing that synagogues didn't yet exist in the first century. But the ground tells another story. Excavations at Magdala in 2009 and at Gamla unearthed synagogue ruins dated precisely to the time of Christ, complete with mosaic floors, ritual baths, and stone benches still in place.[38] These weren't later tributes; they were living sanctuaries. Jesus didn't teach in legend. He walked stone aisles. The Gospels said it first. Now the earth confirms it.[39]

The Ossuary of Caiaphas: A Name in Bone

The Gospels record that Jesus was dragged before Caiaphas, the high priest, in the dead of night.[40] For years, critics dismissed him as invention, no more real than Pilate was once thought to be.[41] Then, in 1990, that argument cracked open. Construction crews digging in south Jerusalem stumbled upon a first-century burial cave. Among the ossuaries inside, one stood apart, ornate, elegant, fit for the elite.[42] Carved into its side, in sharp Aramaic script, were the words:

> *Yehosef bar Qayafa*
> *Joseph, son of Caiaphas.*[43]

This was not speculation. It was archaeology. The inscription, the craftsmanship, the context, everything dated to first-century Jerusalem, the very world of the Gospel narrative.[44] And this was no ordinary tomb. Only a man of high rank could afford limestone carved with care, placed in ceremony. And it bore not just any name, but the very name of the man who presided over Christ's trial. The ossuary does not prove the trial itself. But it proves the man was real. It proves the Gospels named names because they knew the names.

---

38. Aviam, "First Century Jewish Galilee," 58–75; Talgam, *Mosaics of Faith*, 175–79.
39. Zapata-Meza and Sánchez, "First Century Synagogue at Magdala," 27–54.
40. Matt 26:57–68; John 18:12–14.
41. Price, *Incredible Shrinking Son of Man*, 160; Crossan, *Who Killed Jesus?*, 122.
42. Greenhut, "Burial Cave of the Caiaphas Family," 29–36.
43. Greenhut, "Burial Cave of the Caiaphas Family," 29–36.
44. Evans, *Jesus and His World*, 39–42.

PART V. SINGULAR AMONG HISTORY

The box of bones does what skeptics said could never be done: it anchors the Passion narrative in stone. Caiaphas lived, led, judged, and was buried with distinction. The judge of Christ, confirmed by limestone. And the irony still whispers through the dust: the man who condemned the Truth now testifies to it.

The Heel Bone and the Nail: Crucifixion in Stone and Flesh

For centuries, skeptics scoffed that crucifixion was too barbaric to be practiced on Jews in Jerusalem, or doubted that nails were even used at all. Then, in 1968, a tomb was uncovered in Giv'at ha-Mivtar, just outside Jerusalem. Inside lay the ossuary of a young man named Yehohanan. His heel bone still carried the evidence: a seven-inch iron nail, bent and embedded through the bone, with fragments of olive wood from the cross still attached.[45] Here was crucifixion, frozen in time. Not theory. Not legend. Iron through bone. Flesh nailed to wood.

The details matched the Gospel record: victims buried after execution, nails used to fix the feet, wood fragments embedded where the nail struck a knot and bent back. Roman brutality was not literary invention; it was archaeology. Skeptics could no longer deny that nails pierced Jewish flesh in first-century Jerusalem. The discovery does not prove Jesus's crucifixion in isolation. But it proves the practice, in the right place, at the right time, exactly as the Gospels describe. The ground of Jerusalem still bears scars of Rome's crosses. And so the irony deepens: while critics demanded proof, the stones themselves yielded it. A heel bone. A nail. A silent witness whispering the oldest confession: *this happened.*

External Confirmation: Josephus and Tacitus

Skeptics ask: "If Jesus really lived, why don't non-Christian sources mention Him?" The answer: they do. And not just friends, but enemies. Josephus, the Jewish historian, born just after the crucifixion, wrote his *Antiquities of the Jews* around AD 93. He mentions Jesus twice.[46] One passage, the *Testimoni-*

---

45. Haas, "Anthropological Observations," 38–59.
46. Meier, *Marginal Jew* 1:61–62; Theissen and Merz, *Historical Jesus*, 65–66.

um Flavianum in book 18, was later touched by Christian hands, but nearly all scholars agree a core reference is authentic.[47] Reconstructed, it reads:

> *At this time there was a wise man named Jesus. His conduct was good, and he was known to be virtuous. Many Jews and others became his disciples. Pilate condemned him to be crucified. But those who had been his disciples did not abandon him. They reported that he had appeared to them three days after his crucifixion, and that he was alive.*
> *Antiquities* 18.3.3

That is a Jewish historian, no Christian sympathizer, confirming that Jesus lived, had disciples, was crucified under Pilate, and that His followers proclaimed His resurrection.[48] But Josephus also names Him again. In book 20, while describing the stoning of James, he writes:

> *Ananus convened the Sanhedrin of judges, and brought before them the brother of Jesus, who was called Christ, whose name was James, and some others . . . and delivered them to be stoned.*
> *Antiquities* 20.9.1

This second reference is untouched by Christian scribes. Virtually all scholars accept it as authentic. Here, Josephus casually identifies James by his brother, Jesus, who was called Christ.[49] It is a throwaway remark, not a defense. Which makes it all the stronger. The irony runs deep: Tiberius Caesar is accepted as firmly established on slender evidence, while Pilate, far better attested, was long dismissed as a Gospel invention until the Pilate stone surfaced in Caesarea.[50] Bias, not evidence, often drives skepticism. Tacitus, a Roman senator and historian, was no friend of Christians.[51] Writing in his *Annals* around AD 115, he describes Nero's attempt to shift blame for the fire of Rome:

> *Nero fastened the guilt and inflicted the most exquisite tortures on a class hated for their abominations, called Christians by the populace. Christus, from whom the name had its origin, suffered the extreme penalty during the reign of Tiberius at the hands of one of our procurators, Pontius Pilatus . . . and a most mischievous*

---

47. Feldman, "Josephus," 3:990–1017; Evans, *Jesus and His World*, 129–30.
48. Ehrman, *Did Jesus Exist?*, 60–62.
49. Josephus, *Antiquities* 20.9.1.
50. Bond, *Pontius Pilate in History and Interpretation*, 7–10.
51. Bruce, *Jesus and Christian Origins*, 23–24.

PART V. SINGULAR AMONG HISTORY

superstition, thus checked for the moment, again broke out not only in Judea, the first source of the evil, but even in Rome.
Annals 15.44

Tacitus despised Christians. He called their faith a "mischievous superstition." And yet, without meaning to, he confirms the very core: Jesus lived, was executed under Tiberius by Pilate, and His followers refused to die with Him.[52] These are hostile witnesses. Men with every reason to mock or erase, not preserve. Yet they could not ignore Him. When friends testify, it may be loyalty. When enemies testify, it is evidence. Josephus and Tacitus never believed in Christ. But they saw His shadow cross their own histories. And that is the point. Truth does not need cheerleaders. It only needs to be seen, even by those who wish it wasn't there.

Nor was Rome the only witness. By the late second century, the pagan philosopher Celsus wrote one of the earliest full-scale attacks on Christianity. He mocked Jesus as the illegitimate son of a soldier, accused Him of sorcery, and dismissed His followers as deluded peasants. Yet in all his scorn, Celsus never denied that Jesus lived, was crucified, and left behind a movement that shook the empire. Even enemies preserve the bones of truth: they can sneer at meaning, but they cannot erase the fact.[53]

Suetonius: Trouble in Rome

Suetonius, the Roman biographer of emperors, wasn't writing theology. He was writing gossip, scandals, and imperial trivia. And yet, in his *Life of Claudius*, composed around AD 120, he casually notes disturbances among the Jews in Rome "at the instigation of Chrestus."[54] The line is brief, almost throwaway. But it reveals that by Claudius's reign (AD 41 to 54), the message of Christ had already reached the Jewish community of Rome, and was causing enough uproar to draw the emperor's attention. Suetonius probably misunderstood the name, thinking "Chrestus" was a living agitator. But the reference makes sense: debates over Jesus of Nazareth had spilled far beyond Judea, shaking synagogues in the capitol of the empire. This is not Christian testimony. It is an imperial biographer annoyed at Jewish street

---

52. Habermas, *Historical Jesus*, 192–95.
53. Origen, *Against Celsus* 1.28, 2.13.
54. Suetonius, *Twelve Caesars*, "Claudius," 25.4.

fights. And yet, even in Rome, the shadow of the crucified Jew was stirring unrest. Christ was already impossible to ignore.

The Talmud: Hostile Memory

Even Jesus's enemies remembered Him. In the Babylonian Talmud, compiled centuries later but preserving earlier rabbinic traditions, He appears in hostile fragments. One notorious passage reads:

> *On the eve of Passover they hanged Yeshu. . . . He practiced sorcery and enticed Israel to apostasy.*
> *Sanhedrin 43a*[55]

This is no Christian gloss. The Talmud condemns Jesus as a sorcerer who led Israel astray. It acknowledges His execution "on the eve of Passover," aligning with the Gospel timeline, but twists His miracles into charges of magic. The rabbis did not believe in Him. They did not worship Him. They slandered Him. And yet, even in slander, they confirmed the core: Jesus lived, performed works that astonished crowds, was executed at Passover, and left a movement behind. Hostile memory is often the strongest witness. Friends may exaggerate. Enemies have no reason to. And when even enemies preserve the bones of truth, the case grows heavy.

While the Tomb Was Still Warm

The skeptics say: "The Gospels were written decades later. Stories grow. Legends form. The truth was probably simpler."[56] But the early church didn't wait for scrolls before it spoke. Long before Matthew wrote, before Luke investigated, before John declared the Word made flesh, the message was already moving,[57] passed mouth to mouth, not as metaphor, but as resurrection. The first Christians did not begin with theology. They began with testimony. Paul gives us the clearest window. In 1 Cor 15, he reminds the church of what he had "received" and "passed on":

---

55. Babylonian Talmud, *Sanhedrin* 43a.
56. Blomberg, *Historical Reliability of the Gospels*, 192–200, 233–39.
57. Dunn, *Jesus Remembered*, 171–76, 210–20.

PART V. SINGULAR AMONG HISTORY

That Christ died for our sins according to the Scriptures. That He was buried. That He was raised on the third day. That He appeared to Cephas, then to the Twelve.[58]

This is not Paul composing doctrine. This is Paul quoting a creed, a formula already circulating among believers. Scholars across the spectrum, even critics like Bart Ehrman and Gerd Lüdemann, agree it dates within three to five years of the crucifixion.[59] That is not enough time for legends to harden or hallucinations to be canonized. This is the church, while the tomb was still within reach, declaring: He died. He was buried. He rose. We saw Him alive. The raw material of the Gospel, death, burial, resurrection, eyewitness appearances, fulfillment of Scripture, was being preached before the Gospels were written, before any councils met, before Constantine ruled. Before creeds were etched in cathedral stone, they were whispered by men prepared to bleed for them.

Christianity is accused of being a "book religion," as though nothing existed until the canon was sealed. But that is not how it began. The earliest church carried the faith through oral tradition, creeds crafted to be remembered, rhythmic and poetic, impossible to forget.[60] Most were illiterate, but they were not blind. They knew what they had seen. And they carried that truth through prisons, across borders, into the teeth of empire.[61] And this matters for one devastating reason: if the resurrection were a later invention, it would not stand in the earliest creeds. It would not be structured, repeated, and proclaimed while eyewitnesses were still alive. But it is. It was. Which means the confession of the church was forged not in comfort, but in the fire of memory. They proclaimed: He rose, while His tomb was still warm. And no one could stop them.

Stone Synagogues Again: The Places He Preached

The Gospels say again and again that Jesus taught in synagogues across Galilee, from Capernaum to Chorazin, Nazareth to Magdala.[62] For years,

---

58. 1 Cor 15:3-7.
59. Ehrman, *Did Jesus Exist?*, 229; Lüdemann, *Resurrection of Jesus*, 38.
60. Bauckham, *Jesus and the Eyewitnesses*, 264-68.
61. Dunn, *Jesus Remembered*, 171-76, 210-20; Bauckham, *Jesus and the Eyewitnesses*, 34-40, 124-27; Blomberg, *Historical Reliability of the Gospels*, 241-43; Habermas, *Historical Jesus*, 201-5.
62. Mark 1:21; 1:39; Matt 4:23; 9:35; 13:54; Luke 4:16; 4:44.

critics dismissed this as an anachronism. "There were no synagogues in Galilean villages during the first century," they said. The Gospel writers, it was claimed, projected later structures back into Jesus's time. But the stones have spoken. Archaeologists have uncovered multiple first-century synagogues scattered across Galilee, exactly where the Gospels place Him.[63] Among them:

- **Magdala,** hometown of Mary Magdalene. In 2009, excavators uncovered a synagogue complete with stone benches, mosaic floors, and the Magdala stone, carved with menorah imagery, likely used for Torah reading.[64]
- **Gamla,** in the Golan Heights, one of the earliest known synagogues in Israel, dated squarely to the first century.[65]
- **Chorazin,** a village Jesus Himself rebuked.[66] Excavations have exposed the basalt ruins of its synagogue.[67]
- **Mount Arbel,** most recently, a newly discovered synagogue dating to the Second Temple period, built with benches and ritual features, confirming a network of Galilean synagogues in the very age of Jesus.[68]

These were not grand monuments. They were modest halls, rectangular, stone-built, with benches lining the walls. They were not designed for spectacle. They were built for Scripture. For gathering. For teaching. Exactly as the Gospels say. The critics said: "No synagogues in Galilee." But the ruins beneath Galilee say otherwise. The Gospels did not fabricate villages. They did not invent synagogues. They remembered what was there, because they were written while memory still walked those roads.[69]

---

63. Fine, *Art and Judaism*, 142.

64. Aviam, "First Century Synagogue at Magdala," 44–52; Zapata-Meza et al., "Magdala Archaeological Project"; Talgam, "Magdala Stone," 27–46.

65. Meyers and Strange, *Archaeology, the Rabbis, and Early Christianity*, 28.

66. Matt 11:21.

67. Foerster, "Synagogue at Chorazin," 12–17.

68. Vachman, "New Second Temple-Period Synagogue."

69. Levine, *Ancient Synagogue*, 48–50.

PART V. SINGULAR AMONG HISTORY

Martyrdom Records They Could've Lived, But Chose the Flame

Skeptics say: "People die for false things all the time." True. But the apostles and early Christians did not die for abstract beliefs or inherited myths. They died for what they claimed to have seen. These were not distant descendants preserving cultural memory. They were eyewitnesses, or the disciples of eyewitnesses, who had walked with Jesus, touched His wounds, and stood before an empty tomb.[70] When the blade was drawn, they could have recanted. When the fire was lit, they could have fled. But they didn't. And history trembled.

Polycarp, bishop of Smyrna, appointed by John himself,[71] was arrested in old age and dragged before Roman officials. "Swear by Caesar," they demanded. "Deny Christ, and we'll spare you." His reply still thunders: "Eighty-six years I have served Him, and He has done me no wrong. How can I blaspheme my King who saved me?" They bound him to the stake. Eyewitnesses recorded that the flames curled around him like sails in the wind. When fire failed, they killed him with the sword.[72] This was not cultural inertia. It was loyalty to the Risen One.

Ignatius of Antioch, disciple of Peter and John, was marched to Rome around AD 107 to face the beasts. On the way he wrote seven letters, some of the most defiant documents of the early church.[73] He didn't beg for release. He begged no one to intervene: "I am the wheat of God, and let me be ground by the teeth of wild beasts, that I may be found the pure bread of Christ."[74] This is not delusion. It is the voice of a man who had heard the witnesses and chosen to follow them to death.

Justin Martyr began as a philosopher. Around AD 155 he addressed his *First Apology* to the emperor, defending Christianity with reason. Later, under Marcus Aurelius, he was ordered to sacrifice to idols. His answer was simple: "Do what you will. We are Christians. We do not sacrifice to idols."[75] For this, he was beheaded. Justin did not cling to a myth. He followed a faith consistent from fishermen to philosophers, sealed again and again in blood.

---

70. Ignatius, *Apostolic Fathers* 1:185–91, 1: 2:66–85.
71. Polycarp, *Apostolic Fathers* 2:320–45.
72. Polycarp, *Apostolic Fathers* 2:320–45.
73. Ignatius, *Apostolic Fathers* 1:185–91, 1: 2:66–85.
74. Ignatius, *Apostolic Fathers* 1:185–91, 1: 2:66–85.
75. Martyr, *First Apology* and *Acts of the Martyrdom of Justin*, in *First and Second Apologies*, 23–25, 162–69.

Delusion does not breed courage like this. Lies don't endure the flame. These were not anonymous zealots dying for tribal pride. They were the first inheritors of a message passed through scars and carried in memory. They were taught by men who touched the wounds. They chose death because they refused to say it was false. They had everything to gain by walking away. Nothing to gain by staying true, unless it was actually true.

They had everything to gain by walking away. Nothing to gain by staying true, unless it was actually true. Rome thought death would silence them. But in silencing them, it amplified their testimony. The empire turned their voices into echoes that still thunder across history. Their blood became the ink that wrote the church's creed.

The Verdict: When the Five Pillars Face the Nazarene

We've now reached the test. Not of belief, but of evidence. The same five pillars we've laid before every figure now stand before the Nazarene. Not to flatter Him. Not to defend Him. But to see if history itself will bear His name.

1. **Contemporaneity.** Were the claims written near the events, or generations removed? For Jesus, the Gospels were penned within thirty to sixty years of His crucifixion, while eyewitnesses, critics, and killers were still alive.[76] This was before any council, before empires converted, before the story had time to twist. Paul's letters? Even earlier. And the creeds he recited, like 1 Cor 15, are dated within three to five years of the resurrection.[77] These accounts are retrospective, not diaries kept during His ministry. Yet they remain far closer in time to their subject than most ancient biographies, which often emerge centuries later.[78] Meanwhile:

    - Socrates wrote nothing.
    - Alexander's first biography appeared three hundred years after his death.[79]

---

76. Blomberg, *Historical Reliability of the Gospels*, 41–53.
77. Ehrman, *Did Jesus Exist?*, 229–34.
78. Bauckham, *Jesus and the Eyewitnesses*, 5–9.
79. Fox, *Alexander the Great*, 4–6.

PART V. SINGULAR AMONG HISTORY

- Muhammad's biography came 130–200 years later, filtered through oral tradition and redacted copies.[80]
- Confucius's sayings were compiled centuries after his death.

2. **Multiplicity of Sources.** Do we have multiple voices, or one filtered narrative? For Jesus, we have four distinct Gospel accounts, plus letters of Paul, Peter, James, and other leaders.[81] Add to this hostile witnesses, Tacitus, Josephus, the Babylonian Talmud.[82] Not harmony without variation, but convergence without contradiction. Four portraits. One Christ, crucified, buried, risen.

3. **External Confirmation.** Do outsiders affirm what insiders claimed? Tacitus, the Roman senator, scorned Christians, but still named Jesus, His execution, and the reign of Tiberius.[83] Josephus, a Jewish historian, recorded Jesus's death under Pilate and the endurance of His followers.[84] Neither intended to validate Christianity. But neither could write Him away. These external sources are not without dispute: Josephus's passages contain debated interpolations, and Tacitus wrote decades later, but even with those cautions, their very hostility or brevity strengthens the case that Jesus was no invention of Christians. And, decades later, again, is still contemporary.[85]

4. **Archaeology.** Does the dirt match the ink? Yes. Nazareth, long mocked as fiction, was uncovered stone by stone in modern digs.[86] The ossuary of Caiaphas, etched in Aramaic with Yehosef bar Qayafa, confirms the high priest of the Gospels.[87] Synagogues once dismissed as inventions now stand unearthed in Magdala, Chorazin, and Gamla.[88] These finds prove the record of Christ does not float in myth; it leaves footprints in stone.

---

80. Peters, *Muhammad and the Origins of Islam*, 18–24.
81. Bauckham, *Jesus and the Eyewitnesses*, 5–15.
82. Meier, *Marginal Jew* 1:56–59.
83. Tacitus, *Annals* 15.44.
84. Josephus, *Antiquities* 18.3.3, 20.9.1.
85. Feldman, *Josephus and Modern Scholarship*, 681–701; Van Voorst, *Jesus Outside the New Testament*, 39–53.
86. Dark, *Archaeology of Jesus's Nazareth*, 1–10.
87. Greenhut, "Burial Cave of the Caiaphas Family," 230–47.
88. Arav, "Ancient Synagogues in Israel," 44–55.

5. **Chain of Custody.** Can we trust what we read? The New Testament stands unmatched: over 5,800 Greek manuscripts,[89] 10,000 in Latin, and more than 20,000 in other languages. Early fragments like P52 place the Gospel of John in circulation within a generation of its writing.[90] The originals are lost, and variations exist across copies, as is true for every ancient text. Yet the sheer volume and early dating of New Testament manuscripts allow reconstruction with greater confidence than any comparable figure.[91] In contrast: Caesar, 10 manuscripts. Plato, 250. Aristotle, 49. The ancient world has never preserved anything on this scale. Yet paradoxically, Jesus is the one most doubted, not Alexander, not Buddha, not Muhammad, not Socrates. Why? Because His story does not merely ask for agreement. It demands surrender.

The Fire They Chose: The Fork in The Road

The apostles did not suffer for metaphors. They did not scatter across the empire, endure torture, exile, and execution for a parable or a proverb. They bled for a fact: that they had seen Jesus of Nazareth alive after death.[92] These were not distant theologians inheriting abstract creeds. They were firsthand witnesses, men who touched His wounds, walked beside Him, and ate with Him after the tomb was empty. And when the moment came to save themselves by silence, not one of them did.

- Peter was crucified upside down.[93]
- Andrew nailed to a cross in the shape of an X.[94]
- Thomas speared in India.[95]
- Bartholomew flayed alive.[96]
- James beheaded.[97]

---

89. Metzger and Ehrman, *Text of the New Testament*, 51–54.
90. Roberts, *Unpublished Fragment of the Fourth Gospel*, 1–8.
91. Metzger and Ehrman, *Text of the New Testament*, 276–80.
92. Craig, *Reasonable Faith*, 360–62; Habermas, *Historical Jesus*, 200–5.
93. Foxe, *Book of Martyrs*, 1–10.
94. *Acts of Andrew*, in Schneemelcher, *New Testament Apocrypha* 1:435–67.
95. Foxe, *Book of Martyrs*, 1–10.
96. De Voragine, *Golden Legend* 2:15–17.
97. Acts 12:2.

- John plunged in boiling oil, then exiled.[98]
- Simon the Zealot sawn in half.[99]
- Others were beaten, stoned, clubbed, broken.

They had every human reason to recant. Every incentive to walk away. But they didn't. Because it wasn't just belief; it was encounter. It wasn't just conviction; it was memory. You don't let yourself be torn apart for a hallucination. You don't go to the grave singing for a metaphor. These men were not dying for what they believed. They died for what they saw. And that matters. Because the difference between philosophy and witness is the difference between theory and fire.

This testimony is not confined to Christian memory. Around AD 112, Pliny the Younger, governor of Bithynia, wrote to Emperor Trajan describing Christians under interrogation.[100] He noted their habit of meeting before dawn, singing hymns to Christ "as to a god," and refusing to renounce their faith even under threat of death. Though no friend of Christianity, Pliny confirmed what the apostles' fate implies: a courageous community willing to die for what they truly believed.

This Isn't Doubt, It's Evasion

The skeptic accepts Socrates without a single sentence written by his own hand.[101] Accepts Alexander the Great, though his biographies appeared more than three centuries after his death.[102] Accepts Muhammad, though his life comes to us through oral redactions, lost originals, and sectarian contradictions.[103] Accepts Confucius, whose sayings were filtered and canonized long after his passing.[104] But Jesus? Four Gospels, each from an independent author.[105]

---

98. Tertullian, *Prescription Against Heretics*, 36; Eusebius, *Church History* 3.20.

99. Hippolytus, *On the Twelve Apostles* 5:254.

100. Pliny, *Letters* 10.96–97.

101. Laertius, *Lives of Eminent Philosophers* 2.18–47.

102. Plutarch, *Life of Alexander*; Arrian, *Anabasis*; Cartledge, *Alexander the Great*, 29–33.

103. Motzki, "Biography of Muhammad," 1–21.

104. Slingerland, *Confucius*, xvii–xxii.

105. Bauckham, *Jesus and the Eyewitnesses*, 5–12.

- Eyewitness accounts and letters spread across regions.
- Hostile sources, Tacitus and Josephus, confirming His crucifixion.[106]
- Archaeology aligning with Gospel villages, synagogues, and names.[107]
- Over 25,000 manuscripts across languages and continents.[108]
- And martyrs, real men, who could have walked away, but chose to die rather than live a lie.[109]

And still, He is the one most doubted. Why? Because the stakes are not academic. They are eternal. Christ does not stay on the page. He steps off it, looks you in the eye, and commands you to follow. The issue has never been historical credibility. It has always been moral consequence. For if it is true, then nothing remains the same. The Gospels were not written to be admired like Plato. They were not compiled to be studied like Caesar. They were not preserved to be shelved like Confucius. They were written as a summons, sharp, urgent, unyielding. Not merely to declare that He lived. But to proclaim that He lives.

And now, knowing that, what will you do?

---

106. Tacitus, *Annals* 15.44; Josephus, *Antiquities* 18.3.3.
107. Taylor, *Essenes*, 89–92; Aviam, "Synagogues in the Land of Israel," 1–17.
108. Metzger and Ehrman, *Text of the New Testament*, 51–54.
109. Foxe, *Book of Martyrs*, 1–20.

The Double Standard of Truth

WE BEGAN WITH HISTORY in the dock; now, the witnesses have spoken. We have weighed kings against prophets, philosophers against emperors, myths against manuscripts.[1] We have traced the timelines, heard the voices, and marked the silences that greeted us in between. The evidence has been sifted, piece by piece, until the pattern could no longer hide. That is all history requires: a question, an inconsistency noticed, and the courage to follow it. The scales we set in the beginning still stand, and the Nazarene alone bears the weight. Those scales were not arbitrary. They were built on five pillars: contemporaneity, multiplicity, external corroboration, archaeology, and chain of custody. The same measures that exposed the cracks in kings and conquerors now hold firm beneath Him. Where others falter in silence, distance, or decay, His testimony grows stronger the more it is tested.

This is not the place for a new revelation. The end has already been planted, seed by seed, in every chapter. What stands before us now is not a conclusion hastily built, but a tree grown in plain sight, its roots sunk in the past, its branches stretched between what you thought you knew and what you now see. Yes, this book bears the mark of Christianity. The label will cling, whatever the context. Some will dismiss it for that reason alone, and that is their choice. Others may have expected a clash of arguments, sharper weapons, harder blows. But let me be clear: I am not here to win. I am not here to serve myself. I am here to serve Him, and you, my reader. I am here to dig. And what I have unearthed, I lay before you. The pieces are yours to

---

1. Fox, *Alexander the Great*, 27–30; Schiff, *Cleopatra*, 1–10, 19–25; Grant, *Twelve Caesars*, 17–24; Waterfield, *Why Socrates Died*, 1–15, 28–35; Nylan, *Five "Confucian" Classics*, 7–12, 43–50; Armstrong, *Buddha*, xiii–24; Peters, *Muhammad and the Origins of Islam*, 3–10, 181–89; Habermas, *Historical Jesus*, 25–30, 150–55.

The Double Standard of Truth

join or to scatter. For in the end, the weight rests not only in the evidence, but in the intent with which it is received.

At the center stands Jesus, with more evidence than any of them.[2] Yet here lies the paradox: why is He doubted, while they are not? The answer cuts deeper than manuscripts. It was never merely about the evidence. It was about the cost of belief.[3] He claimed to be God, not just a god, but the God. The Maker of all, the One who alone can answer the question, "Why am I here?" To many, that answer, its sheer gravity, is too much to bear.[4]

Man has buried His foundation beneath piles of its own making: trash heaped on truth, filth layered upon stone. And yet the foundation remains. The weight we feel is not illusion but resistance, the crushing press of what has always been there, beneath the grime. To confront Christ is to know what is, and to glimpse what it takes to uncover it. Digging, always digging, both in the world around and in the depths within.[5]

But step back and look. Seriously, take a moment. This is one facet of the reality we inherit: history. And history is not what it seems. It never has been. Yet when younger generations are told, "This is how it was," as though fact, and that story is reinforced by television and film, by books, and by the sanction of academic institutions, the lie ceases to be a lie, so long as it is believed. This is how myth becomes mortar, how distortion is dressed as memory, how illusion is enthroned as knowledge. And perhaps this is one leg of the beast. Perhaps the beast with seven heads is not only future prophecy but present reality, man's own creation, his self-made monster. A chimera raised from vanity and pride, blotting the sun, burying truth beneath its bulk.[6]

Truth Revisited

Let us be clear. Truth is not invention. It is not consensus. It is not what power approves or what culture applauds. Truth is reality as God created it, the order of things as they are, not as we imagine them. To say "This is true" is not merely to describe a fact, but to recognize the Author who set fact in

---

2. Keener, *Historical Jesus of the Gospels*, 87–92, 185–90; Habermas, *Historical Jesus*, 25–30, 150–55.
3. Lewis, *Mere Christianity*, 40–41.
4. Chesterton, *Everlasting Man*, 209–15.
5. Augustine, *Confessions* 10.27–28.
6. Rev 13.

place. Yet the means by which men reach for truth are themselves fallible. Our instruments are warped; our measures crooked.

History comes to us through the pens of victors, the silence of the conquered, the bias of institutions. Evidence is sifted by flawed interpreters, pressed into molds of agenda, ambition, or survival. And so we never see the full honor, or beauty, or intention behind anything. We inherit shadows of what was flayed, fractured, and filtered by human hands. Truly, Plato's allegory of the cave in real life. The boards creak, the measures tilt, the same warnings we saw at the beginning still hold true, the choosing, the compressing, the silencing. But distortion cannot undo what God has made.

God's truth is not undone by flawed vessels. Men may twist it, bury it, or deny it, but they cannot unmake it. Truth is God's handwriting on creation, the pattern by which the world holds together, the system through which we even measure "fact" at all. To strike at truth is to strike at the foundation of being itself, and so the attempt always fails.

History itself proves this. Pilate was dismissed as a myth until stone cried out his name.[7] Nations tried to burn the Scriptures, yet manuscripts multiplied all the more. Skeptics denied cities, peoples, and kings, until spades in the earth uncovered them.[8] And the pattern has not ceased. Stalin's famine was denied until archives bared its cruelty. The Armenian slaughter was buried beneath silence until recognition forced it into the light.[9] Governments ran experiments on their own citizens, concealed for decades until the truth broke through.[10] Men lie, but the world God made does not. Truth is God, and what He breathes cannot be erased.

Mars exists. Whether man looks through a telescope or not, the planet is there. Its mountains rise, its storms rage, its stones lie in silence. Our disbelief does not dissolve it; our ignorance does not erase it. And if two rocks lie side by side on that barren ground, their number is two. Not because we counted them. Not because we agreed to call them so. But because reality itself bears the weight of that fact. Two distinct things, set apart, existing without us. The same is true in time. A sunrise breaks the horizon at a fixed moment, whether we see it or sleep through it. An eclipse traces its shadow whether or not we measure its arc. A man was crucified under

---

7. Millar, *Roman Near East*, 61–62.

8. Kitchen, *On the Reliability*, 464–69.

9. Applebaum, *Red Famine*, 263–75; Akçam, *Young Turks' Crime Against Humanity*, 347–55.

10. Reverby, *Examining Tuskegee*, 201–12.

Pontius Pilate in Judea; whether embraced or dismissed, the event either occurred or it did not. Time does not bend itself to opinion.

And what of morality? To love one's neighbor is good; to betray the innocent is evil. This is not preference, but the grain of reality itself, the moral law written into creation. Even those who deny God stumble into this admission. Sam Harris, an atheist, insists that human flourishing is not arbitrary, that to love is better than to hate, to be healthy is better than to be sick, to be good is better than to be bad.[11] He cannot escape the truth that goodness is better than its negation, though he divorces it from its Author.

The same God who set planets in orbit and numbers in order has also woven justice and goodness into the world. Physical truth, mathematical truth, historical truth, moral truth, they are not different kinds. They are one truth, refracted through different lenses, but indivisible in essence. As water, ice, and vapor are one substance in three forms, so every expression of truth is one reality spoken in many tongues. And as light is wave, particle, and energy all at once, still one light, so truth is manifold in appearance but singular in nature. To fracture truth into compartments is not to weaken it but to reveal our blindness. For truth is not ours. It is God's. To deny it is not to alter reality, but only to blind ourselves to it. Truth is God, and what He breathes cannot be erased.[12]

Truth Tested

From the cave walls to the scroll, from tally to chronicle, humanity has always decided what to preserve and what to forget. But when truth speaks, it is preserved not by choice, but by blood. Speaking of truth, have you ever noticed that those who speak it rarely die quietly? The pattern is older than memory. The prophets of Israel spoke against kings and idols, and the price was exile, imprisonment, stoning.[13] Jeremiah thrown into a cistern. Zechariah struck down in the temple courts.[14]

Yes, others before them must have spoken, voices in forgotten places, cries now buried in dust. But what became of them? Their words dissolved,

---

11. Harris, *Moral Landscape*, 12–20.

12. John 1:1–3; Aquinas, *Summa Theologica* 1.16.1; Augustine, *Confessions* 10.23; Lewis, *Mere Christianity*, 5–8; Einstein, "Fundamental Ideas and Problems"; Tacitus, *Annals* 15.44.

13. Brueggemann, *Prophetic Imagination*, 3–12.

14. 2 Chr 24:20–21; Jer 38:6.

their memory scattered. By contrast, the prophets of Israel thunder still, their words copied across centuries, preserved even by enemies, carried forward at the cost of blood.[15]

And then, every apostle of Jesus. None of the thirteen escaped. Peter crucified upside down, James beheaded, Thomas pierced through in India. Even Judas, consumed by his betrayal, ended himself.[16] Truth, in this world, has never been safe. It never had a chance. From the first marks on stone to the voices of martyrs, what survives is not convenience but conviction. We preserve not decoration, but meaning as if it was from the cave to the cross.

The chain does not end there. Jan Hus, burned at the stake for daring to preach in the language of his people.[17] William Tyndale, strangled and consigned to the flames for translating Scripture into English.[18] Martin Luther King Jr., shot for dreaming of a world not yet realized.[19] Gandhi, felled by a bullet for pressing peace into the fabric of empire.[20] John F. Kennedy, silenced in daylight while calling his nation to a higher path.[21] And at the center, Jesus, crucified under Rome, condemned by Jerusalem, witnessed by history.[22]

This is not anecdote. It is the reflex of power when it collides with truth. Empires crucify it. Movements betray it. Crowds stone it. Institutions erase it. And yet, truth remains. And out of all of this, what is truth? It is the pattern by which God engineered the cosmos and created our world, the grain of reality, the law beneath all laws.

Uneven Scales: Why Evidence Will Never Be Enough

One of the truest lines I have ever heard did not come from a philosopher or celebrity, but from a city manager: "Just because it makes sense, doesn't mean we are going to do it." That story is the parable of humanity. We can have truth staring us in the face, know the cost of ignoring it, and yet pride, politics, or convenience override it. The prophets screamed about Babylon.

15. Childs, *Introduction to the Old Testament*, 67–71.
16. Eusebius, *Church History* 2.25; Foxe, *Book of Martyrs*, 3–12.
17. Fudge, *Fire in the Bones*, 201–12.
18. Daniell, *William Tyndale*, 379–84.
19. Carson, *Martin Luther King Jr.*, 217–23.
20. Fischer, *Gandhi*, 193–97.
21. Schlesinger, *Thousand Days*, 879–85.
22. Tacitus, *Annals* 15.44; Josephus, *Antiquities* 18.3.3.

The Double Standard of Truth

Rome ignored its rot. The generals waved off Pearl Harbor intelligence. The doctors were silenced about cigarettes. The Soviets erased famine from the record. Same logic. Same blindness. The warped boards we stood upon at the beginning creak still beneath our feet. We balance on uneven scales, and the cost is always ruin.

History bears witness to this stubborn refusal. Evidence is not always enough, because men curate even truth when it is handed to them. The warnings are given, the signs stand clear, yet the scales are tilted by will and pride. The prophets warned Judah of Babylon, but their words were mocked until the exile came.[23] Rome dismissed the signs of its own decline, ridiculing reformers, until the Goths battered its gates.[24] Warnings of Japan's approach before Pearl Harbor were ignored, though intelligence was in hand, until the harbor burned.[25] In the years before the First World War, voices cried out about alliances and arms races, but Europe stumbled forward as if blind, until trenches swallowed a generation.[26] Scientists sounded the alarm about cigarettes and lung cancer for decades, but industries scoffed and millions perished.[27] Warnings of famine in Ukraine were buried under propaganda, and the graves came by the millions.[28]

And in our own time, truth is still filtered through the same uneven scales: what does not flatter us, we ignore. What convicts us, we dismiss. This is why evidence alone will never save us. The weight of fact cannot move the heart that has set itself against surrender. We lost lives. We lost dignity. We lost everything. And now truth is here again, this time, your soul for barter. History, for most, feels safe. Decorative. Distant. A museum of men we are allowed to admire because they are dead, harmless, long gone. Then comes Jesus. Not a conqueror. Not a philosopher. Not a cultural symbol. A man who claimed your soul. Who walked into history, was nailed to a Roman cross, and walked out of a sealed tomb. That is not just history. That is judgment. And the moment His name enters the equation, everything shifts. The scrutiny sharpens. The standard rises. Suddenly, Jesus alone must be disproved beyond all possible doubt. Why? Because if He

---

23. Jer 25:8–11.
24. Augustine, *City of God* 1.33.
25. Prange, *At Dawn We Slept*, 541–49.
26. Clark, *Sleepwalkers*, 237–45.
27. Proctor, *Golden Holocaust*, 112–18.
28. Applebaum, *Red Famine*, 263–75.

is who He says He is, then you are not who you think you are. And that is not a historical inconvenience. That is an existential earthquake.

We believe Socrates, a man who wrote nothing, because Plato said so.[29] We believe Alexander the Great not through eyewitness accounts, but through Plutarch, four centuries later, whose biographies were more sermon than history.[30] We believe Cleopatra through Suetonius, a glorified gossip columnist writing rumors a hundred years after her death.[31] We believe Hannibal not through his own people, but through Roman pens dipped in victory and vengeance.[32]

And who are the three men most responsible for this empire of assumption? Plutarch. Suetonius. Tacitus. Plutarch (AD 46 to 120) was a moralist, not a historian. His *Parallel Lives* aimed to shape virtue, not preserve fact. He admitted to smoothing contradictions, reshaping events to fit moral templates.[33] His stories read more like fables than timelines. Suetonius (AD 69 to 122) was a scandal-chasing secretary to emperors. His *Twelve Caesars* is more courtroom whisper than courtroom record: sex, superstition, spectacle. Not evidence, entertainment.[34] Tacitus (AD 56 to 120) is the most respected of the three, yet still a senator with a cynic's pen. In the *Annals*, he rarely cites documents, invents motives, and filters history through his disdain for empire.[35] These are the gatekeepers of Roman memory: no eyewitnesses, no first-person records from the people they describe. And yet, their words are canonized without question.

No one asks if Plutarch exaggerated. No one wonders if Suetonius fabricated. No one demands Tacitus cite his sources. But Luke, who names real cities, rulers, geography, and customs, is dismissed as propaganda.[36] Mark, recording Peter's testimony, is labeled religious fiction. Matthew, with firsthand Jewish knowledge, is tagged "anonymous mythology." John, who stood at the cross and died for the claim, is reduced to theological

---

29. Waterfield, *Why Socrates Died*, 1–15, 28–35.

30. Plutarch, *Life of Alexander*, in *Parallel Lives*; Fox, *Alexander the Great*, 27–30.

31. Schiff, *Cleopatra*, 1–10, 19–25; Suetonius, *Twelve Caesars*.

32. Livy, *History of Rome* V 21.1–22.50; Polybius, *Histories* 3.33–34.

33. Plutarch, *Parallel Lives*; Marincola, *Authority and Tradition in Ancient Historiography*, 62–70.

34. Suetonius, *Twelve Caesars*; Dennison, *Last Empress*, 35–39.

35. Tacitus, *Annals* 1.1–1.10; Mellor, *Tacitus*, 15–20.

36. Hemer, *Book of Acts*, 63–75.

The Double Standard of Truth

poetry. The bar for Jesus is raised to the heavens. For everyone else? The floor is in the basement.

Now consider the manuscript reality. Plato survives in only seven manuscripts. Julius Caesar, ten, written nearly nine centuries after his death. Tacitus, three. Suetonius, under two hundred, all centuries removed. Livy's history is riddled with massive gaps. Meanwhile, the New Testament boasts over 5,800 Greek manuscripts and more than 20,000 in other languages. The earliest fragment, P52, dates within a single generation of Jesus's death.[37] By the early second century, the church fathers were already quoting nearly every verse.[38] Gospel traditions were standardized long before the fall of Rome. No one else in ancient history comes close. No one. And yet, Jesus is the one we are told to doubt.[39] The same five pillars we set at the beginning now bear the final weight. And under them, every empire cracks, except One.

Why? Because the implications are terrifying. To accept Jesus does not revise a footnote; it rewrites your life. It demands repentance. It demands a cross. It demands death to self. And it demands it now. This is not a rejection of reason. It is a rebellion of the will.[40] We do not reject Him for lack of proof. We reject Him because we do not want to kneel. Skepticism becomes a smokescreen. "More evidence" a mirage. "What about contradictions?" a diversion. The truth is clear. It always has been. We just do not want it. Because truth has a face, and it is not yours. History bends for those who ask nothing of us. Alexander kills, and we applaud. Caesar conquers, and we salute. Socrates dies, and we quote him. Buddha meditates, and we smile. Muhammad commands, and we respect. But Jesus? Jesus says, "Follow Me." Jesus says, "Deny yourself." Jesus says, "Take up your cross." Jesus says, "No one comes to the Father except through Me." And suddenly, all the rules change. The standards rise. The scrutiny intensifies. The bar moves. Why? Because Jesus does not fit in the museum of admired men.

He does not flatter your pride; He crucifies it. He does not suggest a path; He claims to be the only one. He does not echo your voice; He calls you to silence your own. What is really on trial here is not Christ; it is you.

---

37. Roberts, *Early Papyrus of the Fourth Gospel*, 8-9; Metzger and Ehrman, *Text of the New Testament*, 39-41.

38. Kelly, *Early Christian Doctrines*, 33-35.

39. Metzger and Ehrman, *Text of the New Testament*, 39-41; Wallace, "Manuscript Evidence for Superior New Testament."

40. Lewis, *Problem of Pain*, 67-69.

Jesus is not the one under scrutiny; your pride is. The question is not "Did He live?" It is "Will you die?" To self, to ego, to control. And that question makes cowards of kings. It turns scholars into skeptics. It turns intellect into armor. It turns evidence into a mirror. Because in the end, this was never about history; it was about lordship.[41] The evidence is in.

Beyond the Trial: The Weight of the Name

The court is adjourned. The witnesses have spoken. The giants of history, conquerors, emperors, prophets, philosophers, have all taken the stand. Their lives cast long shadows, their empires built, their words remembered. But each one faltered under the weight of the five pillars. Each left gaps, silences, contradictions. Each ruled for a time, and then fell to dust. Except One. The Nazarene was not merely placed on trial. He is the trial. His words are not just recorded in ink; they are inscribed into conscience. His death was not the end of a dynasty, but the birth of a kingdom that outlived Rome, Persia, and every empire since.[42] The evidence does not terminate in Him. It opens. It points. It demands. And this is where the fork in the road lies. The question is no longer whether Alexander fought, or Caesar ruled, or Muhammad spoke. The question is whether Christ rose.[43] And if He did, then every throne is temporary, every empire borrowed, every giant already toppled.

The trials were never really about them. They were about Him. Every witness was a mirror. Every silence an echo. Every verdict a shadow cast toward the cross. The giants ruled by force. Christ reigns by truth. And truth is the one empire no power can erase.[44] So now the scales tip to you, the reader. Not as juror. Not as spectator. But as the one in the dock. History has delivered its testimony. The Nazarene still stands. And His question remains the same as it was two thousand years ago:

"Who do you say that I am?"

---

41. Chesterton, *Everlasting Man*, 209–15.
42. Eusebius, *Church History* 2.3–4.
43. Wright, *Resurrection of the Son of God*, 710–19.
44. Chesterton, *Everlasting Man*, 209–15.

The Five Pillars of Historical Confidence

THE FOLLOWING FRAMEWORK IS *built upon established principles of historical inquiry, drawing support from key works cited in the introduction, including Thucydides, Bauckham, Habermas and Licona, Sanders, Meier, Keener, Metzger, and others. Each pillar reflects standards recognized by both secular and faith-based scholars in the historical-critical tradition. What distinguishes this framework is its grounding not in psychological assumptions, but in factual, testable measures that can be applied evenly across all figures of antiquity.*

A Framework for Testing the Trustworthiness of Historical Claims

History is not guesswork, nor is it merely storytelling. It is the discipline of weighing evidence and assessing the reliability of claims made about the past. The following five pillars serve as a teaching framework to evaluate the strength of any historical figure, event, or movement. These pillars are not religious or philosophical; they are academic tools. But when applied with consistency, they reveal a striking truth: few figures withstand the weight of scrutiny as well as the Nazarene.

Pillar 1: Contemporaneity[1]

Was the account written close to the time of the events, or centuries later? The closer a text is to the events it describes, the less room there is for legend to grow unchecked.

---

1. Thucydides, *History* 1.22; Bauckham, *Jesus and the Eyewitnesses*; Licona, *Resurrection*

The Five Pillars of Historical Confidence

Example:

- Jesus of Nazareth: The Gospels were written within 30–60 years of His crucifixion.[2]
- Paul's letters (e.g., 1 Cor 15) date even earlier, within 3–5 years of the resurrection event.[3]
- Contrast: Alexander the Great: His first known biography (by Plutarch) was written nearly three hundred years after his death.[4]

Why it matters: Time amplifies myth. Proximity preserves memory.

Pillar 2: Multiplicity[5]

Do multiple independent sources attest to the same event or person? The more unrelated sources that affirm a claim, the less likely it is to be fabricated. Example:

- Jesus is attested by:
    - Christian sources (Paul, the Gospels, early church fathers)
    - Jewish sources (Josephus, Talmudic references)
    - Roman sources[6] (Tacitus, Pliny the Younger)
        - Compare this to Socrates, who is primarily known only through the writings of Plato and Xenophon,[7] both students.

---

of Jesus, 68–74. (Thucydides lays down the ancient benchmark: reliable history requires eyewitness testimony and proximity to events. Bauckham defends the Gospels as products of living eyewitnesses, not anonymous tradition. Licona uses historiographical analysis to date 1 Cor 15 and other early traditions within years of the resurrection.)

2. Blomberg, *Historical Reliability of the Gospels*, 41–43.
3. Habermas and Licona, *Case for the Resurrection of Jesus*, 221–24.
4. Fox, *Alexander the Great*, 3–4.
5. Meier, *Marginal Jew* 1; Sanders, *Historical Figure of Jesus*, 88–92; Keener, *Historical Jesus of the Gospels*, 185–90. (Meier emphasizes layered traditions and the criteria of authenticity like embarrassment and coherence. Sanders, though not a believer, affirms core facts about Jesus via multiple sources and the unlikely nature of invented suffering. Keener focuses on independent strands of testimony across the Gospels, confirming overlap without collusion.)
6. Ehrman, *Did Jesus Exist?*, 39–53.
7. Johnson, *Socrates: A Man for Our Times*, 20–21.

The Five Pillars of Historical Confidence

Why it matters: One voice may falter. Two may conspire. But when many speak apart and yet echo the same truth, the chorus cannot be ignored.

Pillar 3: External Corroboration[8]

Do outside or even hostile sources confirm the events, even if they disagree on interpretation?

- Early Jewish writings never deny Jesus performed wonders, only that He did so by sorcery.[9]
- Roman records acknowledge a man named "Chrestus" who stirred unrest.[10]
- Pagan critics like Celsus accept Jesus' existence and crucifixion, while mocking His divinity.[11]

Why it matters: A claim without witness beyond itself is vapor. Independent confirmation, especially from unfriendly voices, minimizes bias and secures truth.

Pillar 4: Archaeology[12]

Does the material record align with the written testimony?

- Pilate was dismissed as a myth until a stone inscription confirmed him as prefect of Judea.[13]
- The Pools of Bethesda and Siloam, once thought to be Johannine inventions, have been unearthed with details matching John's account.[14]

---

8. Josephus, *Antiquities* 18.3.1; Tacitus, *Annals* 15.44; Origen, *Against Celsus* 2.13.

9. Schäfer, *Jesus in the Talmud*, 60–62.

10. Suetonius, *Lives of the Caesars* 5.25.

11. Origen, *Contra Celsum* 1.28–32.

12. Mykytiuk, "Archaeology Confirms 50 Real People in the Bible," 42–50; Evans, *Jesus and the Remains*, 25–27; Dever, *What Did the Biblical Writers Know?*, 123–26.

13. Caesarea Maritima inscription naming Pilate, discovered in 1961; see Josephus, *Antiquities* 18.3.1; Tacitus, *Annals* 15.44.

14. John 5:2 and 9:7; excavation reports confirm Bethesda's five porticoes and the Pool of Siloam's first-century structure; see Shanks, *Jerusalem: An Archaeological Biography*, 220–24.

- Nazareth, long claimed to be a later fabrication, has yielded first-century dwellings and synagogue remains.[15]
- The Dead Sea Scrolls revealed astonishing preservation of Jewish Scriptures, strengthening confidence in textual transmission.[16]
- Entire civilizations, like the Hittites, once thought legendary, have been unearthed in overwhelming scale.[17]

Why it matters: The earth remembers what men forget. Fragments pulled from dust and monuments raised from ruin testify with a voice no empire can silence.

Pillar 5: Chain of Custody[18]

Has the source material been reliably preserved over time through textual transmission and archeology? Without preservation, no document can be trusted, no matter how authentic its origin.

Example:

- Over 5,800 Greek manuscripts of the New Testament exist, more than any ancient text.[19]
- Compare: Homer's *Iliad* (643 manuscripts), Caesar's *Gallic Wars* (ten manuscripts).[20]

---

15. Excavations in Nazareth revealed domestic structures and a synagogue from the first century; see Strange, "Nazareth," 4:1050–51.

16. The Dead Sea Scrolls (discovered 1947) confirmed preservation of Isaiah and other texts nearly identical to later manuscripts; see Bruce, *Dead Sea Scrolls and the Bible*, 27–30.

17. The rediscovery of the Hittite Empire in the nineteenth century confirmed its biblical record; see Bryce, *Kingdom of the Hittites*, 1–5.

18. Metzger, *Text of the New Testament*; Wallace, "Majority Text and the Original Text"; Gurry and Hixson, *Myths and Mistakes*.

19. Metzger and Ehrman, *Text of the New Testament*, 51–52.

20. Metzger, *Text of the New Testament*; Wallace, "Majority Text and the Original Text"; Gurry and Hixson, *Myths and Mistakes*. (Metzger is the foundational authority on manuscript transmission and variants. Wallace dismantles common myths about textual instability and affirms the reliability of critical editions. Gurry and Hixson provide up-to-date analysis correcting misunderstandings in popular apologetics while still affirming stability in the textual tradition.)

The Five Pillars of Historical Confidence

- The Dead Sea Scrolls confirm the preservation of Old Testament prophecies[21] and texts.
- Islamic Hadith were compiled over two hundred years after Muhammad's death, with many classified as "weak" or "fabricated" by Muslim scholars themselves.[22]

Why it matters: Words endure only if they are transmitted. Trust rests not in abstraction but in faithful preservation. Where the evidence is thin, confidence weakens; where it is abundant, confidence grows.

Conclusion: A Tool, Not a Verdict

These five pillars are not a theological trick; they are a historical test. Apply them fairly, and you will find some figures collapse under the weight, while others stand firmer. Skeptics, believers, and seekers alike can use this framework to recenter the debate on evidence, not emotion. And when that test is applied to Christ, the real question becomes: *If not Him, then who?*

Those scales were not arbitrary. They were built on five pillars: **contemporaneity, multiplicity, external corroboration, archeology, and chain of custody.** The same measures that exposed the cracks in kings and conquerors now hold firm beneath Him. Where others falter in silence, distance, or decay, His testimony grows stronger the more it is tested.

---

21. VanderKam and Flint, *Meaning of the Dead Sea Scrolls*, 127–35.
22. Brown, *Hadith*, 17–19, 73–76.

Bibliography

"The Acts of Andrew." In *New Testament Apocrypha*, edited by Wilhelm Schneemelcher, translated by R. McL. Wilson, 2:435–67. Louisville: Westminster John Knox, 1991.

Akçam, Taner. *The Young Turks' Crime Against Humanity: The Armenian Genocide and Ethnic Cleansing in the Ottoman Empire*. Princeton, NJ: Princeton University Press, 2012.

Allen, Sarah, and Crispin Williams, eds. *Guodian Bamboo Texts*. Berkeley: Society for the Study of Early China, 2000.

Allison, Dale C. *Resurrecting Jesus: The Earliest Christian Tradition and Its Interpreters*. New York: T. & T. Clark, 2005.

Alter, Robert. *The Art of Biblical Narrative*. New York: Basic, 1981.

Angle, Stephen C. *Contemporary Confucian Political Philosophy: Toward Progressive Confucianism*. Cambridge: Polity, 2012.

Appian. *The Civil Wars*. Translated by Horace White. Loeb Classical Library. Cambridge, MA: Harvard University Press, 1913.

———. *Roman History, Volume III: The Civil Wars, Books 1–3.26*. Translated by Horace White. Loeb Classical Library 2. Cambridge, MA: Harvard University Press, 1913.

———. *Roman History, Volume IV: The Civil Wars, Books 1–2.14*. Translated by Horace White. Loeb Classical Library 4. Cambridge, MA: Harvard University Press, 1912.

———. *Roman History, Volume V: The Civil Wars, Books 2.15–2.92*. Translated by Horace White. Loeb Classical Library 5. Cambridge, MA: Harvard University Press, 1913.

———. *Roman History, Volume IX: The Punic Wars*. Translated by Horace White. Loeb Classical Library 63. Cambridge, MA: Harvard University Press, 1913.

Applebaum, Anne. *Red Famine: Stalin's War on Ukraine*. New York: Doubleday, 2017.

Aquinas, Thomas. *Summa Theologica*. Translated by the Fathers of the English Dominican Province. New York: Benziger Brothers, 1947.

Arav, Rami. "Ancient Synagogues in Israel." In *The Archaeology of the Holy Land: From the Destruction of Solomon's Temple to the Muslim Conquest*, edited by Rami Arav, 44–55. New York: Cambridge University Press, 2013.

Aristophanes. *Clouds. Wasps. Peace*. Translated by Jeffrey Henderson. Loeb Classical Library 488. Cambridge, MA: Harvard University Press, 1998.

Armstrong, Karen. *Buddha*. New York: Penguin, 2001.

Bibliography

Arrian. *Anabasis of Alexander, Volume I: Books 1–4*. Translated by P. A. Brunt. Loeb Classical Library 236. Cambridge, MA: Harvard University Press, 1976.

———. *Anabasis of Alexander, Volume II: Books 5–7. Indica*. Translated by P. A. Brunt. Loeb Classical Library 269. Cambridge, MA: Harvard University Press, 1983.

Assmann, Jan. *Cultural Memory and Early Civilization: Writing, Remembrance, and Political Imagination*. Cambridge: Cambridge University Press, 2011.

Augustine. *The City of God*. Translated by Henry Bettenson. London: Penguin, 2003.

———. *Confessions*. Translated by Henry Chadwick. Oxford: Oxford University Press, 1991.

Augustus. *Res Gestae Divi Augusti*. Translated by P. A. Brunt and J. M. Moore. Oxford: Oxford University Press, 1967.

Aviam, Mordechai. "First Century Jewish Galilee: An Archaeological Perspective." *Journal of the Jesus Movement in Its Jewish Setting* 5 (2018) 58–75.

———. "Magdala—An Overview of Its Architecture and Function." In *Archaeology and the Galilean Jesus: A Re-Examination of the Evidence*, edited by Jonathan L. Reed and Mordechai Aviam, 27–54. Mexico City: Universidad Iberoamericana, 2020.

———. "The Magdala Synagogue: A First Century Synagogue on the Shore of the Sea of Galilee." In *Archaeology and the Galilean Jesus: A Re-Examination of the Evidence*, edited by Jonathan L. Reed, 37–50. Harrisburg, PA: Trinity, 2000.

———. "Synagogues in the Land of Israel: The State of Research." In *Ancient Synagogues: Historical Analysis and Archaeological Discovery*, edited by Dan Urman and Paul V. M. Flesher, 1–17. Leiden: Brill, 1995.

Avshalom-Gorni, Dina. "Migdal: Preliminary Report." *Hadashot Arkheologiyot—Excavations and Surveys in Israel* 121 (2009). https://hadashot.iaa.org.il/report_detail_eng.aspx?id=1236&mag_id=115&utm.

Azami, M. M. *Studies in Early Hadith Literature: With a Critical Edition of Some Early Texts*. Indianapolis: American Trust, 1978.

Bagatti, Bellarmino. *Excavations in Nazareth*. Jerusalem: Franciscan, 1969.

Bailey, Kenneth E. *Jesus Through Middle Eastern Eyes: Cultural Studies in the Gospels*. Downers Grove, IL: IVP Academic, 2008.

Baras, Zvi. "Archaeology and the Historical Jesus." In *Jesus and the Politics of His Day*, edited by Ernst Bammel and C. F. D. Moule, 321–33. Cambridge: Cambridge University Press, 1984.

Barna Group. "Openness to Jesus." Barna, May 17, 2023. https://www.barna.com/research/openness-to-jesus/.

———. "What Do Americans Believe About Jesus?" Barna, April 1, 2015. https://www.barna.com/research/what-do-americans-believe-about-jesus/.

Barnes, Timothy D. *The Sources of the Historia Augusta*. Collection Latomus 155. Brussels: Latomus, 1978.

Bartlett, Robert. *The Making of Europe: Conquest, Colonization and Cultural Change, 950–1350*. Princeton, NJ: Princeton University Press, 1993.

Batey, Richard A. *Jesus and the Forgotten City: New Light on Sepphoris and the Urban World of Jesus*. Grand Rapids: Baker, 1991.

Bauckham, Richard. *Jesus and the Eyewitnesses: The Gospels as Eyewitness Testimony*. Grand Rapids: Eerdmans, 2006.

———. *Jesus and the Eyewitnesses: The Gospels as Eyewitness Testimony*. 2nd ed. Grand Rapids: Eerdmans, 2017.

Beard, Mary. *SPQR: A History of Ancient Rome*. New York: Liveright, 2015.

Bibliography

Bechert, Heinz, and Richard Gombrich, eds. *The World of Buddhism*. London: Thames & Hudson, 1984.
Bell, Daniel A. *China's New Confucianism: Politics and Everyday Life in a Changing Society*. Princeton, NJ: Princeton University Press, 2008.
Ben-Dov, Meir. *Historical Atlas of Jerusalem*. New York: Continuum, 2002.
Bett, H. C. *Propaganda and the Roman Historian*. Oxford: Clarendon, 1924.
Bett, Richard. "Socrates." *Stanford Encyclopedia of Philosophy*, February 16, 2018. Edited by Edward N. Zalta. https://plato.stanford.edu/archives/win2021/entries/socrates/.
———. "The Sophists and Relativism." *Stanford Encyclopedia of Philosophy*, 2019. Edited by Edward N. Zalta. https://plato.stanford.edu/archives/fall2019/entries/sophists-relativism/.
Bloch, Marc. *The Historian's Craft*. Translated by Peter Putnam. New York: Alfred A. Knopf, 1953.
Blomberg, Craig L. *The Historical Reliability of the Gospels*. 2nd ed. Downers Grove, IL: IVP Academic, 2007.
Boardman, John, and Michael D. Coe. *The Oxford History of Classical Art*. Oxford: Oxford University Press, 1993.
Boatwright, Mary T., et al. *The Romans: From Village to Empire*. 2nd ed. New York: Oxford University Press, 2011.
Bond, Helen K. *Pontius Pilate in History and Interpretation*. Cambridge: Cambridge University Press, 1998.
Borrut, Antoine. "Vanishing Scriptures and Ephemeral Writings: On the Transmission of Religious Knowledge in Early Islam." *Jerusalem Studies in Arabic and Islam* 40 (2013) 1–30.
Bosworth, A. B. *Alexander and the East: The Tragedy of Triumph*. Oxford: Clarendon, 1996.
———. *A Historical Commentary on Arrian's History of Alexander. Volume 1: Books I–III*. Oxford: Clarendon, 1980.
———. *A Historical Commentary on Arrian's History of Alexander. Volume 2: Books IV–V*. Oxford: Clarendon, 1995.
Bradley, Keith. *Suetonius' Caesars: A Cultural Commentary*. Oxford: Clarendon, 1991.
Breasted, James Henry. *A History of Egypt*. New York: Charles Scribner's Sons, 1905.
Brickhouse, Thomas C., and Nicholas D. Smith. *Plato's Socrates*. Oxford: Oxford University Press, 1994.
———. *The Trial and Execution of Socrates: Sources and Controversies*. New York: Oxford University Press, 2002.
———. *The Trial and Execution of Socrates: Sources and Controversies*. 2nd ed. New York: Oxford University Press, 2002.
Brooks, E. Bruce, and A. Taeko Brooks. *The Original Analects: Sayings of Confucius and His Successors*. New York: Columbia University Press, 1998.
Brown, Colin. *History and Faith: A Personal Exploration*. Grand Rapids: Zondervan, 1987.
Brown, Jonathan A. C. *Hadith: Muhammad's Legacy in the Medieval and Modern World*. Oxford: Oneworld, 2009.
———. *Hadith: Muhammad's Legacy in the Medieval and Modern World*. 2nd ed. Oxford: Oneworld, 2017.
Brown, Raymond E. *The Death of the Messiah: From Gethsemane to the Grave*. 2 vols. New York: Doubleday, 1994.
Bruce, F. F. *The Dead Sea Scrolls and the Bible*. London: Paternoster, 1955.

BIBLIOGRAPHY

———. *Jesus and Christian Origins Outside the New Testament*. Grand Rapids: Eerdmans, 1974.

———. *The New Testament Documents: Are They Reliable?* 6th ed. Grand Rapids: Eerdmans, 2003.

Brueggemann, Walter. *The Prophetic Imagination*. 2nd ed. Minneapolis: Fortress, 2001.

Bryce, Trevor. *The Kingdom of the Hittites*. Oxford: Oxford University Press, 1998.

Buddhistdoor Global. "Reporting on Buddhism." ReligionLink, 2023. https://religionlink.com/reporting-on/reporting-on-buddhism/?utm.

Bukhari, Muhammad ibn Ismail. *Sahih al-Bukhari*. Translated by Muhammad Muhsin Khan. Riyadh: Darussalam, 1997.

Burnett, Andrew. *Coinage in the Roman World*. London: Seaby, 1987.

Burton, John. *The Collection of the Qur'an*. Cambridge: Cambridge University Press, 1977.

Cadoux, T. J. "Introduction." In *Vellei Paterculi Historiarum Libri Duo*, edited by T. J. Cadoux, 1–40. Leipzig: Teubner, 1982.

Caesar, Julius. *The Civil War*. Translated by Jane F. Gardner. London: Penguin Classics, 1976.

———. *The Gallic War*. Translated by Carolyn Hammond. Oxford: Oxford University Press, 1996.

Canfora, Luciano. *Julius Caesar: The Life and Times of the People's Dictator*. Translated by Marian Hill and Kevin Windle. Berkeley: University of California Press, 2007.

———. *Julius Caesar: The People's Dictator*. Translated by Marian Hill. Berkeley: University of California Press, 2007.

Cantor, Norman. *Inventing the Middle Ages: The Lives, Works, and Ideas of the Great Medievalists of the Twentieth Century*. New York: Morrow, 1991.

Carr, E. H. *What Is History?* New York: Vintage, 1961.

Carson, Clayborne. *Martin Luther King Jr.: A Life*. New York: Penguin, 2001.

Carson, D. A. *The Gospel According to John*. The Pillar New Testament Commentary. Grand Rapids: Eerdmans, 1991.

Carson, D. A., and Douglas J. Moo. *An Introduction to the New Testament*. 2nd ed. Grand Rapids: Zondervan, 2005.

Carter, John M. *Appian and the Romans*. London: Croom Helm, 1983.

Cartledge, Paul. *Alexander the Great: The Hunt for a New Past*. New York: Overlook, 2004.

Casson, Lionel. *Libraries in the Ancient World*. New Haven, CT: Yale University Press, 2001.

Champlin, Edward. "Tiberius the Wise." *Historia: Zeitschrift für Alte Geschichte* 27 (1978) 306–30.

Chauveau, Michel. *Egypt in the Age of Cleopatra: History and Society Under the Ptolemies*. Translated by David Lorton. Ithaca, NY: Cornell University Press, 2000.

Chesterton, G. K. *The Everlasting Man*. San Francisco: Ignatius, 2008.

Childs, Brevard S. *Introduction to the Old Testament as Scripture*. Philadelphia: Fortress, 1979.

Clark, Christopher. *The Sleepwalkers: How Europe Went to War in 1914*. New York: Harper, 2012.

Clayton, Peter A. *Chronicle of the Pharaohs: The Reign-by-Reign Record of the Rulers and Dynasties of Ancient Egypt*. London: Thames & Hudson, 1994.

Coe, Michael D., and Stephen Houston. *The Maya*. 8th ed. London: Thames & Hudson, 2015.

BIBLIOGRAPHY

Columella. *On Agriculture*. Translated by Harrison Boyd Ash. 3 vols. Loeb Classical Library 361, 407, 408. Cambridge, MA: Harvard University Press, 1941–55.

Comfort, Philip W. *The Complete Text of the Earliest New Testament Manuscripts*. Grand Rapids: Baker, 1999.

———. *Encountering the Manuscripts: An Introduction to New Testament Paleography and Textual Criticism*. Nashville: Broadman & Holman, 2005.

Comfort, Philip W., and David P. Barrett. *The Text of the Earliest New Testament Greek Manuscripts*. Wheaton, IL: Tyndale, 2001.

Confucius. *The Analects*. Translated by D. C. Lau. London: Penguin, 1979.

———. *The Analects of Confucius*. Translated by Edward Slingerland. Indianapolis: Hackett, 2003.

Coningham, Robin, et al. "The Earliest Buddhist Shrine: Excavating the Birthplace of the Buddha, Lumbini (Nepal)." *Antiquity* 87 (2013) 1104–23.

Cook, Michael. *Muhammad*. Oxford: Oxford University Press, 1983.

Cook, Scott. *The Bamboo Texts of Guodian: A Study and Complete Translation*. 2 vols. Ithaca, NY: Cornell University East Asia Program, 2012.

Cornell, Timothy J. *The Fragmentary Roman Historians*. 2 vols. Oxford: Oxford University Press, 2013.

Craig, William Lane. *Reasonable Faith: Christian Truth and Apologetics*. 3rd ed. Wheaton, IL: Crossway, 2008.

Creel, Herrlee G. *Confucius: The Man and the Myth*. New York: John Day, 1949.

———. *Confucius and the Chinese Way*. New York: Harper, 1960.

Cressy, David. *England on Edge: Crisis and Revolution 1640–1642*. Oxford: Oxford University Press, 2006.

Crone, Patricia, and Martin Hinds. *God's Caliph: Religious Authority in the First Centuries of Islam*. Cambridge: Cambridge University Press, 1986.

Cross, Frank Moore. *The Ancient Library of Qumran and Modern Biblical Studies*. 3rd ed. Sheffield: Sheffield Academic, 1995.

Crossan, John Dominic. *The Historical Jesus: The Life of a Mediterranean Jewish Peasant*. San Francisco: HarperSanFrancisco, 1991.

———. *Jesus: A Revolutionary Biography*. San Francisco: HarperSanFrancisco, 1994.

———. *Who Killed Jesus? Exposing the Roots of Anti-Semitism in the Gospel Story of the Death of Jesus*. San Francisco: HarperSanFrancisco, 1995.

Cyrino, Monica S., ed. *Rome Season One: History Makes Television*. Malden, MA: Blackwell, 2008.

Daniell, David. *William Tyndale: A Biography*. New Haven, CT: Yale University Press, 1994.

Dark, Ken. *Archaeology of Jesus' Nazareth*. Oxford: Oxbow, 2020.

———. *Archaeology of Nazareth and the Families of Jesus*. London: Oxford Centre for Late Antiquity and Oxford Centre for Byzantine Research, 2020.

———. "The Sisters of Nazareth Convent: A Roman-Period, Byzantine, and Crusader Site in Central Nazareth." *Palestine Exploration Quarterly* 141 (2009) 133–76.

De Voragine, Jacobus. *The Golden Legend: Readings on the Saints* 2. Translated by William Granger Ryan. Princeton, NJ: Princeton University Press, 1993.

Dennison, Matthew. *The Last Empress: The Life and Times of Agrippina*. New York: St. Martin's, 2010.

———. *The Last Empress: The She-Dragon of China*. New York: St. Martin's, 2004.

Bibliography

Destrée, Pierre, and Nicolas D. Smith, eds. *The Cambridge Companion to Socrates.* Cambridge: Cambridge University Press, 2011.
Dever, William G. *What Did the Biblical Writers Know and When Did They Know It?* Grand Rapids: Eerdmans, 2001.
Dio, Cassius. *Roman History.* Vols. 3-4. Translated by Earnest Cary. Loeb Classical Library. Cambridge, MA: Harvard University Press, 1914-27.
———. *Roman History, Volume VI: Books 51-55.* Translated by Earnest Cary. Loeb Classical Library 83. Cambridge, MA: Harvard University Press, 1917.
Donner, Fred M. *Muhammad and the Believers: At the Origins of Islam.* Cambridge, MA: Harvard University Press, 2010.
———. *Narratives of Islamic Origins: The Beginnings of Islamic Historical Writing.* Princeton, NJ: Darwin, 1998.
Dorion, Louis-André. "The Rise and Fall of the Socratic Problem." In *The Cambridge Companion to Socrates*, edited by Donald R. Morrison, 1-23. Cambridge: Cambridge University Press, 2011.
Dover, K. J. *Aristophanic Comedy.* Berkeley: University of California Press, 1972.
Dunn, James D. G. *Jesus Remembered.* Vol. 1 of *Christianity in the Making.* Grand Rapids: Eerdmans, 2003.
Edwards, Catharine. *Death in Ancient Rome.* New Haven, CT: Yale University Press, 2007.
———. *The Politics of Immorality in Ancient Rome.* Cambridge: Cambridge University Press, 1993.
Ehrman, Bart D. *Did Jesus Exist? The Historical Argument for Jesus of Nazareth.* New York: HarperOne, 2012.
———. *Jesus: Apocalyptic Prophet of the New Millennium.* New York: Oxford University Press, 1999.
———. *Misquoting Jesus: The Story Behind Who Changed the Bible and Why.* New York: HarperOne, 2005.
———. *The New Testament: A Historical Introduction to the Early Christian Writings.* 7th ed. New York: Oxford University Press, 2020.
———. *The Triumph of Christianity: How a Forbidden Religion Swept the World.* New York: Simon & Schuster, 2018.
Ehrman, Bart D., ed. and trans. *The Apostolic Fathers. The Epistle of the Church at Smyrna Concerning the Martyrdom of St. Polycarp.* 2nd ed. Loeb Classical Library 25. Cambridge, MA: Harvard University Press, 2003.
Ehrman, Bart D., and Michael W. Holmes, eds. *The Text of the New Testament in Contemporary Research: Essays on the Status Quaestionis.* 2nd ed. Leiden: Brill, 2013.
Einstein, Albert. "Fundamental Ideas and Problems of the Theory of Relativity." Nobel Lecture, Gothenburg, July 11, 1923. https://www.nobelprize.org/prizes/physics/1921/einstein/lecture/.
Eliade, Mircea. *Myth and Reality.* New York: Harper & Row, 1963.
Emanuel, Tov. *Textual Criticism of the Hebrew Bible.* 2nd ed. Minneapolis: Fortress, 2001.
Eusebius. *Church History.* Translated by Kirsopp Lake. 2 vols. Loeb Classical Library 153-54. Cambridge, MA: Harvard University Press, 1926.
Evangelical Alliance UK. "Talking Jesus: The Report." TalkingJesus.org, 2022. https://talkingjesus.org/wp-content/uploads/2023/08/Talking-Jesus-Report-A4-AUG-23-WEB.pdf.
Evans, Craig A. *Jesus and His World: The Archaeological Evidence.* Louisville: Westminster John Knox, 2012.

BIBLIOGRAPHY

———. *Jesus and the Manuscripts: What We Can Learn from the Oldest Texts.* Peabody, MA: Hendrickson, 2020.

———. *Jesus and the Remains of His Day: Studies in Jesus and the Evidence of Material Culture.* Peabody, MA: Hendrickson, 2015.

Evans, Richard J. *In Defence of History.* Rev. ed. New York: Norton, 1999.

Fanti, Giulio. *The Shroud of Turin: First Century After Christ!* Singapore: Pan Stanford, 2015.

Feldman, Louis H. "Josephus." In *The Anchor Bible Dictionary*, edited by David Noel Freedman, 3:990–1017. New York: Doubleday, 1992.

———. *Josephus and Modern Scholarship (1937–1980).* Berlin: Walter de Gruyter, 1984.

Fine, Steven. *Art and Judaism in the Greco-Roman World: Toward a New Jewish Archaeology.* Cambridge: Cambridge University Press, 2005.

Finley, M. I. *Ancient History: Evidence and Models.* New York: Viking, 1985.

Fischer, David Hackett. *Historians' Fallacies: Toward a Logic of Historical Thought.* New York: Harper & Row, 1970.

Fischer, Louis. *Gandhi: His Life and Message for the World.* New York: Mentor, 1954.

Foerster, Gideon. "The Synagogue at Chorazin." *Biblical Archaeologist* 44 (1981) 12–17.

Fox, Robin Lane. *Alexander the Great.* New York: Penguin, 2004.

Foxe, John. *The Book of Martyrs.* Edited by William Byron Forbush. Grand Rapids: Baker, 1967.

Frova, Antonio. "Caesarea Maritima." In *Encyclopedia of Archaeological Excavations in the Holy Land*, edited by Kathleen M. Kenyon and Avraham Negev, 1:244–49. Jerusalem: Israel Exploration Society, 1972.

———. "Caesarea Maritima: The Excavations of 1961 and the Pilate Inscription." In *The New Encyclopedia of Archaeological Excavations in the Holy Land*, edited by Ephraim Stern, 1:256–59. Jerusalem: Israel Exploration Society and Carta, 1993.

Fudge, Thomas A. *Fire in the Bones: Jan Hus and the Birth of Reform.* Eugene, OR: Cascade, 2010.

Futrell, Alison. *The Roman Games: Historical Sources in Translation.* Malden, MA: Blackwell, 2006.

Gabba, Emilio. *Dio's Caesar and the Collapse of the Republic.* Translated by P. J. Cuff. Oxford: Oxford University Press, 1999.

Gabriel, Richard A., and Karen S. Metz. *From Sumer to Rome: The Military Capabilities of Ancient Armies.* Westport, CT: Greenwood, 1991.

Gethin, Rupert. *The Foundations of Buddhism.* Oxford: Oxford University Press, 1998.

Ginzburg, Carlo. *Clues, Myths, and the Historical Method.* Translated by John Tedeschi and Anne C. Tedeschi. Baltimore: Johns Hopkins University Press, 1989.

Goldsworthy, Adrian. *Antony and Cleopatra.* New Haven, CT: Yale University Press, 2010.

———. *Caesar: Life of a Colossus.* New Haven, CT: Yale University Press, 2006.

Gombrich, Richard. *What the Buddha Thought.* London: Equinox, 2009.

Goody, Jack. *The Logic of Writing and the Organization of Society.* Cambridge: Cambridge University Press, 1986.

Grant, Michael. *Cleopatra.* London: Phoenix, 2000.

———. *Greek and Roman Historians: Information and Misinformation.* London: Routledge, 1995.

———. *The Twelve Caesars.* New York: Scribner, 1975.

Bibliography

Greenberg, Raphael, and Adi Erlich. "Arbel (East)." *Hadashot Arkheologiyot—Excavations and Surveys in Israel* 124 (2012). https://hadashot.iaa.org.il/report_detail_eng.aspx?id=2004&mag_id=119.

Greenhut, Zvi. "Burial Cave of the Caiaphas Family." *Biblical Archaeology Review* 18 (1992) 29–36.

———. "Burial Cave of the Caiaphas Family." *Israel Exploration Journal* 43 (1993) 230–47.

Greenleaf, Simon. *The Testimony of the Evangelists: The Gospels Examined by the Rules of Evidence*. Boston: Charles C. Little and James Brown, 1846.

Grierson, Philip. *Numismatics*. Oxford: Oxford University Press, 1975.

Guinness, Os. *Fool's Talk: Recovering the Art of Christian Persuasion*. Downers Grove, IL: InterVarsity, 2015.

Gurry, Peter J., and Elijah Hixson. *Myths and Mistakes in New Testament Textual Criticism*. Downers Grove, IL: IVP Academic, 2019.

Guthrie, W. K. C. *A History of Greek Philosophy* 1. Cambridge: Cambridge University Press, 1962.

Haas, Nicu. "Anthropological Observations on the Skeletal Remains from Giv☒at ha-Mivtar." *Israel Exploration Journal* 20 (1970) 38–59.

Habermas, Gary R. *The Historical Jesus: Ancient Evidence for the Life of Christ*. Joplin, MO: College Press, 1996.

Habermas, Gary R., and Michael R. Licona. *The Case for the Resurrection of Jesus*. Grand Rapids: Kregel, 2004.

Halbwachs, Maurice. *On Collective Memory*. Edited, translated, and with an introduction by Lewis A. Coser. Chicago: University of Chicago Press, 1992.

Hamilton, J. R. *Alexander the Great*. Rev. ed. London: Bristol Classical, 2003.

Hansen, Mogens Herman. *The Athenian Democracy in the Age of Demosthenes: Structure, Principles and Ideology*. Oxford: Blackwell, 1991.

Hanson, Ann Ellis. *Roman Biographies and Historical Distance*. Cambridge: Cambridge University Press, 1997.

Harris, Sam. *The Moral Landscape: How Science Can Determine Human Values*. New York: Free Press, 2010.

Hemer, Colin J. *The Book of Acts in the Setting of Hellenistic History*. Winona Lake, IN: Eisenbrauns, 1990.

Hengel, Martin. *The Four Gospels and the One Gospel of Jesus Christ: An Investigation of the Collection and Origin of the Canonical Gospels*. Harrisburg, PA: Trinity, 2000.

Herodotus. *Histories*. Translated by A. D. Godley. 4 vols. Loeb Classical Library. Cambridge, MA: Harvard University Press, 1920–25.

———. *The Histories*. Translated by Robin Waterfield. Oxford: Oxford University Press, 1998.

Hesiod. *Theogony*. Translated by Glenn W. Most. Loeb Classical Library. Cambridge, MA: Harvard University Press, 2006.

Hippolytus. "On the Twelve Apostles." In *Ante-Nicene Fathers*, edited by Alexander Roberts and James Donaldson, 5:254. Peabody, MA: Hendrickson, 1994.

Hisham, Ibn. *Al-Sīrah al-Nabawiyyah*. Cairo: al-Maṭba'ah al-Kubrā al-Amīriyyah, 1885.

———. *Al-Sīrah al-Nabawiyyah*. Edited by Ferdinand Wüstenfeld. 4 vols. Göttingen: Dieterich, 1858–60.

Holland, Tom. *Dominion: How the Christian Revolution Remade the World*. New York: Basic Books, 2019.

Bibliography

———. *In the Shadow of the Sword: The Birth of Islam and the Rise of the Global Arab Empire.* New York: Doubleday, 2012.

Horace. *Odes and Epodes.* Translated by Niall Rudd. Loeb Classical Library 33. Cambridge, MA: Harvard University Press, 2004.

Horn, Trent. "The Bible Says Jesus Was Real. What Other Proof Exists?" Catholic Answers, September 14, 2023. https://www.catholic.com/magazine/online-edition/jesus-the-pagan-god.

Hoyland, Robert G. *Seeing Islam as Others Saw It: A Survey and Evaluation of Christian, Jewish and Zoroastrian Writings on Early Islam.* Princeton, NJ: Darwin, 1997.

Hoyos, B. Dexter. *Hannibal: Rome's Greatest Enemy.* London: Bristol Classical, 2005.

———. *Hannibal's Dynasty: Power and Politics in the Western Mediterranean, 247–183 BC.* London: Routledge, 2003.

———. *Mastering the West: Rome and Carthage at War.* Oxford: Oxford University Press, 2015.

Hughes-Hallett, Lucy. *Cleopatra: Histories, Dreams and Distortions.* New York: Harper & Row, 1990.

Hughes-Warrington, Marnie. *History Goes to the Movies: Studying History on Film.* London: Routledge, 2007.

Humanists UK. "Less Than Half of Britons Believe in God." May 22, 2023. https://humanists.uk/2023/05/19/new-study-shows-less-than-half-of-britons-believe-in-god/.

Hurley, Donna W. "Suetonius." In *Latin Historians,* edited by C. S. Kraus and A. J. Woodman, 152–70. Oxford: Oxford University Press, 2010.

Hurtado, Larry W. *Lord Jesus Christ: Devotion to Jesus in Earliest Christianity.* Grand Rapids: Eerdmans, 2003.

Ignatius. *The Apostolic Fathers* 1. Translated by Bart D. Ehrman. Loeb Classical Library 24. Cambridge, MA: Harvard University Press, 2003.

Ishaq, Ibn. *The Life of Muhammad: A Translation of Ibn Ishaq's Sirat Rasul Allah.* Translated by A. Guillaume. Oxford: Oxford University Press, 1955.

Johnson, Paul. *Socrates: A Man for Our Times.* New York: Viking, 2011.

Josephus, Flavius. *The Antiquities of the Jews.* Translated by William Whiston. Peabody, MA: Hendrickson, 1987.

———. *The Jewish War.* Translated by H. St. J. Thackeray. 3 vols. Loeb Classical Library. Cambridge, MA: Harvard University Press, 1927–28.

Juynboll, G. H. A. *The Authenticity of the Tradition Literature: Discussions in Modern Egypt.* Leiden: Brill, 1969.

Katz, Brigit. "Oldest-Known Image of Confucius Found in Tomb of Disgraced Emperor." Smithsonian Magazine, March 2, 2017. https://www.smithsonianmag.com/smart-news/oldest-known-image-confucius-found-tomb-disgraced-emperor-180962358/.

Keel, Othmar. *The Symbolism of the Biblical World: Ancient Near Eastern Iconography and the Book of Psalms.* Translated by Timothy J. Hallett. Winona Lake, IN: Eisenbrauns, 1997.

Keener, Craig S. *The Historical Jesus of the Gospels.* Grand Rapids: Eerdmans, 2009.

Keller, Timothy. *The Reason for God: Belief in an Age of Skepticism.* New York: Dutton, 2008.

Kelly, J. N. D. *Early Christian Doctrines.* Rev. ed. London: A & C Black, 1978.

Kennedy, Hugh. *The Great Arab Conquests: How the Spread of Islam Changed the World We Live In.* Philadelphia: Da Capo, 2007.

Bibliography

Kenny, Anthony. *An Illustrated Brief History of Western Philosophy*. 2nd ed. Malden, MA: Blackwell, 2006.

Keown, Damien. *Buddhism: A Very Short Introduction*. Oxford: Oxford University Press, 1996.

Khalidi, Tarif. *The Muslim Jesus: Sayings and Stories in Islamic Literature*. Cambridge, MA: Harvard University Press, 2001.

Kitchen, K. A. *On the Reliability of the Old Testament*. Grand Rapids: Eerdmans, 2003.

Klein, Christopher. "The Bible Says Jesus Was Real. What Other Proof Exists?" History.com, September 11, 2025. https://www.history.com/articles/was-jesus-real-historical-evidence.

Kramer, Joel P. *Where God Came Down: The Archaeological Evidence*. Charlotte, NC: Expedition Bible, 2020.

Kramer, Samuel Noah. *History Begins at Sumer: Thirty-Nine Firsts in Recorded History*. 3rd ed. Philadelphia: University of Pennsylvania Press, 1981.

Kruger, Michael J. *The Question of Canon: Challenging the Status Quo in the New Testament Debate*. Downers Grove, IL: IVP Academic, 2013.

LaBarbera, Daniel. *Truth at the Gate: A Trial of History's Giants*. Eugene, OR: Wipf & Stock, 2025.

Laertius, Diogenes. *Lives of Eminent Philosophers*. Translated by R. D. Hicks. 2 vols. Loeb Classical Library. Cambridge, MA: Harvard University Press, 1925.

Leigh, Matthew. "Suetonius and the Literature of the Spectacle." *The Classical Quarterly* 53 (2003) 210–20.

Lennox, John. *Gunning for God: Why the New Atheists Are Missing the Target*. Oxford: Lion, 2011.

Levick, Barbara. *Tiberius the Politician*. 2nd ed. London: Routledge, 1999.

Levin, Michael. "Scientists Made Xenobots—Tiny Living Robots—That Can Reproduce." Interview by Caroline Delbert. *Popular Mechanics*, January 13, 2021. Podcast. https://www.popularmechanics.com/science/a35204602/xenobots-reproduce-michael-levin-interview/.

Levine, Lee I. *The Ancient Synagogue: The First Thousand Years*. 2nd ed. New Haven, CT: Yale University Press, 2005.

Lewis, C. S. *God in the Dock: Essays on Theology and Ethics*. Edited by Walter Hooper. Grand Rapids: Eerdmans, 1970.

———. *Mere Christianity*. New York: HarperOne, 2001.

———. *The Problem of Pain*. New York: HarperOne, 2001.

Lewis, Michael. *The Big Short: Inside the Doomsday Machine*. New York: Norton, 2010.

Lewis-Williams, David. *The Mind in the Cave: Consciousness and the Origins of Art*. London: Thames & Hudson, 2002.

Licona, Michael R. *The Resurrection of Jesus: A New Historiographical Approach*. Downers Grove, IL: IVP Academic, 2010.

Lieu, Samuel N. C. *Manichaeism in the Later Roman Empire and Medieval China*. Tübingen: Mohr Siebeck, 1992.

Lings, Martin. *Muhammad: His Life Based on the Earliest Sources*. Rochester, VT: Inner Traditions, 2006.

Lintott, Andrew. "The Value of Plutarch's *Lives* as Historical Evidence." In *Plutarch and History*, by Christopher Pelling, 1–20. Swansea: Classical Press of Wales, 2002.

Livy. *History of Rome, Volume V: Books 21–22*. Translated by B. O. Foster. Loeb Classical Library 295. Cambridge, MA: Harvard University Press, 1929.

Bibliography

———. *History of Rome, Volume VI: Books 23–25*. Translated by B. O. Foster. Loeb Classical Library 355. Cambridge, MA: Harvard University Press, 1929.

———. *History of Rome, Volume VII: Books 26–27*. Translated by Frank Gardner Moore. Loeb Classical Library 366. Cambridge, MA: Harvard University Press, 1940.

———. *History of Rome, Volume VIII: Books 28–30*. Translated by Frank Gardner Moore. Loeb Classical Library 396. Cambridge, MA: Harvard University Press, 1949.

———. *History of Rome, Volume XIV: Summaries. Fragments. Julius Obsequens. General Index*. Translated by Alfred C. Schlesinger. Loeb Classical Library 404. Cambridge, MA: Harvard University Press, 1959.

Loewe, Michael. *Chinese Ideas of Life and Death: Faith, Myth and Reason in the Han Period (202 BC–AD 220)*. London: George Allen & Unwin, 1982.

Lopez, Donald S. *Buddhism and Science: A Guide for the Perplexed*. Chicago: University of Chicago Press, 2008.

———. *The Story of Buddhism: A Concise Guide to Its History and Teachings*. New York: HarperOne, 2001.

Lucian. "The Death of Peregrine." In *The Works of Lucian of Samosata*. Translated by H. W. Fowler and F. G. Fowler. Oxford: Clarendon, 1905.

Lüdemann, Gerd. *The Resurrection of Jesus: History, Experience, Theology*. Minneapolis: Fortress, 1994.

Luxenberg, Christoph. *The Syro-Aramaic Reading of the Koran: A Contribution to the Decoding of the Language of the Koran*. Berlin: Hans Schiler, 2007.

Macy, Beth. *Dopesick: Dealers, Doctors, and the Drug Company That Addicted America*. New York: Little, Brown, 2018.

Makeham, John. *Lost Soul: "Confucianism" in Contemporary Chinese Academic Discourse*. Cambridge, MA: Harvard University Press, 2008.

Marincola, John. *Authority and Tradition in Ancient Historiography*. Cambridge: Cambridge University Press, 1997.

Martyr, Justin. *The First and Second Apologies*. Translated by Leslie William Barnard. New York: Paulist, 1997.

McDowell, Josh. *The New Evidence That Demands a Verdict: Evidence for the Bible*. Nashville: Thomas Nelson, 1999.

McDowell, Josh, and Sean McDowell. *Evidence That Demands a Verdict: Life-Changing Truth for a Skeptical World*. Nashville: Thomas Nelson, 2017.

McDowell, Sean. *The Fate of the Apostles: Examining the Martyrdom Accounts of the Closest Followers of Jesus*. New York: Routledge, 2015.

McRay, John. *Archaeology and the New Testament*. Grand Rapids: Baker Academic, 1991.

Meier, John P. *In the Fullness of Time: A Historian Looks at Christmas, Easter, and the Early Church*. New York: Doubleday, 1991.

———. *A Marginal Jew: Rethinking the Historical Jesus 1*. New Haven, CT: Yale University Press, 1991.

Mellor, Ronald. *Tacitus*. London: Routledge, 1993.

Mettinger, Tryggve N. D. *The Riddle of Resurrection: Dying and Rising Gods in the Ancient Near East*. Stockholm: Almqvist & Wiksell, 2001.

Metzger, Bruce M. *The Early Versions of the New Testament: Their Origin, Transmission, and Limitations*. Oxford: Clarendon, 1977.

———. "The Nazareth Inscription Once More." *Journal of Biblical Literature* 70 (1951) 233–35.

Bibliography

Metzger, Bruce M., and Bart D. Ehrman. *The Text of the New Testament: Its Transmission, Corruption, and Restoration*. 4th ed. Oxford: Oxford University Press, 2005.

Meyers, Eric M., and James F. Strange. *Archaeology, the Rabbis, and Early Christianity*. Philadelphia: Fortress, 1981.

Miles, Richard. *Carthage Must Be Destroyed: The Rise and Fall of an Ancient Civilization*. New York: Viking, 2011.

Millar, Fergus. *The Emperor in the Roman World (31 BC–AD 337)*. Ithaca, NY: Cornell University Press, 1977.

———. *The Roman Near East, 31 BC–AD 337*. Cambridge, MA: Harvard University Press, 1993.

———. *A Study of Cassius Dio*. Oxford: Clarendon, 1964.

Momigliano, Arnaldo. *The Classical Foundations of Modern Historiography*. Berkeley: University of California Press, 1990.

Montgomery, John Warwick. *Faith Founded on Fact*. Nashville: Thomas Nelson, 1978.

Morley, Neville. *The Roman Empire: Roots of Imperialism*. London: Pluto, 2010.

Morrison, Donald R., ed. *The Cambridge Companion to Socrates*. Cambridge: Cambridge University Press, 2011.

Motzki, Harald. "The Biography of Muhammad: The Issue of the Sources." *Der Islam* 68 (1991) 1–21.

———. "The Biography of Muhammad: The Issue of the Sources." In *The Prophet Muhammad in History, Thought, and Culture: An Encyclopedia of the Sirah*, edited by Coeli Fitzpatrick and Adam Hani Walker, 68–70. Santa Barbara, CA: ABC-CLIO, 2014.

———. "The Collection of the Qur'an and the Compilation of the Hadith." In *The Cambridge Companion to the Qur'an*, edited by Jane Dammen McAuliffe, 60–77. Cambridge: Cambridge University Press, 2006.

———. "The Musannaf of ʿAbd al-Razzāq al-Ṣanʿānī as a Source of Authentic Aḥādīth of the First Century A.H." *Journal of Near Eastern Studies* 50 (1991) 1–21.

Muslim ibn al-Hajjaj. *Sahih Muslim*. Translated by Nasiruddin al-Khattab. Riyadh: Darussalam, 2007.

Mykytiuk, Lawrence J. "Archaeology Confirms 50 Real People in the Bible." *Biblical Archaeology Review* 40 (2014) 42–50.

Nagel, Thomas. *The Last Word*. New York: Oxford University Press, 1997.

Nails, Debra. *The People of Plato: A Prosopography of Plato and Other Socratics*. Indianapolis: Hackett, 2002.

Nasr, Seyyed Hossein. *The Heart of Islam: Enduring Values for Humanity*. New York: HarperOne, 2004.

Neusner, Jacob, trans. *Babylonian Talmud*. Peabody, MA: Hendrickson, 2011.

Neuwirth, Angelika. *Scripture, Poetry, and the Making of a Community: Reading the Qur'an as a Literary Text*. Oxford: Oxford University Press, 2014.

———. *Scripture, Poetry, and the Making of a Community: The Qur'an and the Bible in the Light of the Qur'an*. Oxford: Oxford University Press, 2014..

Nora, Pierre. "Between Memory and History: Les Lieux de Mémoire." *Representations* 26 (1989) 7–24.

Norton, Mary Beth. *In the Devil's Snare: The Salem Witchcraft Crisis of 1692*. New York: Vintage, 2003.

Nylan, Michael. *The Confucian Tradition*. Washington, DC: Catholic University of America Press, 2010.

Bibliography

———. *The Five "Confucian" Classics*. New Haven, CT: Yale University Press, 2001.
Office for National Statistics. "Religion by Age and Sex, England and Wales: Census 2021." January 30, 2023. https://www.ons.gov.uk/.
Open Science Collaboration. "Estimating the Reproducibility of Psychological Science." *Science* 349 (2015) aac4716. https://doi.org/10.1126/science.aac4716.
Origen. *Against Celsus*. Translated by Henry Chadwick. Cambridge: Cambridge University Press, 1980.
Orwell, George. *Nineteen Eighty-Four*. London: Secker & Warburg, 1949.
P52 (Rylands Library Papyrus P52). The Rylands Fragment of John 18:31–33, 37–38. ca. AD 125. Manchester: John Rylands Library.
Paterculus, Velleius. *Roman History*. Translated by Frederick W. Shipley. Loeb Classical Library 152. Cambridge, MA: Harvard University Press, 1924.
Pelling, C. B. R. "Caesar's Narrative and the Ideology of History." *Greece & Rome* 45 (1998) 186–202.
———. *Characterization and Individuality in Greek Literature*. Oxford: Clarendon, 1990.
———. *Plutarch and History: Eighteen Studies*. Swansea: Classical Press of Wales, 2002.
———. "Plutarch and Roman Politics." In *Plutarch and History: Eighteen Studies*, by C. B. R. Pelling, 145–64. Swansea: Classical Press of Wales, 2002.
———. "Plutarch's Caesar: A Moralist with a Taste for Politics." *Greece & Rome* 30 (1983) 147–54.
Peters, F. E. *Islam: A Guide for Jews and Christians*. Princeton, NJ: Princeton University Press, 2003.
———. *Muhammad and the Origins of Islam*. Albany: State University of New York Press, 1994.
Pew Research Center. "The Future of World Religions: Population Growth Projections, 2017–2050." April 2, 2015. https://assets.pewresearch.org/wp-content/uploads/sites/11/2015/03/PF_15.04.02_ProjectionsFullReport.pdf?utm.
———. "What Americans Know About Religion." July 23, 2019. https://www.pewresearch.org/religion/2019/07/23/what-americans-know-about-religion/.
Pfann, Stephen J. *Nazareth Village Farm: A Case Study in Historical Archaeology*. Jerusalem: Nazareth Village, 2001.
Philo. *On the Embassy to Gaius*. Translated by F. H. Colson. Loeb Classical Library 379. Cambridge, MA: Harvard University Press, 1962.
Plantinga, Alvin. *Warranted Christian Belief*. New York: Oxford University Press, 2000.
Plato. *Apology, Crito, and Phaedo*. Translated by G. M. A. Grube. Indianapolis: Hackett, 2001.
———. *Five Dialogues*. Edited by John M. Cooper. Translated by G. M. A. Grube. Indianapolis: Hackett, 2002.
———. *Plato: Complete Works*. Edited by John M. Cooper. Indianapolis: Hackett, 1997.
———. *Republic*. Translated by G. M. A. Grube. Revised by C. D. C. Reeve. Indianapolis: Hackett, 1992.
———. *Symposium*. Translated by Alexander Nehamas and Paul Woodruff. Indianapolis: Hackett, 1989.
Pliny. *Letters*. Translated by Betty Radice. London: Penguin Classics, 1963.
Plutarch. *Life of Crassus*. In *Parallel Lives*, translated by Bernadotte Perrin, 8–11. Vol. 3 of the Loeb Classical Library. Cambridge, MA: Harvard University Press, 1916.

Bibliography

———. *Life of Julius Caesar.* In *Plutarch's Lives,* translated by John Dryden and revised by Arthur Hugh Clough, 130–55. Modern Library Classics. New York: Modern Library, 2001.

———. *Lives.* 11 vols. Translated by Bernadotte Perrin. Loeb Classical Library. Cambridge, MA: Harvard University Press, 1914–26.

———. *The Lives of the Noble Grecians and Romans.* Translated by Thomas North. Reprinted with introduction by Brian Vickers. London: Everyman's Library, 1993.

Polybius. *Histories.* Translated by W. R. Paton. 6 vols. Loeb Classical Library. Cambridge, MA: Harvard University Press, 1922–27.

———. *The Histories.* Translated by Ian Scott-Kilvert. London: Penguin Classics, 1979.

Polycarp. *The Apostolic Fathers* 2. Translated by Bart D. Ehrman. Loeb Classical Library 25. Cambridge, MA: Harvard University Press, 2003.

Pomeroy, Sarah B. *Women in Hellenistic Egypt: From Alexander to Cleopatra.* New York: Schocken, 1984.

Prange, Gordon W. *At Dawn We Slept: The Untold Story of Pearl Harbor.* New York: Penguin, 1982.

Price, Martin Jessop. *Coinage in the Name of Alexander the Great and Philip Arrhidaeus* 1. Zurich: Swiss Numismatic Society, 1991.

Price, Robert M. *The Christ-Myth Theory and Its Problems.* Cranford, NJ: American Atheist, 2011.

———. *The Incredible Shrinking Son of Man: How Reliable Is the Gospel Tradition?* Amherst, NY: Prometheus, 2003.

Proctor, Robert. *Golden Holocaust: Origins of the Cigarette Catastrophe and the Case for Abolition.* Berkeley: University of California Press, 2011.

Propertius. *Elegies.* Translated by G. P. Goold. Loeb Classical Library 18. Cambridge, MA: Harvard University Press, 1990.

Puin, Gerd R. "Observations on Early Qur'an Manuscripts in San'a." In *The Qur'an as Text,* edited by Stefan Wild, 107–11. Leiden: Brill, 1996.

Qian, Sima. *Records of the Grand Historian: Shiji.* Translated by Burton Watson. 2 vols. New York: Columbia University Press, 1993.

Reeve, C. D. C. *Socrates in the Apology: An Essay on Plato's Apology of Socrates.* Indianapolis: Hackett, 1989.

Reverby, Susan M. *Examining Tuskegee: The Infamous Syphilis Study and Its Legacy.* Chapel Hill: University of North Carolina Press, 2009.

Reynolds, Gabriel Said. *The Emergence of Islam: Classical Traditions in Contemporary Perspective.* Minneapolis: Fortress, 2012.

Reynolds, L. D., and N. G. Wilson. *Scribes and Scholars: A Guide to the Transmission of Latin and Greek Literature.* 3rd ed. Oxford: Oxford University Press, 1991.

Richardson, J. S. *Appian in Context: Political Commentary on the Civil Wars.* Cambridge: Cambridge Philological Society, 1991.

Ricoeur, Paul. *Time and Narrative* 1. Chicago: University of Chicago Press, 1984.

Riggsby, Andrew. *Caesar in Gaul and Rome: War in Words.* Austin: University of Texas Press, 2006.

Roberts, C. H. *An Early Papyrus of the Fourth Gospel.* Manchester: Manchester University Press, 1935.

———. *An Unpublished Fragment of the Fourth Gospel in the John Rylands Library.* Manchester: Manchester University Press, 1935.

Bibliography

Rodkinson, Michael L., trans. *The Babylonian Talmud: Translated into English with Notes, Glossary and Indices* 8. Boston: New Talmud, 1918.

Rogers, Raymond N. "Studies on the Radiocarbon Sample from the Shroud of Turin." *Thermochimica Acta* 425 (2005) 189–94.

Roller, Duane W. *Cleopatra: A Biography*. Oxford: Oxford University Press, 2010.

Rollston, Christopher A. "Forging History: From Antiquity to the Modern Period." In *Archaeologies of Text: Archaeology, Technology, and Ethics*, edited by Matthew T. Rutz and Morag M. Kersel, 176–90. Oxford: Oxbow, 2014.

Rose, Charles Brian. *Dynastic Commemoration and Imperial Portraiture in the Julio-Claudian Period*. Cambridge: Cambridge University Press, 1997.

Rosenstone, Robert A. *History on Film/Film on History*. 3rd ed. London & New York: Routledge, 2006.

Rufus, Quintus Curtius. *Histories of Alexander*. Translated by John C. Rolfe. 2 vols. Loeb Classical Library. Cambridge, MA: Harvard University Press, 1946.

Sallust. *The Jugurthine War*. Translated by J. C. Rolfe. Loeb Classical Library 116. Cambridge, MA: Harvard University Press, 1931.

Sanders, E. P. *The Historical Figure of Jesus*. London: Penguin, 1993.

Scarre, Chris. *Chronicle of the Pharaohs: The Reign-by-Reign Record of the Rulers and Dynasties of Ancient Egypt*. London: Thames & Hudson, 1995.

Scarre, Chris, ed. *The Human Past: World Prehistory and the Development of Human Societies*. 3rd ed. New York: Norton, 2005.

Schachter, Jacob, trans. "Sanhedrin 43a." In *The Babylonian Talmud: Tractate Sanhedrin*. London: Soncino, 1935.

Schäfer, Peter. *Jesus in the Talmud*. Princeton, NJ: Princeton University Press, 2007.

Schiff, Stacy. *Cleopatra: A Life*. New York: Little, Brown and Company, 2010.

Schlesinger, Arthur M. *A Thousand Days: John F. Kennedy in the White House*. Boston: Houghton Mifflin, 1965.

Schmandt-Besserat, Denise. *Before Writing* 1. Austin: University of Texas Press, 1992.

Schmidt, Alvin J. *How Christianity Changed the World*. Grand Rapids: Zondervan, 2004.

Schwartz, Benjamin I. *The World of Thought in Ancient China*. Cambridge, MA: Harvard University Press, 1985.

Scullard, H. H. *From the Gracchi to Nero: A History of Rome from 133 BC to AD 68*. 5th ed. London: Routledge, 1982.

Seager, Robin. *Julius Caesar*. 2nd ed. London: Bloomsbury Academic, 2006.

Shakespeare, William. *Antony and Cleopatra*. Edited by Emrys Jones. London: Penguin Classics, 2005.

———. *Antony and Cleopatra*. Edited by Emrys Jones. New York: Penguin Classics, 2005.

Shanks, Hershel. *Jerusalem: An Archaeological Biography*. New York: Random House, 1995.

Shea, Neil. "Oldest Known Image of Confucius Found in Tomb of Disgraced Emperor." *Smithsonian Magazine*, March 2, 2017. https://www.smithsonianmag.com/smart-news/oldest-known-image-confucius-found-tomb-disgraced-emperor-180962193/.

Sherwin-White, A. N. *Roman Society and Roman Law in the New Testament*. Oxford: Clarendon, 1963.

Shoemaker, Stephen J. *The Death of a Prophet: The End of Muhammad's Life and the Beginnings of Islam*. Philadelphia: University of Pennsylvania Press, 2012.

Shotter, David. *The Fall of the Roman Republic*. London: Routledge, 2005.

———. *Tiberius Caesar*. 2nd ed. London: Routledge, 2004.

BIBLIOGRAPHY

Siculus, Diodorus. *Library of History*. Translated by C. H. Oldfather et al. 12 vols. Loeb Classical Library. Cambridge, MA: Harvard University Press, 1933–67.

Sinai, Nicolai. *The Qur'an: A Historical-Critical Introduction*. Edinburgh: Edinburgh University Press, 2017.

Slick, Matt. "Manuscript Evidence for Superior New Testament Reliability." CARM, December 10, 2008. https://www.carm.org/article/manuscript-evidence-for-superior-new-testament-reliability/.

Slingerland, Edward. *Confucius: Analects with Selections from Traditional Commentaries*. Indianapolis: Hackett, 2003.

Smith, Jonathan Z. *Drudgery Divine: On the Comparison of Early Christianities and the Religions of Late Antiquity*. Chicago: University of Chicago Press, 1990.

Snyder, Frankie. "The Magdala Stone: Another Suggestion for the Square Object Under the Menorah." *Near East Archaeological Society Bulletin* 69 (2024) 65–75.

Spencer, Robert. *Did Muhammad Exist? An Inquiry into Islam's Obscure Origins*. Wilmington, DE: Intercollegiate Studies Institute, 2012.

Stern, Ephraim, ed. *The New Encyclopedia of Archaeological Excavations in the Holy Land*. Jerusalem: Israel Exploration Society and Carta, 1993

Stone, I. F. *The Trial of Socrates*. New York: Anchor, 1989.

Stone, Oliver, dir. *Alexander*. 2004; Warner Bros. Pictures.

Strange, James F. "Nazareth." In *Anchor Bible Dictionary*, edited by David Noel Freedman, 4:1050–51. New York: Doubleday, 1992.

Strong, John S. *The Buddha: A Short Biography*. Oxford: Oneworld, 2001.

Suetonius. *Lives of the Caesars*. 2 vols. Translated by J. C. Rolfe. Loeb Classical Library 31, 38. Cambridge, MA: Harvard University Press, 1913–14.

———. *The Twelve Caesars*. Translated by Robert Graves. Revised by James B. Rives. London: Penguin Classics, 2007.

Syme, Ronald. *Roman Papers* 4. Edited by E. Badian. Oxford: Clarendon, 1988.

———. *The Roman Revolution*. Oxford: Oxford University Press, 1939.

Tacitus. *The Annals*. Translated by Alfred John Church and William Jackson Brodribb. New York: Modern Library, 1942.

———. *The Annals of Imperial Rome*. Translated by Michael Grant. London: Penguin, 2003.

———. *The Complete Works of Tacitus*. Translated by Alfred John Church and William Jackson Brodribb. New York: Random House, 1942.

Talgam, Rina. "The Magdala Stone and the Synagogue as a House of Study." *Journal of Jewish Art* 38 (2012) 27–46.

———. *Mosaics of Faith: Floors of Pagans, Jews, Samaritans, Christians and Muslims in the Holy Land*. Jerusalem: Yad Ben-Zvi, 2014.

Taylor, C. C. W. *Socrates: A Very Short Introduction*. Oxford: Oxford University Press, 2000.

Taylor, Joan E. *The Essenes, the Scrolls, and the Dead Sea*. Oxford: Oxford University Press, 2012.

Tertullian. *Apology*. Translated by T. R. Glover. Loeb Classical Library 250. Cambridge, MA: Harvard University Press, 1931.

———. *Prescription Against Heretics*. Translated by T. R. Glover. Loeb Classical Library 305. Cambridge, MA: Harvard University Press, 1954.

Thapar, Romila. *Aśoka and the Decline of the Mauryas*. Oxford: Oxford University Press, 1961.

Bibliography

Theissen, Gerd, and Annette Merz. *The Historical Jesus: A Comprehensive Guide.* Minneapolis: Fortress, 1998.
Thucydides. *History of the Peloponnesian War.* Translated by Charles Forster Smith. Vol. 1 of the Loeb Classical Library. Cambridge, MA: Harvard University Press, 1919.
———. *The Peloponnesian War.* Translated by Richard Crawley. New York: Modern Library, 1951.
Toplin, Robert Brent. *Reel History: In Defense of Hollywood.* Lawrence: University Press of Kansas, 2002.
Topol, Eric J. *Deadly Medicine: Why Tens of Thousands of Heart Patients Died in America's Worst Drug Disaster.* New York: Knopf, 2004.
Tov, Emanuel. *Textual Criticism of the Hebrew Bible.* 3rd ed. Minneapolis: Fortress, 2012.
Vachman, David. "A New Second Temple-Period Synagogue Discovered Near Mount Arbel." Israel Antiquities Authority, 2021.
Van Seters, John. *In Search of History: Historiography in the Ancient World.* New Haven, CT: Yale University Press, 1983.
VanderKam, James C., and Peter Flint. *The Meaning of the Dead Sea Scrolls.* San Francisco: HarperSanFrancisco, 2002.
Van Voorst, Robert E. *Jesus Outside the New Testament: An Introduction to the Ancient Evidence.* Grand Rapids: Eerdmans, 2000.
Virgil. *Aeneid.* Translated by H. Rushton Fairclough. Revised by G. P. Goold. Loeb Classical Library 63. Cambridge, MA: Harvard University Press, 1999.
Vitz, Paul. *Faith of the Fatherless: The Psychology of Atheism.* San Francisco: Ignatius, 2013.
Vlastos, Gregory. *Socrates: Ironist and Moral Philosopher.* Ithaca, NY: Cornell University Press, 1991.
Walbank, F. W. *A Historical Commentary on Polybius.* 3 vols. Oxford: Clarendon, 1957–79.
———. *Polybius.* Berkeley: University of California Press, 1972.
Walker, John. *A Catalogue of the Arab-Byzantine and Post-Reform Umaiyad Coins.* London: British Museum, 1956.
Wallace, Daniel B. "Majority Text and the Original Text." In *The Majority Text: Essays and Reviews in the Continuing Debate,* edited by Theodore P. Letis, 157–73. Fort Wayne, IN: Institute for Reformation Biblical Studies, 1987.
———. *Manuscript Evidence for Superior New Testament Reliability.* Dallas: Biblical Studies, 2001.
———. *Revisiting the Corruption of the New Testament: Manuscript, Patristic, and Apocryphal Evidence.* Grand Rapids: Kregel Academic, 2011.
———. "Some Second Thoughts on the Majority Text." Bible.org, 2004. https://bible.org/article/some-second-thoughts-majority-text.
Wallace-Hadrill, Andrew. *Suetonius: The Scholar and His Caesars.* New Haven, CT: Yale University Press, 1983.
Wansbrough, John. *Quranic Studies: Sources and Methods of Scriptural Interpretation.* Oxford: Oxford University Press, 1977.
Waterfield, Robin. *Why Socrates Died: Dispelling the Myths.* New York: Norton, 2009.
Watt, W. Montgomery. *Muhammad at Mecca.* Oxford: Oxford University Press, 1953.
White, Hayden. *Metahistory: The Historical Imagination in Nineteenth-Century Europe.* Baltimore: Johns Hopkins University Press, 1973.
White, Horace. *Appian's Roman History.* London: Macmillan, 1899.
Wilson, Emily R. *The Death of Socrates.* Cambridge, MA: Harvard University Press, 2007.

Bibliography

Wineburg, Samuel S. *Historical Thinking and Other Unnatural Acts: Charting the Future of Teaching the Past*. Philadelphia: Temple University Press, 2001.

Wiseman, T. P. *The Invention of History in Ancient Rome*. Exeter: University of Exeter Press, 1994.

———. *The Myths of Rome*. Exeter: University of Exeter Press, 2004.

Woodman, A. J. *Rhetoric in Classical Historiography: Four Studies*. London: Croom Helm, 1988.

Wright, N. T. *Jesus and the Victory of God*. Vol. 2 of *Christian Origins and the Question of God*. Minneapolis: Fortress, 1996.

———. *The Resurrection of the Son of God*. Minneapolis: Fortress, 2003.

Wyke, Maria. *Projecting the Past: Ancient Rome, Cinema and History*. London: Routledge, 1997.

Wynne, Alexander. *Buddhism: An Introduction*. London: I. B. Tauris, 2010.

———. *The Origin of Buddhist Meditation*. New York: Routledge, 2007.

Xenophon. *Anabasis*. Translated by Carleton L. Brownson. Loeb Classical Library 90. Cambridge, MA: Harvard University Press, 1922.

Apology. In Memorabilia. Translated by E. C. Marchant. Loeb Classical Library 168. Cambridge, MA: Harvard University Press, 1923.

———. *Memorabilia*. Translated by Amy L. Bonnette. Ithaca, NY: Cornell University Press, 1994.

———. *Memorabilia*. Translated by E. C. Marchant. Loeb Classical Library. Cambridge, MA: Harvard University Press, 1923.

Yao, Xinzhong. *An Introduction to Confucianism*. New York: Cambridge University Press, 2000.

Zangenberg, Jürgen K. "Archaeological Evidence of Pontius Pilate." In *Pontius Pilate: Portraits of a Roman Governor*, edited by Helen K. Bond and David W. Chapman, 29–36. Tübingen: Mohr Siebeck, 2003.

Zangenberg, Jürgen. "Archaeological Evidence of Pontius Pilate." In *The World of Jesus and the Early Church*, edited by Craig A. Evans, 229–42. Peabody, MA: Hendrickson, 2011.

Zanker, Paul. *The Mask of Socrates: The Image of the Intellectual in Antiquity*. Berkeley: University of California Press, 1995.

Zapata-Meza, Marcela, and Jesús García Sánchez. "The First-Century Synagogue at Magdala, Galilee." *Journal of Ancient Judaism* 12 (2021) 145–74.

———. "The First-Century Synagogue at Magdala—An Overview of Its Architecture and Function." In *Archaeology and the Galilean Jesus*, 27–54. Mexico City: Universidad Iberoamericana, 2020.

Zapata-Meza, Marcela, et al. "The Magdala Archaeological Project (2010–2012): A Preliminary Report of the Excavations at Migdal." *'Atiqot* 90 (2018) 83–125. https://www.anahuac.mx/mexico/EscuelasyFacultades/educacion/sites/default/files/inline-files/The-Magdala-Archaeological-Project.pdf

Ziliang, Liu. "Excavating the Marquis of Haihun's Tomb." Fairbank Center for Chinese Students (blog), January 29, 2018. https://fairbank.fas.harvard.edu/blog/excavating-the-marquis-of-haihuns-tomb/.

Zinn, Howard. *A People's History of the United States*. New York: Harper Perennial, 2003.

Zürcher, Erik. *The Buddhist Conquest of China: The Spread and Adaptation of Buddhism in Early Medieval China*. 2nd ed. Leiden: Brill, 2007.

Index

Alexander the Great (Alexander III of Macedon), 13
  coins as testimony, 13, 20–21, 23
  contrasted with Christ, Jesus (The Nazarene), 16, 18, 20–23, 166
  contrasted with the Gospels, 14, 17, 19–20, 23–24
  conquest vs. confession, 23
  evaluation under Five Pillars, 21, 166
  myth and reception
    myth-makers and echoes, 21, 23
    Hollywood film, 18–19
    prototype of divine kingship, 15–16, 19–20, 23
  sources and historiography, 16–28
    Arrian, 13–16, 28
    Apologists for Arrian, 16
    Aristobulus, 15
      Ptolemy I Soter, 14
    Diodorus Siculus, 19
      Cleitarchus, 19
    Plutarch, 17
    Quintus Curtius Rufus, 18
    what Rome gained through Alexander, 19–20
Alexandria, 14–15, 26, 32, 41, 46, 93, 139, 142
Apostles
  Andrew, 153
  Bartholomew, 153
  James, 153
  John, 154
  Paul, 147–48
  Peter, 153
  Simon, 154
  Thomas, 153
  Others, 154
Appian of Alexandria
  compared to five pillars, 93
  Hannibal narrative design, 33
  Julius Caesar in The Civil Wars, 93
  Roman history, 32
Augustus (Octavian)
  omitting Cleopatra from Res Gestae, 40, 47
  creating villains and virtue, 44, 46
  Augustus as Rome's savior, 45

Buddha (Siddhartha Gautama), 50
  Ananda, 51
  Ashokan Pillars, 56–57, 59
  contrasted with mythological gods, 57
  contrasted with The Gospels, 51–53
  contrasted with Christ, Jesus (The Nazarene), 52, 55, 57–58, 60, 153
  evaluation under Five Pillars, 59, 153
  merged with Confucian ethics and Daoist cosmology, 54–55, 59
  myth and reception, 53–57
  sources and historiography, 52, 54, 56, 58–59
    Han Dynasty, 54

Index

Buddha (continued)
    Pali Canon, 52–53, 59
    Sutras, 55
    Theravāda, Mahāyāna, and Vajrayāna tradition, 53, 59

Caesar, Julius, 87
    Brutus, 95
    Cato suicide, 94–95
    Civil War and Gallic War, 87–88
    coins, 90, 97
    contrasted with Christ, Jesus (The Nazarene), 88, 90, 92–97
    evaluation under Five Pillars, 87, 90, 94, 97
    love interest of Cleopatra, 44
    manuscripts, 140, 163
    myth and reception, 90
    siege of Alexandria, 46
    self-made narrative, 88, 94
    sources and historiography, 90–96
        Appian, 93
        Cassius Dio, 92
        Cicero, 94–96
        Plutarch, 91
        Suetonius, 90
Christ, Jesus (The Nazarene), 137
    archaeology, 141–44, 148–49
    census under Quirinius, 106
    contrasted with
        Alexander, 16, 18, 20–23, 140, 154, 166
        Buddha, 52, 55, 57–58, 60, 153
        Caesar (Julius) 88, 90, 94, 97
        Caesar (Tiberius), 105, 107–8
        Cleopatra, 48–49
        Confucius, 62–63, 66–72, 154
        Hannibal, 25–27, 29, 36–38
        Muhammad, 124, 126, 129–30, 133–34, 154
        Socrates, 79–84, 140
    crucifixion under Pilate during Tiberius's reign, 100–102, 104, 106
    dangerous Christ, 60, 82–83, 92, 117
    evaluation under Five Pillars, 138, 151–52, 166–67
    martyrdoms, 150, 153–54
    historical persistence, 7
    hostile corroboration, 144–47
        Celsus, 146, 167
        Josephus, 144
        Suetonius, 146
        Tacitus, 146
        Talmud, 147
    The Gospels, 138, 141, 147
        archeological support, 143–44
    P52, 140
Cleopatra, 39
    Antony, Mark, 44–45
    Asp at her breast, 41, 48
    coins, 44
    circular reasoning, 43
    contrasted with Christ, Jesus (The Nazarene), 48–49
    erased by Rome, 40, 45–47
    evaluation under Five Pillars, 40
    Hollywood, 47
    myth and theater, 44, 47–48
    last Pharaoh, 39
    political strategist, 39, 44, 46, 48
    sources and historiography, 40–45
        Augustus, 40, 44–45
        Cassius Dio, 42–43
        dramatized by Shakespeare, 41
        Plutarch, 41–42
        Suetonius, 43–44
        siege of Alexandria, 46
    temptress, 42, 44, 47–48
    two Cleopatra's, 46
Confucius (Kong Fuzi), 61
    Analects, 62–65, 71
    archeology, 67
    contrasted with The Gospels, 63, 66, 69–70
    contrasted with Christ, Jesus (The Nazarene), 62–63, 66–72
    evaluation under Five Pillars, 65, 71
    legacy compiled later by disciples, 67
    Han Dynasty as state orthodoxy, 64–65
    Song Dynasty as state orthodoxy, 68
    Sima Qian, 76

Five Pillars, 2, 9–10, 165

Index

Alexander, 18, 21
Caesar, Julius, 87, 90, 92–94, 97
Caesar, Tiberius, 100, 102
Christ, Jesus, 138, 151
Confucius, 65, 71
Cleopatra, 40
establishing framework, 3
Hannibal, 40
Muhammad, 131–33
Pilate, 114
Socrates, 75
The Double Standard, 156, 163–64
why do they exist?, 5

Gandhi, 160

Hannibal Barca, 25
  becoming a narrative, 30, 34–35, 37
  campaigns against Rome, 25, 32
  contrasted with The Gospels, 29, 34, 37
  contrasted with early Christian writings, 26
  contrasted with Christ, Jesus (The Nazarene), 25–27, 29, 36–38
  erased by Rome, 26–28, 35
  salting of Earth, 26
  sources and historiography, 27–33
    Appian, 32–33
    Livy, 29, 33
    Plutarch, 31, 33
    Polybius, 27–28, 33
    Scipio Aemilianus, 28, 33
Harris, Sam, 159
Hus, Jan, 160

Ignatius of Antioch, 150
Irenaeus of Lyons, 54

Jugurtha of Numidia, 43
Justin Martyr, 150

Kennedy, John F., 160
King, Martin Luther Jr., 160

Magdalene, Mary, 149
Mithridates VI of Pontus, 42–43

Muhammad ibn Abdullah ibn Abdul-Muttalib, 123
  archeology, 132
  biography, 124, 132–33, 152–53
  coins, 132–34
  contrasted with The Gospels, 125–28, 130, 134
  contrasted with Christ, Jesus (The Nazarene), 124, 126, 129–30, 133–34
  conflicting sources, 125, 128, 154
  coins, 133
  evaluation under Five Pillars, 131–33
  Josephus compared to Hadith, 128–29
  militarized faith, 129–30
  Old Testament vs Qur'an, 131
  removal of certain information, 124, 127–28, 130
  Seal of the Prophets, 123
  sources and historiography, 124–34
    external sources, 134
    Ibn Hisham, 124–25
    Ibn Ishaq, 127, 133
    Hadith, 125, 127, 130
    Qur'an, 126, 133

Pilate, Pontius, 109
  believed to be myth, 110
  coins, 112, 116
  condemned Christ, Jesus (The Nazarene), 105–6, 116
  confirmed by Pilate Stone, 56, 111–12
  inscription, 111
  cost of belief, 118
  contrasted with The Gospels, 112–13
  evaluation under Five Pillars, 152, 167
  facing God, 117
  sources and historiography, 114–19
    hostile corroboration, 114–17
    Josephus, 114–15
    Philo, 111
    Tacitus, 115
    unique to other historical giants, 118–19
Pliny the Younger, 80, 154, 166
Polycarp, 150

Index

Pressures on public inheritance of the past
   market incentive, 2
   narrative compression, 1
   selection and presentism, 1

Socrates, 75
   contrasted with The Gospels, 78
   contrasted with Christ, Jesus (The Nazarene), 79–84
   evaluation under Five Pillars, 8, 81–82, 166
   no external confirmation, 80
   three faces of one man, 76–78, 84
   sources and historiography, 75–166
      Aristophanes, 75, 78, 113
      Aristotle, 75, 81, 140, 153
      Plato, 75–77, 79, 113, 162–63, 166
      Thucydides, 78
      Xenophon, 75, 77, 113
Stalin, Joseph, 158
Status and Power Building
   Alexander, 19–20, 23
   Buddha, 52
   Caesar, Julius, 88–90, 94–95
   Caesar, Tiberius, 99, 101, 106
   Confucius, 64–65
   Hannibal, 45
   Jesus and Power, 139, 160, 164
   Muhammad, 123, 125, 130–31, 133–34

Thucydides, 78, 165
Tiberius, Caesar, 99
   Capri retreat, 100, 102
   coins, 107
   contrasted with The Gospels, 104
   contrasted with Christ, Jesus (The Nazarene), 105, 107–8
   emperor during crucifixion of Christ, 100–102, 104, 106
   evaluation under Five Pillars, 102
   sources and historiography, 101–7
      Suetonius, 102
      Tacitus, 101, 106
      Pilate, Pontius, 100, 104
      Tiberius vs Julius, 105
      Velleius Paterculus, 103
   three faces of one man, 104, 107
Tyndale, William, 160